Essentials of EU Law

Students new to the study of EU law can find knowing what questions to ask to be as much of a challenge as answering them. This book clearly sets the scene: it explores the history and institutions of the EU, examines the interplay of its main bodies in its legislative process, and illustrates the role played by the EU courts and the importance of fundamental rights. The student is also introduced to the key principles of the internal market, in particular the free movement of goods and the free movement of workers. In addition a number of other EU policies, such as the Common Agricultural Policy, Environmental Protection, and Social Policy are outlined, while a more detailed inquiry is made into European competition law. This book is an essential first port-of-call for all students of European law.

AUGUST REINISCH is Professor of International and European Law and Dean for International Relations of the Law School at the University of Vienna.

Essentials of
EU Law

AUGUST REINISCH

CAMBRIDGE UNIVERSITY PRESS
Cambridge, New York, Melbourne, Madrid, Cape Town,
Singapore, São Paulo, Delhi, Mexico City

Cambridge University Press
The Edinburgh Building, Cambridge CB2 8RU, UK

Published in the United States of America by
Cambridge University Press, New York

www.cambridge.org
Information on this title: www.cambridge.org/9781107025660

© Cambridge University Press 2012

First edition published 2009
Second edition published 2012

Printed and bound by the MPG Books Group, UK

A catalogue record for this publication is available from the British Library

Library of Congress Cataloguing in Publication data
Reinisch, August.
Essentials of EU law / August Reinisch. – 2nd ed.
p. cm.
Includes index.
Rev. ed. of: Essential questions in EU law. c2009.
ISBN 978-1-107-02566-0 (hardback)
1. Law – European Union countries. 2. Law – European Union countries –
Miscellanea. 3. European Union – History. I. Reinisch, August.
Essential questions in EU law. II. Title.
KJE949.R45 2012
349.24–dc23
2012014210

ISBN 978-1-107-02566-0 Hardback
ISBN 978-1-107-60894-8 Paperback

Contents

Preface	*page* vii
List of abbreviations	x
1	History of European integration	1
2	The institutional framework	15
3	The making of Union law	38
4	The effect of Union law	58
5	Judicial control within the Union	77
6	Protecting fundamental rights within the EU	99
7	The free movement of goods	121
8	The free movement of persons	139
9	EU competition law	170
10	Selected EU policies	209
11	The EU as an international actor	238
	Index	265

Preface

This book owes its existence to a number of factors, most importantly the persistent requests of my students both at the Bologna Center of Johns Hopkins University and at Bocconi University in Milan for a simple and readable, and preferably short, introduction to the law of the European Union. It was, and remains, a particular challenge to teach EU law in institutions with mostly economics and political science students, who are not always wholly enthusiastic about learning the law. That made me realise that there is a lack of available academic resources for this particular purpose. Of course, there are the excellent treatises such as *EU Law* by Craig and De Burca, now already in its fifth edition (2011), and the second edition of *European Union Law* by Chalmers, Hadjiemmanuil, Monti and Tomkins (2010), as well as a number of other first-rate law books – needless to say, not always a light fare even for law students. The students at my home law school at the University of Vienna equally demanded access to learning the law in a most time-efficient manner.

Being brief on EU law is, of course, like squaring the circle, with the additional, hermeneutic complication that it is almost impossible to understand anything fully without first understanding everything, at least a little. This book has been written against all these odds. It aims at explaining the most important institutional aspects of the European Union, the interplay of its main bodies in the process of European legislation, the control of legality exercised by the two EU courts, the importance of fundamental rights in this context and the role of the EU as an international actor. It equally tries to familiarise the reader with the most important aspects of so-called substantive EU law, that is, the law of the four freedoms, in particular, the free movement of goods in the internal market and the freedom rights of EU citizens as workers, self-employed and family members. In addition, a number of other EU policies, such as the Common Agricultural Policy (CAP), environmental and consumer protection, Social Policy and Police and Judicial Cooperation in Criminal Matters (PJCC) are outlined, while a more detailed inquiry is made into European competition law.

In all these areas, the main principles stemming from the original 1957 Rome Treaty Establishing the European Community (TEC) to the most recent amendments after the Lisbon Treaty 2009, are outlined and discussed together with the major rules contained in EU legislation. When discussing the law, particular emphasis is laid on the case law of the Court of Justice (ECJ) and the General Court, which should make the sometimes rather tedious rules and principles livelier and more accessible.

The specific Questions and Answers format was deliberately chosen in order to move away from the usual textbook structure and provide easy access to the core issues of EU law. Instead of lengthy footnotes or endnotes and ample indices and tables of cases, instruments, etc., a light system of cross-references will guide the users through this book, remind them of content they have already read in earlier chapters, or alert them to further explanations in subsequent chapters. Additionally, bold print is used where necessary in order to indicate the most important terms and concepts used in EU law.

Thanks go to many friends and colleagues who advised me and gave helpful comments. I am particularly grateful to Christina Knahr and Jakob Wurm for their assistance in preparing the first edition of this book under the name of *Essential Questions in EU Law*. Equally, Melanie Fink's help in updating the book was of crucial value. Last, but not least my thanks go to Sinead Moloney at CUP for accompanying this project since its beginning.

A final disclaimer is warranted: do not use this little book as a substitute for further and more detailed study of EU law! It is intended only to provide a first and general introduction into a fascinating and ever growing body of law and should encourage the reader to do so. If it does, it has been successful.

August Reinisch
Vienna, January 2012

Abbreviations

ACP	African, Caribbean and Pacific
ALDE	Alliance of Liberals and Democrats for Europe
BvE	Decision on constitutional disputes between federal organs (German Constitutional Court)
BvR	Decision on complaint of unconstitutionality (German Constitutional Court)
CAP	Common Agricultural Policy
CCP	Common Commercial Policy
CFI	Court of First Instance
CFR	Charter of Fundamental Rights of the European Union
CFSP	Common Foreign and Security Policy
CIS	Commonwealth of Independent States
CMLR	Common Market Law Reports
COREPER	Permanent Representatives Committee
CSFR	Czech and Slovak Federal Republic
DG	Directorate-General
EC	European Community
ECHR	European Convention on Human Rights
ECJ	European Court of Justice
ECOFIN	Council for Economic and Financial Affairs
ECR	European Court Reports
ECR	European Conservatives and Reformists Group
ECSC	European Coal and Steel Community
ECtHR	European Court of Human Rights
EEA	European Economic Area
EEC	European Economic Community
EESC	European Economic and Social Committee

EFD	Europe of Freedom and Democracy Group
EFTA	European Free Trade Agreement
EHRR	European Human Rights Reports
EMU	European Monetary Union
EP	European Parliament
EPC	European Political Cooperation
EPP	Group of the European People's Party – Christian Democrats
ERTA	European Road Transport Agreement
ESC	Economic and Social Committee
ESDP	European Security and Defence Policy
EU	European Union
EURATOM	European Atomic Energy Community
GATS	General Agreement on Trade in Services
GATT	General Agreement on Tariffs and Trade
GNP	Gross national product
GUE/NGL	Confederal Group of the European United Left/ Nordic Green Left
JHA	Cooperation in Justice and Home Affairs
Les Verts/EFA	Group of the Greens/European Free Alliance
MEP	Member of European Parliament
NATO	North Atlantic Treaty Organization
OECD	Organization for Economic Cooperation and Development
OEEC	Organization for European Economic Cooperation
OJ	Official Journal
PJCC	Police and Judicial Cooperation in Criminal Matters
QMV	Qualified majority voting
S&D	Group of the Progressive Alliance of Socialists and Democrats in the European Parliament
SEA	Single European Act
TEC	Treaty establishing the European Community
TEU	Treaty on European Union
TFEU	Treaty on the Functioning of the European Union
TRIPs	Agreement on Trade Related Intellectual Property Rights

UNCTAD	United Nations Conference on Trade and Development
VAT	Value added tax
WEU	Western European Union
WLR	Weekly Law Reports
WTO	World Trade Organization

1 History of European integration

For centuries, the history of the small continent, or quasi-continent, of Europe has been a history of war and peace, where rival political entities, predominantly in the form of **nation-states**, have tried to dominate each other. The terrible twentieth-century experience of two World Wars, fought mainly on European territory, provided the necessary impetus to seek alternative ways of political survival, co-existence, or even cooperation. In its historic context, European integration must be understood as an attempt primarily motivated by the desire to secure peace and stability through establishing appropriate institutions. The institutions created in post-war Europe were based on ideas, partly dating back to the Middle Ages. However, it was the situation after 1945 which made it possible to think about actually setting up new structures which would make war in Europe, if not impossible, then at least much less likely. The creation of a **European Coal and Steel Community** (ECSC) in 1951, by which two strategically important industry sectors of rival nations like France and Germany were pooled, was such an important and highly pragmatic first step. It was soon followed by the establishment of two further organisations, the **European Economic Community** (EEC) and the **European Atomic Energy Community** (EURATOM) in 1957, which were designed as open regional organisations with a long-term goal of a yet undefined European unity.

Until today the process of European integration has been characterised by a constant tension between the maintenance of individual Member State power and further **integration**, leading to 'an ever closer union among the peoples of Europe', as promised in the opening lines of the 1957 Treaty of Rome's preamble. This introductory chapter is intended to provide an overview of European integration. In the course of this process, the three initially rather specialised, supranational organisations, the ECSC, the EEC and EURATOM, developed into a single comprehensive and highly integrated entity called the **European Union** (EU).

? 1.1 Does the history of ideas provide antecedents for European integration?

European political philosophy provides numerous examples of political concepts transgressing the nation-state. Some commentators have referred back as far as Pierre Dubois, the late medieval Frenchman, who suggested an assembly of delegates presided over by the French king in order to realise the old dream of the crusaders to recapture the Holy Land (*De recuperatione terrae sanctae*, 1306). The proposal by Dubois' contemporary, the Italian poet Dante Alighieri, demonstrates that the history of ideas has always been highly influenced by day-to-day politics. As a staunch supporter of the Ghibbelines and opponent of the Guelfs who supported the Papacy, Dante preferred the leadership of the (German) Holy Roman Emperor (*Monarchia*, 1308 or later).

Quite concrete and surprisingly 'modern' suggestions were made: for instance, by William Penn, who proposed a 'European Union' with decision making on the basis of weighted voting (*An Essay Towards the Present and Future Peace of Europe*, 1693); or by the Abbé de Saint Pierre, who advocated a sophisticated institutional framework including elements such as unanimity and qualified majority voting (→ *2.3*), and an internal dispute settlement mechanism (*Projet pour rendre la paix perpétuelle en Europe*, 1713). This principal purpose of guaranteeing a perpetual peace remained central to the plans of Jean Jacques Rousseau (*Extrait du projet de paix perpétuelle*, 1761) and Immanuel Kant (*Zum ewigen Frieden*, 1795).

In these early phases, however, **European integration plans** could hardly be separated from larger concepts such as world confederation and world government. It was only after the First World War that a specific regional integration concept for Europe was developed. Both the vision of the **Pan-European Movement** by Count Richard Nikolaus Coudenhove-Kalergi (*Das Pan-Europäische Manifest*, 1923) and the specific proposals by the French Foreign Minister, Aristide Briand, in 1929, which even led to a 'Study Group on European Union' set up by the League of Nations, proved to be utopian in the face of rising nationalism and fascism.

The Second World War, while destroying any hopes for Pan-Europa, at the same time demonstrated the necessity of European integration in order to avoid future wars. In his famous Zurich speech in 1946 Winston Churchill proposed a sort of 'United States of Europe'. The time was ripe to actually start thinking about how to bring about European integration.

> **? 1.2 Explain the philosophies underlying the concepts of federalism and functionalism in the context of European integration**

There were essentially two rival concepts concerning the actual steps which were required in order to reach the common goal of European integration: **federalism** and **functionalism**.

On the one hand, the 'federalists', building on various political movements formed in (Western) Europe in the late 1940s, pursued a more 'radical' path with a view to forming a United States of Europe by designing a constitution for a federal Europe in which political union was a logical first step.

'Functionalists', on the other hand, took a more 'pragmatic' approach. Their leading advocates, the French politicians Robert Schuman and Jean Monnet, thought that integrating strategically important sectors of the economy, and thereby removing them from national control, would not only make military confrontation among the Members materially impossible, but also – in the long run – lead to further economic and other integration. Ultimately, as neo-functionalist theory stressed, the **'spill-over effect'** of economic integration could even lead to political union (→ *1.8*).

The **Schuman Plan**, presented in May 1950, used these ideas and proposed the merger of the French and German coal and steel industries by putting them under shared control and inviting other European nations to join.

1.3 Outline the early history of European supranational integration

European integration closely followed what the functionalists had expected. The Schuman Plan led to the 1951 **Paris Treaty** establishing the European Coal and Steel Community (ECSC) comprising France, Germany, Italy and the Benelux countries (Belgium, the Netherlands and Luxembourg). This treaty entered into force in July 1952 for a period of fifty years, and it set up the first truly **supranational** (→ *1.5*) organisation with a 'High Authority', its main organ, having far-reaching powers in order to create a common market in coal and steel.

The ECSC was a useful blueprint for further economic integration and in 1955 – after the unsuccessful attempts to set up a **European Defence Community** (→ *1.8*) – the ECSC Member States at their conference in Messina decided to turn 'back to economics'. They entrusted the task of elaborating proposals for further integration to an expert committee, headed by the Belgian politician, Paul Henri

Spaak. By March 1957, the ECSC founding states had convened to sign the **Treaties of Rome**, establishing a European Economic Community (EEC) and a European Atomic Energy Community (EURATOM), which both entered into force on 1 January 1958.

1.4 Which other post-war European organisations could have served as a framework for further integration?

European integration via the three Communities is embedded in the larger context of a number of 'European' international organisations founded after the Second World War.

Among the **'transatlantic'** organisations, the **Organization for European Economic Cooperation** (OEEC), founded in 1948, served primarily to administer the delivery of the United States Marshall Plan aid to Europe (European Recovery Program). In 1960, it was transformed into the **Organization for Economic Cooperation and Development** (OECD).

The most important military – equally 'transatlantic' – organisation is the North Atlantic Treaty Organization (NATO) founded in 1949. Its European counterpart was the **Western European Union** (WEU), which was established in 1954, based on the 1948 Brussels Treaty originally concluded between France, the United Kingdom and the Benelux countries. Though the WEU was expected to become the defence arm of the EU after the Amsterdam Treaty, it was formally terminated in 2010 following the transfer of its functions to the EU.

Among the **'general political'** organisations, the **Council of Europe**, founded in 1949, covers a broad variety of issues, excluding defence. Its weak decision-making procedures, however, have prevented it from gaining a role competing with the European Union. Still, in the field of human rights, the Council of Europe successfully elaborated the 1950 **European Convention on Human Rights** (ECHR) as well as later protocols amending it. It also provided an institutional mechanism of supervision through the European Commission and the **European Court of Human Rights** (ECtHR). The rights and freedoms contained in the ECHR are considered to form part of EU law as expressions of general principles of law (→ *6.2, 6.5*). They also feature prominently in the (originally non-binding) EU Charter of Fundamental Rights solemnly adopted at the Nice Conference in 2000 (→ *6.14*). Only after the entry-into-force of the Lisbon Treaty (→ *1.11*), the Charter has become legally binding and the EU was formally empowered to accede to the ECHR. On the ECHR side, Protocol No. 14, which finally entered into force in 2010, paved the way for the accession of a non-state entity like the EU.

1.5 Describe the characteristics of a supranational organisation

The term **'supranational'** was first expressly used in the ECSC Treaty characterising the High Authority until this institution was merged with the Commission in the 1965 **Merger Treaty**. This Treaty in effect replaced the three distinct sets of Community institutions under the three legally separate Communities (ECSC, EEC and EURATOM) by a single set of institutions. There have been many attempts to define the notion of a **'supranational'** – as opposed to a weaker 'international' or **'intergovernmental'** – organisation. Since none of them is completely satisfactory, the prevailing view nowadays prefers to identify a number of characteristic elements, the combined existence of which should allow one to speak of a 'supranational' organisation.

These elements include, most importantly, **majority voting** in the decision-making institutions (→ *2.3*) with the power to **bind outvoted Members** (→ *3.7*), a system of **obligatory dispute** settlement (→ *5.4*), the **direct effect** (→ *4.1*, *4.4*) and **supremacy** (→ *4.10*, *4.11*) of EU law in/over national law, and the existence of **'own resources'** (→ *2.18*) of the organisation. All these elements will be explained in more detail in later sections of this book.

> ### 1.6 What was the widening vs. deepening debate about?

The **widening vs. deepening** debate concerns the question of whether **enlargement** or **internal enhancement** of the Communities/Union should come first. With the geopolitical changes of 1989 this ceased to be an academic question, and instead became one of the central issues dominating the political debate of the 1990s.

It was felt that widening may lead to a lowering of the speed of integration, while deepening could create a **'fortress Europe'** locking out the Eastern half of the continent. The political choice made was to try to avoid both situations and, thus, to aim for both widening and deepening at the same time.

Attempts have been made to tackle the problem of losing common ground when opening the Union to more Members by introducing such concepts as 'variable geometry', **'flexibility'** or 'multiple speed' of European integration. The Maastricht Treaty on European Union, for instance, provided a basis for the United Kingdom to opt-out of the Social Policy Chapter (→ *10.14*), for the United Kingdom and Denmark to opt-out of the European Monetary Union (EMU), as well as allowing neutrals to opt-out of defence agreements, while the Nice Treaty contained reformed provisions on **'enhanced cooperation'** between smaller circles of EU Member States. This, of course, may clearly jeopardise the ideal of a coherent **'acquis communautaire'**, that is, the entire body of EU law, comprising the treaties, legislation, the case law of the ECJ, as well as unwritten law such as general principles of EU law. In practice 'enhanced cooperation' has been rarely resorted to. The new conditions under the Lisbon Treaty facilitating its use and broadening its scope to include Common Foreign and Security Policy (CFSP) matters may change that.

? 1.7 Which steps have been undertaken to widen the Community since the 1990s?

After the first enlargements of the three Communities in 1973 (Denmark, United Kingdom and Ireland), 1981 (Greece), and 1986 (Portugal and Spain), the accession of Austria, Finland and Sweden in 1995 brought the European Union to a membership of fifteen countries.

The true widening debate, however, related to the wave of membership applications of the 1990s by Turkey and Morocco (already in 1987), Cyprus and Malta (1990), Switzerland (1992), Hungary and Poland (1994), Bulgaria, Romania, Slovakia, Estonia, Lithuania and Latvia (1995), the Czech Republic and Slovenia (1996).

The rules governing the **accession** of new Members to the EU provide that any 'European State' that respects the principles of freedom, democracy, human rights and the rule of law may apply for membership. After a preliminary assessment by the Commission (**'avis'**), the Council decides on the opening of formal negotiations. There is not much substantive leeway involved here because the EU regularly insists on the acceptance by the accession candidates of the entire '*acquis communautaire*' (→ 1.6). Basically the negotiations may result in the provision of transitional periods, effectively postponing the entry-into-force of certain parts of the *acquis*. Next, the European Parliament, by an absolute majority of the MEPs, and the Council, by a unanimous vote, have to agree before all EU Member States have to ratify the accession treaty.

In practice, the EC/EU has used various forms of **pre-accession** treaties to prepare candidates for membership. The **Agreement on the European Economic Area** (EEA) with six European Free Trade

Association (EFTA) states, which entered into force after protracted negotiations in 1994, is a – very sophisticated – example of an **association agreement** (→ *11.3, 11.4*) concluded by the EC. Only a year later, three states, namely Austria, Finland and Sweden, joined the EU, while Iceland, Liechtenstein and Norway remain 'associated' with the EC/EU through the EEA.

Between 1991 and 1996, another wave of association agreements, the so-called **Europe Agreements**, with the Eastern European countries in transition and **partnership agreements** with the Baltic States, Albania, the Russian Federation, Ukraine and other CIS states were concluded.

The Europe Agreements led to the biggest enlargement of the EU ever when ten new countries, namely Cyprus, the Czech Republic, Estonia, Hungary, Latvia, Lithuania, Malta, Poland, the Slovak Republic and Slovenia joined the Union in 2004. In 2007, Romania and Bulgaria acceded to the Union bringing its total membership to twenty-seven states.

The accession of Turkey, with which the EC has been linked through an association agreement since 1963, remains the most controversial politically. Turkey's application for membership dates back to 14 April 1987.

Other candidate countries for accession include Croatia (since 2004), the Former Yugoslav Republic of Macedonia (since 2005), Montenegro (since 2010) and Iceland (since 2010). By the end of 2011, the accession negotiations with Croatia have proceeded to a formal approving vote by the Parliament and the Council.

1.8 Which were the major steps towards political union?

The grand political designs of the **'federalists'** fared less well than the functional approach (→ *1.2*). In particular, the early plans for a European Defence and Political Community were unsuccessful.

In 1952, after the outbreak of the Korean War and under American pressure for German rearmament, the Treaty establishing a **European Defence Community** was signed. It was based on the French Pleven Plan and its intention was to integrate German military power in a way modelled on the ECSC structure. However, it never entered into force, because its ratification by France had become impossible after the French National Assembly rejected it in 1954. At the same time, early plans to set up a European Political Community ultimately failed. Also, later attempts to revive such ideas for a union of European States remained unsuccessful. While the Member States commissioned proposals for political union, the resulting Fouchet Plans (1961, 1962) were not adopted. Instead, again in a more pragmatic fashion, the EC Member States assumed a voluntary political cooperation on the basis of unanimity, which has been called **European Political Cooperation** (EPC) since the 1970s (→ *11.17*). In this framework the heads of state or government of the Member States began to meet regularly in what was to be called the **European Council** (→ *2.1*).

Other important steps on the way to **European political union** were the Tindemans Report of 1975 (which called for economic and monetary union, institutional reform, a common foreign policy, etc.), the first direct elections to the European Parliament and the creation of a European Monetary System in 1979, the Genscher–Colombo Plan of 1981 for the establishment of a European Union, and the Spinelli draft Treaty establishing the European Union adopted by the Parliament in 1984.

These events led to the two **intergovernmental conferences** on economic and monetary union, on the one hand, and on political union, on the other, opened in 1990 and concluded by the 1992 **Maastricht Treaty on European Union.** This in turn provided the impetus for further intergovernmental conferences in 1996–1997 and in 2000, leading to the adoption of the **Amsterdam Treaty** in 1997, which entered into force in 1999, and then the **Nice Treaty** in 2001, which entered into force on 1 February 2003.

? 1.9 What happened to the EU Constitution?

All these developments served as input for the currently abandoned process of adopting a **constitution for Europe**. While a
Constitutional Convention, a body composed of representatives
of EU institutions as well as of national parliaments and governments both of Member States and accession candidates, produced a
Draft Treaty establishing a Constitution for Europe, which was
adopted by an Intergovernmental Conference of the Union's Member
States and signed by them in 2004, French and Dutch voters openly
rejected this further treaty amendment in national referenda.

The starting points for the deliberations in the Constitutional
Convention were the 'left-overs' from the Nice Treaty, as laid down
in the 2001 **Laeken Declaration** of the European Council: the division of powers between the EU and its Member States (→ *3.2, 3.6*);
the status of the EU Fundamental Rights Charter (→ *6.14*); the sim-
plification of the Treaties; and the role of national parliaments. The
Draft Constitution Treaty suggested the merger of the separate pillars (→ *1.10*) and the creation of one single EU with a more effective decision-making process and broader powers.

? 1.10 Outline the development of the institutional structure of the EU up to the Lisbon Treaty

There has always been much confusion about the true subject(s) of
European integration. Everything was originally quite simple and
straightforward. The **Treaties of Rome** (→ *1.3*) added the **European
Economic Community** (EEC) and the **European Atomic Energy
Community** (EURATOM) to the existing **European Coal and
Steel Community** (ECSC) (→ *1.3*). In 1965, these three separate
supranational organisations pooled their institutions in the so-called

Merger Treaty (→ *1.5*), but otherwise they remained legally distinct entities. Over the years the short label **'European Community'** (EC) gained acceptance not only for the EEC but also for all three Communities.

As so often happens, changes in the law followed the factual ones. In 1992, the Member States agreed to officially rename the European Economic Community (EEC) the **European Community** (EC). The treaty by which they did so provided for a number of other very significant structural changes. After many failed attempts in the past, the **Maastricht Treaty (Treaty on European Union** (TEU)) (→ *1.6, 11.17*) established a **European Union** (EU), which was based on three different **pillars**:

(1) the three **supranational** (→ *1.3, 1.5*), pre-existing European Communities, as well as the two **intergovernmental** (→ *1.5, 11.19*) **pillars**;

(2) Common Foreign and Security Policy (CFSP); and

(3) Co-operation in Justice and Home Affairs (JHA).

The latter initially covered such diverse fields as asylum, immigration, international crime issues, as well as judicial, customs and police cooperation. In 1997, some of these tasks were shifted to the supranational EC pillar by the Treaty of Amsterdam, which also renamed the third pillar **Police and Judicial Cooperation in Criminal Matters** (PJCC) (→ *10.23*).

A number of common provisions provided the roof structure of this 'European House'. It should not come as a surprise that the quasi-official classical image of a **'temple with three pillars'** never gained universal acceptance and that some prefer to speak of the bizarre structure of a Gothic cathedral.

This structure was abolished with the Treaty of Lisbon (→ *1.11*). The Treaty of Lisbon merged the European Union and the European Community into a **single European Union**, replacing and succeeding to the European Community. The new institutional structure is outlined in Chapter 2 (The institutional framework).

? 1.11 What is the Lisbon Treaty?

In June 2007, the plans to adopt the Constitution Treaty were finally abandoned. Instead, a **Reform Treaty** was elaborated, which incorporated many features of the Draft Constitution but represented a clearly scaled-down version of the former. In December 2007, the Member States agreed on the **Lisbon Reform Treaty**, which amended both the Treaty on European Union (TEU) and the Treaty on the European Community (TEC), renaming the latter **'Treaty on the Functioning of the European Union'** (TFEU) and replacing the EC by the EU.

The ensuing ratification process was initially well under way in most Member States. However, it was slowed down when, in June 2008, Irish voters rejected the treaty in a popular referendum. After concessions to the Irish, the reluctant approval by the German Constitutional Court, and the final readiness to ratify the Treaty on the part of the Polish and the Czech presidents, the **Lisbon Reform Treaty** entered into force on 1 December 2009.

The **Lisbon Treaty** brought a number of significant amendments, aimed at the streamlining of the EU's activities and eventually overcoming the three pillar structure, coupled with another round of unfortunate renumbering of Treaty provisions (in the following the old 'pre-Lisbon' Treaty provisions will be quoted in brackets as ex Articles). Major substantive changes brought about by the Treaty of Lisbon include the granting of more powers to the Parliament, especially through the extension of the former co-decision procedure to a broad range of new areas, renaming it the 'ordinary legislative procedure' (→ *3.9*). Furthermore, in several policy areas the Council voting system changed from unanimity to qualified majority voting, calculated on the basis of double majority of Member States and inhabitants (→ *2.4*). The visibility and coherence of the EU's external action was to be enhanced by the establishment of a new High

2 The institutional framework

The organisational structure of the EU may, with all its complexity, seem Byzantine to outsiders. One will recognise an interesting mix between the traits of a traditional **international organisation** and those of a **state-like entity** with typical **separation-of-powers** issues. According to Article 13 TEU (ex Article 7 TEC), the EU possesses the following institutions:

- the European Parliament
- the European Council
- the Council
- the European Commission
- the Court of Justice of the European Union
- the European Central Bank
- the Court of Auditors.

In addition, advisory institutions, such as the **European Economic and Social Committee** or the **Committee of the Regions,** shall assist the European Parliament, the Council and the Commission. While the 'institutional triangle', consisting of the Council, Commission and Parliament which are largely responsible for the Union's legislation, will be described in some detail in this chapter, the courts of the EU, the European Court of Justice, the European General Court as well as the Civil Service Tribunal, will be explained in Chapter 5 (Judicial control within the Union). This section aims at explaining the **composition** and **internal decision making** of the Union's institutions, while their interaction in the context of **European legislation** will be analysed in Chapter 3 (The making of Union law).

? 2.1 What is the difference between the 'European Council' and the 'Council of the EU'?

The **'European Council'** ($\rightarrow$ *11.17*) evolved through a series of heads of government meetings since the 1960s, which were institutionalised at the Paris Summit in 1974. The 'European Council' was first mentioned in the Community treaties as a result of the 1986 **Single European Act** (SEA). It is now legally based on the TEU. According to Article 15 TEU (ex Article 4 TEU), it consists of the heads of state or government of the Member States, together with its President, an office which was created by the Treaty of Lisbon, and the President of the Commission. The newly established High Representative of the Union for Foreign Affairs and Security Policy ($\rightarrow$ *11.2*) shall take part in the work of the European Council. If the questions under discussion require it, the members of the European Council may decide each to be assisted by a minister and, in the case of the President of the Commission, by a member of the Commission.

The European Council meets at least twice every six months and is entrusted with the broad **policy definition** of the Union. In the words of the TEU, it 'shall provide the Union with the necessary impetus for its development and shall define the general political directions and priorities thereof' (Article 15(1) TEU). The European Council is an important actor in the Common Foreign and Security Policy ($\rightarrow$ *11.18*) and plays a prominent role in the context of politically sensitive matters.

The 'European Council' is not identical with the **'Council of the EU'**. That Council – originally the 'Council of the EC' or just the **'Council'** – is rather mainly concerned with adopting legislation, which is done jointly with the Parliament. According to Article 16

TEU (ex Article 203 TEC), the Council consists of a **representative** of each **Member State** 'at **ministerial level**, who may commit the government of the Member State in question and cast its vote'. Such a formulation was added by the Maastricht Treaty in order to allow also representatives of provinces of federal states to sit on the Council.

The **Presidency** ($\rightarrow$ *11.18*, *11.20*) of the Council is responsible for organising and chairing **Council**, **COREPER** (Permanent Representatives Committee) ($\rightarrow$ *2.6*) and **working group** meetings. Except for the Foreign Affairs Council, which is chaired by the High Representative of the Union for Foreign Affairs and Security Policy, it is held by each Member State for a period of six months. The work programmes the Presidency's actions are based on are agreed between three consecutive presidencies, meaning that they cover 18 months in total.

? 2.2 Who represents the Member States in the Council?

The **'Council of the EU'**, while always consisting of exactly the same Member States, is not always made up of the same representatives. Rather, the Member States are represented in this institution according to the **subject matter** under consideration by 'a representative of each Member State at ministerial level' (Article 16(2) TEU).

Thus, the **finance ministers** of the Member States meet as the **'Council for Economic and Financial Affairs'**, commonly referred to as **'ECOFIN'**, the environmental ministers as **Environmental Council**, while the foreign ministers meet either as **General Affairs** or as **Foreign Affairs Council**. As **Foreign Affairs Council** they deal with the EU's action abroad while ensuring compliance with the strategic guidelines of the European Council as well as consistency and coherence ($\rightarrow$ *11.18*). As **General Affairs Council** they perform a mostly **coordinating** role in the context of the Council in its various configurations and deal with cross-cutting policies of the Union, such as enlargement or budgetary questions. Together with the President of the European Council and the European Commission they prepare and follow up the European Council Meetings. In total, the Council now meets in ten **'configurations'**, comprising, in addition to the four mentioned above: 'Justice and Home Affairs'; 'Employment, Social Policy, Health and Consumer Affairs'; 'Competitiveness'; 'Transport, Telecommunications and Energy'; Agriculture and Fisheries'; and 'Education, Youth and Culture'.

As a result of this multiplication, it may happen that a number of Council meetings take place simultaneously in different meeting rooms in Brussels or Luxembourg. Council meetings are always attended by Commission representatives, who are assisted by a Secretariat headed by the Secretary-General of the Council (→ *11.2*). In order to increase the transparency of the Council's work, the Lisbon Treaty introduced a provision according to which the 'Council shall meet in public when it deliberates and votes on a draft legislative act' (Article 16(8) TEU).

? 2.3 Which voting procedures are followed in the Council?

As lawyers probably know, the correct answer to legal questions is almost invariably: 'It depends.' This is also true for the procedure to be followed by the Council, which depends upon the precise legal basis on which it is empowered to act.

Broadly speaking, there are three main voting procedures available to the **Council**:

(1) simple majority;
(2) qualified majority; and
(3) unanimity.

According to Article 16(3) TEU, the Council shall act by qualified majority, except where the Treaties provide otherwise. Even
though unanimity is still required in a number of areas, the Treaty
of Lisbon increased the application of the qualified majority procedure. However, even where formally qualified majority would be
sufficient, the practice of the Council shows that most of the time it
is attempted to take decisions by consensus.

Simple majority voting requires the votes of fourteen out of the
twenty-seven Member States. This voting procedure applies where
the Treaties so provide. It is only used for less sensitive areas and
mainly procedural questions, such as the adoption of the Council's
rules of procedure or requests for studies or proposals from the
Commission (Article 241 TFEU).

Qualified majority voting (QMV) ($\rightarrow$ *2.4, 3.11*) has become the
most important form of decision making within the Council. Today,
most legislative acts, especially those adopted in the 'ordinary legislative procedure' ($\rightarrow$ *3.8, 3.9*), have become subject to QMV.

Unanimity presently applies only in very sensitive and important
areas. In the context of the ordinary legislative procedure, unanimity is only required in cases where the Commission cannot accept
the amendments introduced into its proposal ($\rightarrow$ *3.9*). Most other
instances of unanimity apply in the context of a 'special legislative procedure' ($\rightarrow$ *3.10*). Unanimity also applies when laying down
principles and guidelines in the areas of common foreign and security policy ($\rightarrow$ *11.18*) or police and judicial cooperation in criminal
matters ($\rightarrow$ *10.25*), furthermore, in cases concerning membership of
the Union, taxation, finances of the Union and citizenship. Article
238(4) TFEU (ex Article 205(3) TEC) provides that Members, either
present in person or represented, may abstain without preventing the
adoption of acts requiring unanimity. This formulation, therefore,
indicates that unanimous decisions may not be taken if one of the
Members is absent. In the past, the predecessor rule to this provision
has been used by some Members, most notably by France exercising

its 'empty chair' policy in the 1960s by which it prevented the Community from adopting acts, in particular, in the controversial **Common Agricultural Policy (CAP)** (→ *2.5, 10.1–3*).

? 2.4 Outline the development and prospects of qualified majority voting

The bargaining about the allocation of votes and the precise technique of QMV remains one of the most contentious negotiating issues, not only at each round of enlargement but also whenever Treaty amendments are discussed. The **number of votes** each Member State can cast, as well as the number of votes constituting a qualified majority, is set by the Treaty. While the allocation of votes to individual Member States roughly corresponds to such **'objective'** factors as economic power, population and geographical size, the precise figures remain subject to **political bargaining**. Therefore, the method of calculating the qualified majority was subject to considerable changes in the course of the amendments to the Treaties. Until the new method introduced by the Treaty of Lisbon enters into force on 1 November 2014, the system of weighted votes will continue to be applied.

After the 1995 accession of three more Member States (→ *1.7*), QMV was defined as sixty-two out of a total of eighty-seven votes, cast by all (then) fifteen EC Members. Under this system of weighted voting the largest Members (Germany, France, Italy and the UK) had ten votes, Spain eight, Belgium, Greece, the Netherlands and Portugal five, Austria and Sweden four, Denmark, Ireland and Finland three and Luxembourg two votes. Where, exceptionally, a vote was not taken on the basis of a Commission proposal an additional requirement was that ten Member States had to vote in favour.

As a result of the 2004 accession of ten new EU Member States the allocation of votes and the required voting quorums had to be amended again. The Enlargement Protocol inserted the necessary changes to former Article 205 TEC, which distributed votes ranging between three (for Malta) and twenty-nine (for Germany, France and the UK). The new quorum for a qualified majority was 232 votes, cast by a majority of Members in the case of a vote on a Commission proposal. In other cases, a two-thirds majority of Member States was additionally required.

The 2004 enlargement has also introduced the idea of a so-called **triple majority** in certain cases. A new paragraph 4 was inserted into former Article 205 TEC according to which, in the case of a qualified majority voting, 'a member of the Council may request verification that the Member States constituting the qualified majority represent at least 62% of the total population of the Union. If that condition is shown not to have been met, the decision in question shall not be adopted.'

As of 1 January 2007, after the accession of Romania and Bulgaria (with fourteen and ten votes, respectively), the total number of votes has risen to 345. A **qualified majority** is reached by 255 votes in favour, which amounts to approximately **74 per cent** of the total number of votes. In addition, a **majority of Member States** – in some cases even a two-thirds majority of Member States – is required to adopt a Council measure.

This system of weighted votes will continue to apply until 1 November **2014**, when the new method of calculating the **qualified majority**, introduced by the Treaty of Lisbon, will enter into force. The Treaty of Lisbon introduces a complex system defining a qualified majority. The basic provision is Article 16(4) TEU, stipulating that a qualified majority 'shall be defined as at least **55% of the members** of the Council, comprising at least fifteen of them and representing Member States comprising at least **65% of the population** of the Union'. This system is called **'double majority system'**. Article 16(4) TEU adds that '[a] blocking minority must at least include four Council members, failing which the qualified majority shall be deemed attained'.

The politically most sensitive issue of blocking minorities led to a complex bargaining outcome. Between 1 November 2014 and 31 March 2017, 75 per cent of the required blocking minority may request negotiations for a 'satisfactory solution' – a mild euphemism for unanimity. As from 1 April 2017, this figure will even decrease to 55 per cent of the normally required blocking minority.

The complex and time-consuming transition to QMV in ever more areas of EU law reflects the inherent tension between the wish to create a more efficient supranational organisation and the desire of Member States to retain their sovereignty. Thus, the history of European integration is full of setbacks to the majority voting.

? 2.5 What did the 'Luxembourg Compromise' achieve?

By the 'Luxembourg Compromise' or 'Luxembourg Accord', the Member States managed to solve a severe political crisis in 1966, when France exercised its so-called empty chair policy (→ *2.3*) preventing Council decisions from being made on **Common Agricultural Policy** (CAP) issues.

The political compromise achieved basically enabled a single Member State to request a departure from majority voting (→ *2.3, 2.4*) by invoking its essential interests. In diplomatic language it provided:

> "Where, in the case of decisions which may be taken by majority vote on a proposal of the Commission, very important interests of one or more partners are at stake, the Members of the Council will endeavour, within a reasonable time, to reach solutions which can be adopted

by all the members of the Council while respecting their mutual interests and those of the Community, in accordance with Article 2 of the EEC Treaty.''

France added that discussions should continue until unanimity can be reached, while other Member States thought that prolonged inability to arrive at a mutually acceptable solution would lead back to majority voting.

The legal implications of this undertaking, which has not at any time become part of treaty or secondary EC law, were never formally tested. While it probably constituted just a non-binding, political agreement (a gentlemen's agreement), some have argued that it might have had an *estoppel* effect, preventing Member States from suddenly changing their voting behaviour. The Luxembourg Accord was invoked a few times in the context of the CAP during the 1980s; however, it is no longer directly relevant today. It did find some re-incarnation in the so-called **Ioannina formula** which provided for an informal strengthening of the blocking minority after the 1995 accession round. A similar formula was adopted with regard to the new majority voting rules under the Lisbon Treaty to be applied after 2014. Where flexibly decreasing blocking minorities indicate their opposition to a Council measure, the Council shall do all in its power to reach a 'satisfactory solution' (→ *2.4*).

The 'Luxembourg Compromise' continues to serve as an important reminder of the inherent tension between QMV and unanimity decision-making procedures (→ *1.3*, *1.5*). Thus, it is not surprising that it found a re-incarnation in the context of the CFSP's first timid attempts to introduce QMV in its decision-making procedures in former Article 23(2) TEU. Also this provision survived the entry into force of the Treaty of Lisbon and can now be found in Article 31(2) TEU (→ *11.19*).

2.6 Explain the structure and tasks of COREPER

The Permanent Representatives Committee, better known under its French acronym **'COREPER'**, consists of the diplomatic representatives of the Member States to the EU in Brussels. It is their task to prepare the work of the Council.

As a subsidiary body of the **Council**, COREPER meets at two levels: COREPER II, usually consisting of the permanent representatives of the Member States at ambassador level, deals with the most important matters such as economic and finance issues or external relations; and COREPER I, normally staffed by the deputies of the permanent representatives, addresses issues such as the environment, social affairs or the internal market.

If the representatives within COREPER reach **consensus**, that is, an informal agreement, then there will be no deliberation of these items, so-called **A-points**, in the Council. Rather, they will be adopted through a simplified bloc vote. The remaining issues, so-called **B-points**, will be discussed and decided upon in the Council by the ministers according to the voting procedures provided for in the Treaty (→ *2.3*).

COREPER in turn is assisted by a number of **working groups**, composed of government officials from the Member States, as well as by many committees established under the **'comitology'** scheme of the Treaties (→ *2.13*).

The technical and organisational details of COREPER II meetings are prepared by the so-called *Antici* Group, the personal assistants of the permanent representatives and, in the case of COREPER I, by the so-called *Mertens* Group.

All these groupings on a sub-ministerial level are crucial for the functioning of the Council; they serve to integrate Member States' interests in the EU's decision-making process and they help to transmit European interests back to the Member State level.

2.7 How many nationals of the same Member State can serve on the Commission?

Though the members of the Commission serve in their **personal capacity** and are **not** supposed to **represent Member State interests**, the question of whether all Member States would continue to have the right to nominate their 'national Commissioner' has been one of the most controversial issues during the enlargement negotiations of the 1990s and in the early years after the turn of the millennium.

Until the 2004 accession of ten new Members, the five largest Member States, namely France, Germany, Italy, Spain and the UK, had in fact kept their right to nominate two members of the Commission. Since 2004 the Commission has included only one national of each of the Member States.

The 2004 Enlargement Protocol provides, however, that after the accession of the twenty-seventh Member State the number of members of the Commission shall be less than the number of Member States. The decision on a rotation system could not be agreed upon in 2004 and was therefore deferred to a later stage. The **Lisbon Treaty** also opted for a slimmed down Commission. According to Article 17(4) TEU, until 31 October **2014**, the Commission 'shall consist of one national of each Member State, including its President and the High Representative of the Union for Foreign Affairs and Security Policy'. After that date, however, Article 17(5) stipulates that it 'shall consist of a number of members [...] corresponding to **two thirds** of the number of Member States'. A rotation system is supposed to be implemented in order to ensure that there would be a Commissioner from each Member State in two out of any three consecutive Commission periods of office.

This is, however, subject to a reservation. The European Council, acting unanimously, can decide to alter the number of Commissioners. It in fact adopted such a decision in July 2009. This was a concession to Ireland before it held a second referendum on the Lisbon Treaty.

The current twenty-seven Commissioners are chosen on the 'ground of their **general competence** and European commitment from persons whose **independence** is beyond doubt', as Article 17(3) TEU (ex Article 213(1) TEC) puts it. According to the same provision, they serve **renewable five-year terms**. The members of the Commission are assisted by a personal staff, called a **'cabinet'**, of seven to eight (for the President, eleven) people and by permanent officials working in the **Directorates-General** (DGs) organised according to subject-matter areas similar to ministries at the national level.

? 2.8 How are the members of the Commission selected?

Over the years, the procedure of setting up the Commission has been significantly refined. In particular, the role of the Parliament in the process of choosing Commissioners has been strengthened.

According to Article 17(7) TEU, the European Council, acting by a qualified majority, proposes a candidate for President of the Commission to the European Parliament. The European Parliament then **elects the President** by majority of its component members. This procedure is repeated, if the candidate does not obtain the required majority in the Parliament.

As regards the other members of the Commission, the Member States draw up a list of candidates. This list is to be adopted by the Council by **common accord** with the President-elect. The whole body of Commissioners is then subject to a **'vote of consent'** by the Parliament. The final step is their formal appointment by the European Council, acting by a qualified majority.

In practice, the Parliament has conducted hearings with nominees and, if dissatisfied with individual candidates, threatened to veto the entire Commission. In 2004 this led to the replacement of three nominees of the Barroso Commission.

2.9 How is a Commission proposal adopted?

According to Article 250 TFEU (ex Article 219 TEC), the Commission takes decisions by **simple majority** voting. In practice, formal votes are taken in the weekly Commission meetings only very rarely and only in regard to important matters. Rather, there are three other procedures that are regularly used in order to adopt Commission decisions. Pursuant to the **written procedure**, proposals are communicated to the Commission members, who may raise reservations and/or amendments. Otherwise, the proposal will be adopted as suggested. This is usually used where all points have been agreed by the relevant Directorates-General beforehand. According to the **empowerment procedure**, the college of Commissioners may empower one or more of its members to make a decision, while the **delegation procedure** allows a transfer of decision-making powers to directors-general and heads of service.

Since the Commission is a **collegiate body**, once decisions are taken they have to be backed by the entire Commission. This is sometimes referred to as the principle of collegiality or of collective responsibility.

2.10 Describe the elements of the Commission's 'right of initiative'

Article 17(2) TEU accords the Commission the **exclusive right** to formulate **proposals** with respect to 'Union legislative acts' (→ *3.1*). Exceptions to this rule can only be provided for in the Treaties.

A major exception are the special rules concerning the former third pillar (PJCC), where the Commission shares the right of initiative with one-quarter of the Member States. This gives the Commission enormous influence not only on the actual formulation, but ultimately also on the content of Union legislation.

The Council (Article 241 TFEU) and the Parliament (Article 225 TFEU) may request the Commission to submit proposals. The Commission has no corresponding duty to act upon any such requests. However, it has to give reasons if it decides not to submit a proposal. A new form of initiative introduced by the Lisbon Treaty is the so-called **'citizens' initiative'**, whereby a group of not less than one million EU citizens of a significant number of Member States may invite the Commission to draw up a proposal (Article 11(4) TEU).

In practice, the importance of the Commission's right of initiative is reinforced by the fact that Council amendments of such proposals usually require unanimity, and by the right of the Commission to amend or withdraw proposals at any time before actual Council adoption.

? 2.11 How does the Commission fulfil its tasks of supervision and control?

The Commission acts as the **'guardian of the treaties'** ensuring that EU law is complied with. For this purpose, the TFEU endows the Commission with a number of specific supervisory powers, ultimately comprising the power to institute legal proceedings before the ECJ in a variety of cases such as:

- the **right to sue a Member State** according to Article 258 TFEU (ex Article 226 TEC) (→ *5.11*);
- the **right to sue other Community organs** according to Article 263 TFEU (ex Article 230 TEC) (→ *5.5*); and

- the **right to request a lump sum or penalty payment** from Member States failing to implement a decision of the ECJ according to Article 260(2) TFEU (ex Article 228(2) TEC) (→ *5.12*).

Furthermore, for a long time the Commission was directly responsible for 'enforcing' competition law under former Articles 81 and 82 TEC (now Articles 101 and 102 TFEU) (→ *9.16*). Even after the reform of EU competition law, the Commission has retained certain supervisory powers under Regulation 1/2003/EC.

2.12 What is the Commission's role in the Union's external relations?

In the field of the Union's 'foreign affairs', called 'external relations' in EU jargon, the Commission shares powers with the Council which, with different degrees of involvement of the Parliament, retains the power to conclude **international agreements** entered into by the EU (→ *11.3*).

Such agreements are, however, **negotiated** by the **Commission**, albeit under certain Council influence laid down in Article 218 TFEU (ex Article 300 TEC): basically, the Council must authorise the Commission to open negotiations. In addition, the Council may appoint a special committee to assist the Commission and it may issue directives to the Commission for the conduct of negotiations. The Commission's negotiating role is particularly important in the high-profile case of the accession of new Member States (→ *11.3*).

Further, the **Commission represents** the EU in the World Trade Organization (WTO) and in other **international organisations**, such as the United Nations and its specialised agencies, the Council of Europe, OECD and others (→ *11.4*); it also maintains diplomatic ties with more than 140 countries accredited to the EU.

Based on the **Common Commercial Policy** powers under Article 207 TFEU (ex Article 133 TEC), the Commission is also in charge of enforcing the EU's trade protection legislation, such as anti-dumping and countervailing duty legislation or the Trade Barriers Regulation (→ *11.5*).

> ## ? 2.13 What is the 'comitology' system and how was it affected by the entry into force of the Lisbon Treaty?

The notion of **'comitology'** basically signifies a complicated system of law-making under the supervision of specialised committees, which represent Member States and assist the Commission in areas of law-making delegated by the Council. To a considerable extent, comitology applied in the fields of agriculture (→ *10.1*), fisheries (→ *10.6*) and competition law (→ *ch. 9*).

Though there was no authority for 'comitology' in the original Treaty text, the ECJ upheld the legality of this system in 1970 in Case 25/70 *Einfuhr- und Vorratsstelle* v. *Köster et al.* [1970] ECR 1161. Basically, the Court found that if the Treaty gave the Council the power to delegate law-making powers it could do so with conditions. This reasoning was integrated into the text of the Treaty by the **SEA** (→ *2.1*) which amended the predecessor rule to former Article 202 TEC (now Article 291 TFEU). In addition to its authority to confer on the Commission certain rule-making powers, it expressly stated that the Council 'may impose certain requirements in respect of the exercise of these powers'.

According to the Comitology Decision 1999/468/EC, one has to distinguish between so-called:

- **advisory committees**, which have only consultative functions;
- **management committees**, whose qualified majority rejection of a Commission draft refers the matter to the Council; and

- **regulatory committees**, whose approval is required for the Commission.

Because of the vast transfer of law-making powers from the Council to the Commission (more than two-thirds of all regulations are adopted under delegated law-making procedures), comitology has been questioned repeatedly from a constitutional point of view. A first concern was the lack of transparency in the comitology system. Hence, a clearer hierarchy of norms as well as standardisation of procedures seemed necessary. Another major concern was the potential threat comitology posed to the Union's institutional balance. This involved the relationship between the Council and the Commission as well as the problem of the lack of parliamentary control over the Commission, since the comitology committees only included representatives of Member States.

In an attempt to simplify the complicated system that had gradually developed, the Lisbon Treaty introduced the distinction between 'legislative acts' and 'non-legislative acts' of the Union ($\rightarrow$ *3.1*). The new comitology restricts the Commission's powers to 'non-legislative acts'. These are further divided into two categories – 'delegated acts' (Article 290 TFEU) and 'implementing acts' (Article 291 TFEU). Pursuant to Article 290(1) TFEU a 'legislative act may delegate to the Commission the power to adopt non-legislative acts of general application to supplement or amend certain non-essential elements of the legislative act'. The same Article further provides that the 'objectives, content, scope and duration' of the delegation of power shall be explicitly defined in the underlying legislative acts. Article 290(2) TFEU expressly states that a delegated act may enter into force only if no objection has been expressed by the European Parliament or the Council within a period set by the legislative act.

With regard to 'implementing acts' Article 291(3) TFEU envisages the adoption of rules and general principles concerning 'mechanisms for control by Member States of the Commission's exercise of implementing powers'. This formulation is based on former

Article 202 TEC and allows the continuation of the existing system of comitology in the area of implementing acts. The rationale for the control of the Member States in this area is that they are primarily responsible for the implementation of EU law.

? 2.14 Describe the structure of the European Parliament

The **'Assembly'**, as it was originally referred to in the ECSC and EC Treaty, began to refer to itself as **'Parliament'** in 1962. Since the 1986 SEA it has officially been known as the **'European Parliament'** (EP).

According to Article 14(2) TEU, the Parliament shall not exceed the number of 750 members (MEPs), plus the President. At the moment, it consists of 754 seats. This has been accepted for the current legislative period, running from 2009–2014, as the already elected members cannot lose their seats. For the next elections, however, the total number of 751 must be adhered to.

The minimum number of members per country is six; the maximum number is 96 (Article 14(2) TEU). Currently, Malta, Luxembourg, Cyprus and Estonia send six members, whereas Germany sends 99 members, exceeding the maximum number by three members.

Since 1979, the MEPs have been directly elected for a **five-year term** on the basis of the respective national election laws. Though there are no genuine European political parties as yet, MEPs are organised not according to national but rather according to **transnational party affiliations**. Currently, there are seven political groups: the EPP (Group of the European People's Party – Christian Democrats); the S&D (Group of the Progressive Alliance of Socialists and Democrats in the European Parliament); the ALDE (Alliance of Liberals and Democrats for Europe); ECR (European

Conservatives and Reformists Group); Les Verts/The Greens/EFA (Group of the Greens/European Free Alliance); the GUE/NGL (Confederal Group of the European United Left/Nordic Green Left); and the EFD (Europe of Freedom and Democracy Group).

After some disagreement and rivalry over the official seat of the Parliament, in 1992 the Member States decided that plenary sessions would take place in Strasbourg, committee meetings in Brussels and that the Secretariat should be seated in Luxembourg.

Parliamentary sessions are chaired by an elected president and by fourteen vice-presidents (each for a term of 2½ years), who form the EP's **'Bureau'**, the Parliament's executive body in charge of internal financial, administrative and organisational matters. In addition, the president chairs the Conference of Presidents, composed of the leaders of the political groups, a body which decides, among other things, on the agenda for plenary meetings, bringing suit against another institution before the European Court of Justice (ECJ) (→ *5.6*) and settling conflicts of jurisdiction between different parliamentary committees.

Most of the work of the EP is carried out in its twenty specialised standing **committees** (for example: legal affairs; civil liberties, justice and home affairs; foreign affairs; petitions; etc.), wherein MEPs serving as rapporteurs will draft parliamentary resolutions expressing the EP's opinion on Commission proposals. These parliamentary committees of twenty-eight to eighty-six members meet once or twice a month in public sessions in Brussels in order to discuss legislative proposals.

2.15 What are the legislative 'powers' of the European Parliament?

Enacting legislation has become one of the central functions of the European Parliament. Whereas prior to the SEA it was generally merely consulted, with the entry into force of the Lisbon Treaty, the former co-decision procedure, now called the **'ordinary legislative procedure'**, was extended to a whole range of new issues. This means that the Council and the Parliament decide together on the enactment of legislation. Article 14(1) TEU states that the EP 'shall, jointly with the Council, exercise legislative […] functions'.

Apart from the ordinary legislative procedure, the Lisbon Treaty introduced the so-called **'special legislative procedure'**. This indicates a deviation from the ordinary legislative procedure and could for example mean that the EP is only to be consulted or that the EP adopts the legal act on its own, after approval of the Council. Important procedures in this regard are the **'consent procedure'**, formerly known as 'assent procedure' and the **'consultation procedure'**. The former makes the adoption of a legislative act subject to the EP's consent; it cannot, however, amend the proposal. The latter reduces the involvement of the EP to being consulted, without rendering its opinion legally binding for the Council.

In the Common Foreign and Security Policy the EP enjoys a less important role. According to Article 36 TEU, '[t]he High Representative of the Union for Foreign Affairs and Security Policy shall regularly consult the European Parliament on the main aspects and the basic choices' of the CFSP (→ *11.2*). Nevertheless, the Treaty of Lisbon significantly enhanced the role of the EP in the conclusion of international agreements, as it has to give its consent to all agreements mentioned in Article 218(6)(a) TFEU (→ *11.3, 2.17*).

2.16 How does the Parliament exercise control vis-à-vis the other European institutions?

The Parliament enjoys a full range of **supervisory powers**, similar to those that can be found in national parliaments. In particular, the EP has the right to:

- **elect** the President of the Commission (Article 14(1) TEU), which, however, has to be read in conjunction with Article 17(7) TEU on the influence of the European Council in this process (→ *2.8*);
- **approve** the nominations of **Commission** members by way of a 'vote of consent' with regard to the whole body of Commissioners (Article 17(7) TEU; ex Article 214 TEC) (→ *2.8*);
- cast a vote of no-confidence, a so-called **motion of censure**, by a two-thirds majority on the Commission 'as a body' (Article 234 TFEU; ex Article 201 TEC);
- **question** the Commission (Article 230 TFEU) and to some extent the Council;
- bring an **action for annulment** or **failure to act** (Articles 263 and 265 TFEU; ex Articles 230 and 232 TEC) (→ *5.6, 5.4*); and
- set up a temporary **Committee of Inquiry** (Article 226 TFEU; ex Article 195 TEC).

In addition, the EP has appointed an **Ombudsman** (Article 228 TFEU; ex Article 195 TEC) to receive complaints concerning 'instances of maladministration' within the EU institutions, bodies, offices or agencies. Further, the Treaty provides for the right of any individual to petition the EP (Article 227 TFEU; ex Article 194 TEC) on matters within the Union's fields of activity and which directly affect him or her.

2.17 Which situations require the consent of the European Parliament?

The **consent**, formerly assent, procedure (→ *2.15, 3.10*) is required for a number of highly important matters such as:

- the **accession** of new Member States under Article 49 TEU (→ *1.7, 11.3*);
- the conclusion of international agreements pursuant to Article 218(6)(a) TFEU (→ *11.3, 2.15*); and

• the **investiture** of the whole body of Commissioners according to Article 17(7) TEU (→ *2.8*).

? 2.18 What is the Parliament's role in the Union's budgetary process?

Apart from its legislative and supervisory functions, the EP according to Article 14 TEU, jointly with the **Council**, exercises budgetary functions. The complex procedure is outlined in Article 314 TFEU (ex Article 272 TEC). The EP **approves** the annual **budget** based on a **Commission proposal** in a special legislative procedure during which it may make changes and amendments to the initial proposal. The annual budget is funded from so-called **'own resources'** of the Union, which comprise: **customs duties** based on the Common Customs Tariff (→ *11.5*); **agricultural levies**, charged on agricultural imports according to the CAP (→ *10.3*); the so-called **'VAT resource'**, a contribution by the Member States equivalent to 1 per cent of the final selling price of a common base of goods and services, and the so-called **'GNP resource'**, a maximum of 1.27 per cent of a Member's GNP.

? 2.19 What does the Court of Auditors do?

The Court of Auditors consists of one national from each Member State appointed after consultation with the EP by the Council for a renewable six-year term. Pursuant to Article 287 TFEU (ex Article 248 TEC), it **examines** the accounts of all **revenue and expenditure** of the Union on the basis of the principles of **legality, regularity and sound financial management**. At the end of each fiscal year the Court of Auditors prepares the Annual

Report on the basis of which the EP will give a discharge to the Commission.

2.20 What are the tasks of the European Economic and Social Committee as well as of the Committee of the Regions?

The Economic and Social Committee (ESC), which has started to call itself **European Economic and Social Committee** (EESC), is not an 'institution' according to Article 13 TEU (ex Article 7 TEC), but rather an advisory body of the EU. Pursuant to Article 300 TFEU (ex Article 257 TEC), it consists of 'representatives of organisations of employers, of the employed, and of other parties representative of civil society, notably in socioeconomic, civic, professional and cultural areas'. The number of representatives shall not exceed 350 (Article 301 TFEU). The idea is to have an input from these various fields of organised civil society into the law-making process of the EU. The TFEU contains sometimes obligatory or optional **consultation** rights of the ESC, which also has the right of issuing opinions on its own initiative.

Like the ESC the **Committee of the Regions** may be consulted by the Commission, the Council or the EP during the law-making process of the EU, particularly on matters of **cross-border cooperation**. In practice, its influence appears to be rather low.

3 The making of Union law

Union law consists of so-called primary and secondary law. The concept of **primary law** relates to law made by the Member States via their international law treaty-making powers. Therefore, it comprises the initial 1957 Treaty of Rome plus various treaty amendments, such as the SEA, the Maastricht, Amsterdam, Nice and Lisbon Treaties, the Charter of Fundamental Rights as well as the accession treaties. **Secondary law**, on the other hand, refers to law **made by** the Union's **institutions** based on the authorisation contained in the Treaties (the primary law). Articles 288 to 292 TFEU outline the different categories of legal acts of the Union. Whereas Article 288 TFEU refers to the instruments to be used by the Union, Articles 289–292 TFEU establish a hierarchy of norms between legislative and non-legislative acts. Article 294 TFEU specifies the most important form of law-making, the ordinary legislative procedure, whereas various special legislative procedures are found throughout the Treaty.

3.1 What kind of instruments are used for Union law-making?

The instruments at the disposal of the Union for law-making are regulations, directives and decisions, as well as soft-law instruments such as recommendations and opinions. Article 288 TFEU briefly characterises the legal quality of these **legal acts**:

" "To exercise the Union's competences, the institutions shall adopt regulations, directives, decisions, recommendations and opinions.

"A **regulation** shall have **general application**. It shall be **binding** in its entirety and **directly applicable** in all Member States.

"A **directive** shall be **binding**, as to the **result to be achieved**, upon each Member State to which it is addressed, but shall leave to the national authorities the choice of form and methods.

"A **decision** shall be **binding** in its entirety. A decision which specifies those to whom it is addressed shall be binding only on them.

"**Recommendations** and **opinions** shall have **no binding force**. " "

Regulations, directives and decisions can constitute legislative acts, delegated acts, implementing acts and other legal acts. According to Article 289(3) TFEU, legal acts adopted pursuant to the ordinary legislative procedure or to a special legislative procedure constitute **'legislative acts'**. In such acts, it can be foreseen to delegate to the Commission the power to 'adopt **non-legislative acts** of general application to supplement or amend certain non-essential elements of the legislative act' (Article 290(1) TFEU) ($\rightarrow$ *2.13*). These are the so-called **delegated acts**. Article 291 TFEU introduces another type of non-legislative acts, **'implementing acts'**. The primary responsibility to implement Union legislation rests within the Member States. However, according to Article 291(2) TFEU, '[w]here uniform conditions for implementing legally binding Union acts are needed, those acts shall confer implementing powers on the Commission' or in certain instances on the Council.

Despite the abolition of the former pillar structure through the entry into force of the Treaty of Lisbon, the **Common Foreign and**

Security Policy is subject to distinct rules as regards the legal acts of the Union. Article 25 TEU specifies that the CFSP is pursued through general guidelines to be defined by the European Council, decisions adopted mainly by the Council and the strengthening of systematic cooperation between Member States (11.18).

In addition to the **non-binding recommendations** and **opinions**, a number of **soft law instruments** have been used. They range from **Action Plans**, outlining intended legislation, **Notices**, such as those laying down competition law enforcement policies (→ *9.8*), and **Declarations**, laying down certain procedures or values to be respected, to soft law-making procedures, such as the **'open method of coordination'** used in various fields not covered by Union competence. Through this method of policy coordination 'best practices' are identified, which other Member States are encouraged to emulate, and their performance is then often 'benchmarked' against that of the most successful. The open method of coordination has frequently been applied, particularly in the field of **social and employment policy**.

3.2 What does the 'principle of conferral' stand for?

The Treaties do not contain a general grant of legislative powers to the EU. Instead, the principle of **'enumerated'** or **'conferred powers'** means that all powers enjoyed by the Union are 'derived powers', which have been transferred from the Member States in the Treaties (→ *5.4*, *5.8*). This idea is codified in Article 5(2) TEU (ex Article 5(1) TEC), which states:

> "Under the principle of conferral, the Union shall act only within the limits of the competences conferred upon it by the Member States in the Treaties to attain the objectives set out therein. Competences not conferred upon the Union in the Treaties remain with the Member States."

The same concept of a limited transfer of powers is expressed in Article 13(2) TEU (ex Article 7(1) TEC) which provides that '[e]ach institution shall act within the limits of the powers conferred on it in the Treaties' and in Article 1(1) TFEU according to which '[t]his Treaty organises the functioning of the Union and determines the areas of, delimitation of, and arrangements for exercising its competences' (→ *5.8*).

This fairly obvious principle requiring delegated law-making by the EU institutions to be based on a Treaty authorisation is, however, complicated by the fact that the Treaty does not only contain express authorisations. Instead – and the ECJ has confirmed this position – Union legislation may also be based on **'implied powers'** or on the broad authorisation contained in **Article 352 TFEU** (ex Article 308 TEC) (→ *3.4*).

According to the **implied powers doctrine**, as developed primarily in the institutional law of the United Nations, international organisations are deemed to have such **powers** as are **necessary** for the **fulfilment** of their **functions or tasks**. Sometimes an even broader version of implied powers is used when, instead of 'functions', general 'treaty objectives' are taken as a yardstick to determine the scope of implied powers. The implied powers doctrine is also often relied upon in the area of **EU treaty-making powers** (→ *11.8–13*).

Despite a rather broad interpretation of Union powers – intended to give the Treaty the most effective application (*effet utile*) – the ECJ, in principle, seems to adhere to the narrower interpretation of implied powers. This can be seen in the case concerning *Migration Policies*, Joined Cases C-281, 283–285 and 287–285 *Germany and others* v. *Commission* [1987] ECR 3203, in which the ECJ held that 'where an Article of the EEC Treaty … confers a specific task on the Commission it must be accepted, if that provision is not to be rendered wholly ineffective, that it confers on the Commission necessarily and *per se* the powers which are indispensable in order to carry out that task'.

The Court has demonstrated that it is willing to call a halt on too sweeping interpretations of Union powers by the institutions themselves. In the case concerning the Tobacco Advertising Directive, Case C-376/98 *Germany* v. *European Parliament and Council* [2000] ECR I-8419, it held that the Community legislature had no power to adopt that directive on the basis of the harmonisation provisions relating to the establishment of the internal market contained in what was then Article 100a TEC (now Article 114 TFEU) (→ *3.11*). Thus, in a very rare move, the Tobacco Advertising Directive was annulled (→ *5.8*).

3.3 How do we know whether a specific act should be adopted by the EU or by its Member States?

Ever since the beginning of European integration under the framework of the Treaty of Rome, the distribution of powers between the EU and its Member States has been a highly complex issue which reflected the political struggle between the centripetal forces of ever closer integration and the centrifugal forces of protecting Member State sovereignty. The limits of Community/Union powers were thus often judicially tested and defined by the jurisprudence of the ECJ.

The Draft Constitution Treaty as well as the Treaty of Lisbon attempted to clarify matters by, for the first time, spelling out specific **'categories and areas of Union competence'** in Articles 2 to 6 TFEU. Based on the Court's jurisprudence, the TFEU distinguishes between **exclusive** and **shared** Union competences and circumscribes the role of Member State coordination and Union support in various policy fields.

Article 2(1) TFEU provides that '[w]hen the Treaties confer on the Union **exclusive competence** in a specific area, only the Union may legislate and adopt legally binding acts, the Member States being able to do so themselves only if so empowered by the Union or for the implementation of Union acts'. The Union possesses exclusive competence only in a limited number of areas, laid down in Article 3 TFEU, among them, the **customs union**, the establishing of the **competition rules** necessary for the functioning of the internal market, **monetary policy** for the Member States whose currency is the euro, the **conservation of marine biological resources** under the common fisheries policy, and most importantly in the field of the **common commercial policy (CCP)** (→ *11.5*). In addition, Article 3(2) TFEU 'codified' the judge-made principle that the Union has 'exclusive competence for the conclusion of an international agreement when its conclusion is provided for in a legislative act of the Union or is necessary to enable the Union to exercise its internal competence, or in so far as its conclusion may affect common rules or alter their scope' (→ *11.11*).

Pursuant to Article 4 TFEU, **shared competences** comprise the following areas: the **internal market, social policy, cohesion** policy, **agriculture and fisheries**, **environment**, **consumer protection, transport**, trans-European networks, **energy, freedom, security and justice**, and common safety concerns in public health matters. Article 2(2) TFEU clarifies that in the case of **shared competences**, both 'the Union and the Member States may legislate and adopt legally binding acts in that area' and that only when the Union is exercising its competence the Member States are pre-empted to adopt national measures. Thus, in the area of **shared competences** a specific act may be adopted both by the EU and its Member States. Where the former has exercised its shared powers, the Member States are not permitted to act. Conversely, where the EU has ceased to exercise them, the Member States may act again.

? 3.4 Does the 'flexibility clause' enlarge the EU's powers?

In addition to implied powers as accepted by the ECJ, the Treaty contains a very broad law-making authorisation in **Article 352**

TFEU (ex Article 308 TEC), the so-called **flexibility clause**. Its first paragraph runs as follows:

> "If action by the Union should prove necessary, within the framework of the policies defined in the Treaties, to attain one of the objectives set out in the Treaties, and the Treaties have not provided the necessary powers, the Council, acting unanimously on a proposal from the Commission and after obtaining the consent of the European Parliament, shall adopt the appropriate measures."

In the past, this provision has been used repeatedly by the EC in order to legislate in fields not yet covered by express authorisation, such as environmental policy measures (→ *10.8*). The fears that the EC would expand its competence through reliance on this Article have been captured in the 2001 Laeken Declaration on Future Reform of the EU (→ *1.9*). It opened up the possibility of a review of former Article 308 in the light of preventing 'creeping expansion of competences' of the EU, and it enabled the Union to 'continue to be able to react to fresh challenges and developments and to explore new policy areas'.

As a reaction to these concerns, the Treaty of Lisbon codified a catalogue of **Union competences** and reaffirmed the **'principle of conferral'** in Article 5(2) TEU, as well as the, originally judge-made, differentiation between **exclusive Union competences**, **shared competences** and **Member State competences** (→ *3.3, 11.11, 11.12*).

Furthermore, Article 352 TFEU, as opposed to its predecessor Article 308 TEC, directly addresses these concerns. As a response to the often articulated criticism that Article 308 TEC only required consultation of the Parliament, Article 352 TFEU introduced the requirement of **consent** of the Parliament. In addition, paragraphs (2)–(4) of Article 352 outline conditions for competences resulting from Article 352(1), including an obligation of the Commission to 'draw national Parliaments' attention to proposals based on this Article', a prohibition of the use of Article 352 for the purpose of harmonising Member States' laws in cases where the Treaties exclude such harmonisation and an express exclusion of the use of the flexibility clause in the CFSP.

Also the ECJ has reaffirmed the principal idea that **Article 352 TFEU** 'being an integral part of an institutional system based on the principle of conferred powers, **cannot** serve as a basis for **widening** the scope of **Community powers** beyond the general framework created by the provisions of the [TFEU] as a whole' (Joined Cases C-402/05 P and C-415/05 P *Kadi and Al Barakaat* v. *Council and Commission* [2008] ECR I-6351). The idea's actual application in this case demonstrates, however, that the Court is willing to interpret the flexibility clause in a wide fashion.

The case concerned, among others, the question of whether the Community had the power to adopt so-called **targeted sanctions**, such as **asset freezing**. Since the Treaty only conferred an express power to adopt restrictive measures 'with one or more third countries' (ex Article 301 TEC; now Article 215 TFEU) the measures targeting individuals and groups were adopted on the basis of Article 308 TEC, the predecessor provision to Article 352 TFEU. In *Kadi*, the Court did not have a problem to uphold the freezing regulation. It was of the opinion that the express power to adopt country sanctions was 'the expression of an implicit underlying objective, namely, that of making it possible to adopt such measures through the efficient use of a Community instrument'.

Article 75 TFEU now contains an express **anti-terrorism competence** to adopt 'measures with regard to capital movements and payments, such as the freezing of funds, financial assets or economic gains belonging to, or owned or held by, natural or legal persons, groups or non-State entities' (→ *10.29, 11.21*).

3.5 May the Council base a specific legal act on the Treaty as a whole?

The policy rationale of the principle of enumerated or conferred powers could be easily circumvented in practice if EU institutions invoked the Treaty in general as a legal basis of their law-making activities. Article 296 TEU (ex Article 253 TEC) aims at preventing such abuse by imposing a **duty to state the reasons** on which specific legislation is based (→ 5.9). The ECJ interpreted this obligation to require either specific reference to a Treaty article, or at least a possibility of identification from the context. In the case concerning *Tariff Preferences*, Case 45/86 *Commission v. Council* [1987] ECR 1493, the Court annulled (→ 5.5, 5.8) a Council measure the legal basis of which had not been sufficiently identified.

The Treaty requirement to give reasons is intended to facilitate **judicial review** by the European courts and to foster transparency of law-making, which includes the opportunity for the parties to defend their rights and interests, as the ECJ has already found in Case 24/62 *Germany v. Commission* [1963] ECR 63 (→ 5.9).

3.6 Explain the meaning of subsidiarity

To some extent as a response to the ever increasing scope of Union legislation, the principle of **subsidiarity** was introduced into the Treaties by the Maastricht amendments in 1992 in order to alleviate Member States' fears of the perceived creeping **expansion** of EU **competences**.

The Treaties distinguish between the existence of competence on the one hand, and the use of competence on the other hand. Whereas the existence is governed by the principle of conferral (→ 3.2), the use 'is governed by the principles of **subsidiarity** and

proportionality' (Article 5(1) TEU). These two principles are further explained in Article 5(3) and (4):

> "3. Under the principle of subsidiarity, in areas which do **not** fall within its **exclusive competence**, the Union shall act only if and in so far as the objectives of the proposed action **cannot** be **sufficiently achieved** by the Member States, either at central level or at regional and local level, but can rather, by reason of the scale or effects of the proposed action, be **better achieved** at **Union level**.

> "The institutions of the Union shall apply the principle of subsidiarity as laid down in the Protocol on the application of the principles of subsidiarity and proportionality. National Parliaments ensure compliance with the principle of subsidiarity in accordance with the procedure set out in that Protocol.

> "4. Under the principle of proportionality, the content and form of Union action shall not exceed what is necessary to achieve the objectives of the Treaties."

This has to be read in conjunction with Protocol No 2 to the Lisbon Treaty on the application of the principles of subsidiarity and proportionality. Protocol No 2 requires the Commission to 'consult widely' before proposing legislative acts (Article 2). It furthermore includes the obligation that '[a]ny draft legislative act should contain a detailed statement making it possible to appraise compliance with the principles of subsidiarity and proportionality' (Article 5 Protocol No 2). In addition, the Commission is required to publish annual reports on the application of the principle (Article 9 Protocol No 2).

Although the ECJ has affirmed its power to annul Union acts adopted in violation of the principle of subsidiarity, and thereby accepted the latter's so-called **justiciability**, it has been very **reluctant** to second-guess the political agreement underlying Union legislation. This may have been one of the reasons why the Lisbon Treaty has provided the national parliaments with an enhanced role in this regard. The most important changes introduced in this context is the early warning mechanism according to which national parliaments can request the Union institutions to reconsider proposed legislation they believe to be in violation of subsidiarity (Articles 6 and 7 Protocol No 2). In the ordinary legislative procedure such concerns may end the EU law-making process where specific Council or Parliament majorities share this assessment.

3.7 Outline the general principles of Union law-making

As a rule, Union legislation begins with a **Commission proposal** (this is usually referred to as the Commission's 'right of initiative' (→ *2.10*)), followed by Council deliberations with different degrees of **involvement** on the part of the **European Parliament** (→ *2.15*) and **advisory bodies**, such as the Economic and Social Committee or the Committee of the Regions (→ *2.20*). What is ultimately required is the formal **adoption** of the proposal **by the Council** through qualified majority or unanimity (→ *2.5, 2.6*) and, in most cases now, by the **Parliament**.

For a long time, the Treaty of Rome contained a complex web of different **law-making procedures,** and it was often very difficult to ascertain which would have been the correct one to apply for a specific legislative proposal. In theory at least, the Treaty itself determines which of the different procedures applies to a particular subject matter. Though there are a considerable number of different procedures in total, the Treaty of Lisbon has substantially reduced the uncertainties and streamlined the main procedures. These are now the **ordinary legislative procedure** (→ *3.9*) and the **special legislative procedures** (→ *3.10*). Among the special legislative procedures, in particular the **consent procedure** and the **consultation procedure** are important (→ *3.10*).

? 3.8 Outline the main stages in the shift from the consultation procedure to the ordinary legislative procedure

In the history of law-making of the EU, there have been a variety of different procedures to adopt legislation. The main difference between them, as well as the main impetus for change, was the power that the respective procedure afforded to the Parliament.

The major law-making procedure under the original 1957 Rome Treaty was the **consultation procedure**, which gave only a modest role to the EP in Community law-making. It basically required the **Council**, before adopting a Commission proposal, either by QMV or unanimity, to obtain an **opinion** from the **Parliament**, although it did **not have to follow** it. Today, the consultation procedure where the Council acts unanimously is a form of the special legislative procedure (→ *3.10*).

In 1986, the SEA (→ *2.1*) introduced the **cooperation procedure**. This could be seen as an acknowledgement of the EP's increased democratic legitimacy after the first direct elections in 1979 giving the Parliament a greater say in Community legislation (→ *2.15*). In a complex procedural system the cooperation procedure provided for **two readings**: a **'common position'** to be adopted by the Council on the basis of the Parliament's opinion on the **Commission proposal**; and the requirement of **unanimity** in the Council if **Parliament** should be **overruled**.

The cooperation procedure initially applied to a considerable number of legislative measures to be adopted in the field of the single market, as well as to environmental measures, health and safety

for workers and social policy measures under the Social Policy
Protocol (→ *10.17*).

With the Maastricht and the Amsterdam Treaty these areas have all
become subject to the **co-decision procedure**, leaving only certain
issues concerning the European Monetary Union for cooperation.
The co-decision procedure, introduced with the Maastricht Treaty,
was the first procedure effectively making the EP a co-legislator.
Hence, this was the most significant increase of the power of the
EP.

With the entrance into force of the Lisbon Treaty, the co-operation
procedure was completely abolished. The co-decision procedure was
renamed **'ordinary legislative procedure'** in order to indicate that
the standard procedure for Union legislation shall divide the legislative authority between the Council and the Parliament. The gradual
shift towards more involvement of the Parliament in the adoption of
EU legislation partly remedied the deficiencies in democratic legitimacy of the Union (→ *3.12*).

3.9 How does the ordinary legislative procedure work?

With the amendments of the Treaty of Amsterdam a large portion of
important Community law-making became subject to the so-called
co-decision procedure according to former Article 251 TEC. The
importance of this procedure is underlined by the fact that the Lisbon
Treaty simply refers to it as the **'ordinary legislative procedure'**
which consists 'in the joint adoption by the European Parliament
and the Council of a regulation, directive or decision on a proposal
from the Commission' (Article 289(1) TFEU). The ordinary legislative procedure is defined in **Article 294 TFEU**. It basically provides
for **two successive readings**, by Parliament and the Council, of a
Commission proposal and the convocation, if the two co-legislators

cannot agree, of a **'Conciliation Committee'**. This is composed of Council and Parliament representatives, with the participation of the Commission, and should help to reach an agreement which may then be finalised in a **third reading**. Parliament may ultimately block the adoption through its veto.

Under this procedure a **Commission proposal** is sent to both the Parliament and the Council to a first reading. If the Parliament does not propose any amendments, or, if it does so, and the Council accepts them all, the proposal may be adopted accordingly. Otherwise, the Council shall adopt its position and communicate it to the Parliament. In the second reading, the Parliament then has three months after which it may either:

(1) approve of the position of the Council;

(2) reject the position of the Council by majority of its members; or

(3) propose amendments to the position of the Council equally by majority of its members.

In the first case, the act will be deemed to have been adopted in accordance with the position of the Council. In the second case, if Parliament exercises its **'veto power'**, the proposed act will be deemed not to have been adopted. In the case of parliamentary amendments, on which the Commission shall deliver its opinion, the following steps may occur:

(1) If the Council approves of all amendments by qualified majority, the act will be deemed to have been adopted accordingly (subject, however, to the qualification that the adoption of amendments on which the Commission has delivered a negative opinion is only possible by a unanimous vote).

(2) If, however, the Council does not approve of all the amendments of the EP, the President of the Council, in agreement with the President of the EP, shall convene within six weeks a meeting of the **Conciliation Committee**. This committee, consisting of an equal number of representatives of the Council and the EP, has

the task of reconciling the disagreement and agreeing on a joint text. Failure to reach such a joint text will lead to the lapse of the legislative proposal.

(3) If the Conciliation Committee does, however, approve a joint text within six weeks, Parliament and Council have another six weeks for a third reading in which they may, by absolute majority of votes cast and by qualified majority, respectively, adopt the act in accordance with the joint text.

The former co-decision procedure was initially intended for measures in the fields of harmonisation, free movement of workers, the freedom of establishment, education, culture, public health and consumer protection. After the changes introduced by the Treaty of Amsterdam it became applicable to a wide variety of areas. Today, as indicated by its designation as 'ordinary legislative procedure', it is certainly the **most important law-making procedure**.

? 3.10 Briefly outline the most important forms of the special legislative procedure

The **special legislative procedure** applies where this is provided for in the Treaties (Article 289(2) TFEU). However, according to Article 48(7) TEU, where the TFEU envisages a legislative act to be adopted according to a special legislative procedure, 'the European Council may adopt a decision allowing for the adoption of such acts in accordance with the ordinary legislative procedure'. This shall take effect if national Parliaments do not oppose the decision within six months.

The special legislative procedure can take various forms, the most important of which are the following:

In the **consultation procedure**, a legislative act is adopted by the **Council acting unanimously or by qualified majority after**

consultation with the Parliament. The meaning of consultation is determined by the case-law on the former consultation procedure ($\rightarrow$ *3.8*). The ECJ has tried to interpret the procedural requirements in a strict manner to the advantage of the Parliament. In the *Isoglucose* Case, Case 138/79 *Roquette Frères* v. *Council* [1980] ECR 3333, it held, for instance, that the Council's obligation to wait for the EP's opinion constituted an **'essential procedural safeguard'**, disregard of which led to the annulment of Council legislation ($\rightarrow$ *5.9*). In another case, the so-called *Generalised Tariff Preferences* case, Case C-65/93 *Parliament* v. *Council* [1995] ECR I-643, it held that, although there were no fixed deadlines, **sufficient time** is **required** for the EP so that only in urgent cases would the Council be allowed not to await the Parliament's opinion. In the *Road Taxes* case, Case C-21/94 *Parliament* v. *Council* [1996] ECR I-1827, the ECJ further clarified that there was a **duty** to **re-consult** the EP 'when the text finally adopted, viewed as a whole, departs substantially from the text on which the Parliament has already been consulted, except where the amendments essentially correspond to [its] wishes'.

Today the most important use of this procedure is the Union's harmonisation powers, officially called the 'approximation of laws ... as directly affect the establishment or functioning of the internal market', provided for in Article 115 TFEU, harmonisation of indirect taxation (Article 113 TFEU), rights to vote and stand in municipal and EP elections (Article 22 TFEU), furthermore social security and social protection (Article 21(3) TFEU), protection by diplomatic and consular authorities of any Member State (Article 23 TFEU) and measures regarding operational police cooperation (Article 87(3) TFEU) ($\rightarrow$ *10.30*).

Another form of the special legislative procedure is the adoption of a legislative act by the **Council acting unanimously with the consent of the Parliament**. This procedure, previously referred to as **assent procedure** and now called the **consent procedure**, applies to sensitive issues, for example action to combat various forms of

discrimination (Article 19(1) TFEU), the enhancement of citizens'
rights (Article 25 TFEU), the establishment of a European Public
Prosecutor (Article 86(1) TFEU), the creation of a uniform method
for electing MEPs (Article 223(1) TFEU), implementing measures
for the system of own resources of the EU (Article 311 TFEU) and
actions on the basis of the 'flexibility clause' (→ *3.4*) (Article 352
(1) TFEU).

The **EP can also adopt a legislative act with the approval of
the Council**. This is the case for measures regarding regulations and
general conditions governing the performance of the duties of its
members (Article 223 (1) TFEU), the exercise of the inquiry by the
temporary Committee of Inquiry (Article 226 TFEU) and regulations and conditions regarding the performance of the Ombudsman's
duties (Article 228(4) TFEU).

? 3.11 Explain the choice of legislative procedures if more than one legal basis is available

By selecting a particular legal basis for Union legislation, the EU
institutions may try to avoid 'problems' either in the Council, for
example, by using a procedure requiring QMV instead of unanimity,
or in the Parliament, for example, by opting for a procedure where
Parliament has less influence. In order to prevent such **'procedure
shopping'**, the ECJ has exercised its annulment power (→ *5.8*).

According to settled ECJ case law, as expressed in the *Indirect
Tax Recovery* Case, Case C-388/01 *Commission* v. *Council* [2004]
ECR I-4829, 'the choice of the legal basis for a Community measure must rest on objective factors amenable to judicial review,
which include in particular the aim and the content of the measure'.
Where the Court is able to identify a primary purpose and content
of Community legislation, 'the act must be based on a single legal

basis, namely that required by the main or predominant purpose or component'.

The ECJ's search for the **primary purpose** of Union legislation in order to determine its legal basis has already been pursued in the so-called *Waste Directive* Case. In Case C-155/91 *Commission* v. *Council* [1993] ECR I-939, the Court stipulated that the 'nature, aim and context of the act in question' should be analysed. In the Court's view the main focus of the directive was environmental, implementing such ecological principles as rectification at source and waste transport minimisation, and not the internal market principle of free movement of waste. It, thus, found that the environmental basis for legislation under Article 130s TEC (now Article 192 TFEU) was correct and prevailed over the internal market basis of Article 100a TEC (now Article 115 TFEU).

Where it is not possible to identify a primary purpose and content of Union legislation, the ECJ will apply a **hierarchical test**, establishing which of the Treaty articles serving as possible legal basis prevails over the other. The use of this different test can be seen in the *Titanium Dioxide* Case as well as subsequent jurisprudence, and it explains why the outcome was different. Case C-300/89 *Commission* v. *Council* [1991] ECR 1991 I-2867, concerned the use of the correct legislative procedure by the Community's institutions, in particular, whether a directive, that is, Council Directive 89/428/EEC of 21 June 1989 on procedures for harmonising the programmes for the reduction and eventual elimination of pollution caused by waste from the titanium dioxide industry, was to be adopted in accordance with Article 100a TEC (calling for the co-operation procedure) or according to Article 130s TEC (providing for unanimity and EP consultation). The ECJ annulled the 1989 directive which had been adopted unanimously by the Council on the basis of then Article 130s TEC (now Article 192 TFEU). While acknowledging that both provisions could serve as the legal basis for the Community act in question, the Court held that the 'use of both provisions as a joint legal basis would divest the cooperation procedure of its very substance' and that it was thus necessary to determine the appropriate legal basis. The ECJ held that this would have been then Article 100a TEC (now Article 114 TFEU) calling for the co-operation procedure and thus a larger role of EP. In the Court's view the internal market harmonisation power under Article 100a TEC could pursue environmental purposes and was thus hierarchically superior to Article 130s TEC.

? 3.12 What does the notion of 'democratic deficit' stand for?

Since the 1990s the debate about the **democratic legitimacy** of the EU has focused on a number of actual and perceived deficiencies, mostly under the concept of 'democratic deficit'. It stands for a lack of direct democratic law-making as a result of less than fully representative decision making, for a 'bypassing of democracy' through **comitology** (→ *2.13*) and other legislative techniques where the executive dominates, and for the 'transparency and complexity issue' resulting from Council voting behind closed doors, etc.

One of the possible answers to the lack of direct democratic legitimacy is usually found in the **'indirect legitimacy'** through representatives of the Member States in the Council. These are government officials who are selected on the basis of a democratic consensus in the Member States. This dual form of democratic representation is expressed in the new 'provisions on democratic principles' of the post-Lisbon TEU. Article 10(2) TEU states that '[c]itizens are directly represented at Union level in the European Parliament' and that 'Member States are represented in the European Council by their Heads of State or Government and in the Council by their governments, themselves democratically accountable either to their national Parliaments, or to their citizens'. The increased role of the

EP in EU law-making (→ *3.8*), whose members have been directly elected since 1979 (→ *2.14*), may equally counterweight the present 'democratic deficit'.

The Treaty of Lisbon also tried to counter the democratic deficit by enhancing the role of national parliaments. Article 12 TEU in combination with Lisbon Treaty Protocols provides for enhanced direct **information** of national parliaments with regard to draft legislative acts of the Union, as well as the possibility to **intervene** in draft EU legislation for failure to comply with the principle of **subsidiarity** (→ *3.6*).

Finally, the Lisbon Treaty introduced the European citizens' initiative as a new form of participatory democracy. Pursuant to Article 11(4) TEU '[n]ot less than one million citizens who are nationals of a significant number of Member States may take the initiative of inviting the European Commission, within the framework of its powers, to submit any appropriate proposal on matters where citizens consider that a legal act of the Union is required for the purpose of implementing the Treaties'.

4   The effect of Union law

Union law, that is, the treaties and secondary law made according to the different legislative procedures, is **directly applied** and **enforced** by **EU institutions** only exceptionally. The most important exception relates to the Commission's power to enforce EU **competition law** (Articles 101 and 102 TFEU (ex Articles 81 and 82 TEC), as well as Regulation 17, now Regulation 1/2003). In addition, the Commission also exercises other treaty-based or delegated powers.

Most Union law, however, is **applied** and **enforced** in a **decentralised fashion** by **national authorities**. As a rule, the **courts** and **administrative agencies** of the Member States apply and enforce 'directly applicable' EU law as well as nationally implemented non-directly applicable Union law.

This chapter will explain how the European Court of Justice has made Union law ever more effective by declaring not only **regulations**, but also **Treaty provisions** and provisions in **directives** – under certain circumstances – **directly applicable/effective** in the legal systems of the Member States and by stating that, in case of conflict with national law, EU law enjoys **primacy/supremacy**.

4.1 What do we understand by 'direct effect'?

A norm of international or supranational law is said to have 'direct effect' if it is sufficiently **clear**, **precise** and **unconditional** to be invoked before national courts or administrative agencies.

In EU law 'direct effect' may attach to provisions of the Treaty, of international agreements of the Union and secondary legislation, including, under certain circumstances, even to directives.

As opposed to **general international law**, where states are considered to be **free** as to **how** they **implement** international obligations and where direct effect, thus, normally depends upon national constitutional law governing the 'incorporation' of international law into the national legal order, the ECJ developed case law according to which the **direct effect** of **Union law** is an **inherent characteristic** of, and required by, EU law. The Court has already stated in the famous *Van Gend* Case, Case 26/62 *Van Gend en Loos* v. *Nederlandse Administratie der Belastingen* [1963] ECR 1 (→ *4.4*), that:

> "independently of the legislation of Member States, Community law therefore not only imposes obligations on individuals but is also intended to confer upon them rights which become part of their legal heritage."

4.2 What is the difference between 'direct applicability' and 'direct effect'?

To a large extent these two terms are used **interchangeably**. Even early ECJ cases such as *Van Gend* used them synonymously. There is one distinction that may be derived directly from the text of the EU Treaty. While Article 288 TFEU (ex Article 249 TEC) (→ *ch. 3*) states that regulations are 'directly applicable in all Member States', the Treaty does not use the term 'direct effect' at all. It also does not provide for the 'direct applicability' of certain Treaty norms or rules contained in directives. Therefore, 'direct effect' can be seen as a substitute for a largely similar concept and is mostly used in respect of Treaty provisions and directives.

In a number of ECJ cases, 'direct effect' is used when emphasising that rights are conferred upon **individuals**; it thus mainly implies that individuals can rely upon or **invoke** a norm having direct effect before national courts and tribunals.

? 4.3 What is the rationale for 'direct effect'?

The major policy rationale behind 'direct effect' of Union law norms lies in the fact that this strongly enhances the effectiveness (*'effet utile'*; → 3.2) and **uniform application** of EU law, and thereby contributes to the ideal of legal integration by creating a homogeneous legal order in which all market participants enjoy the same legal rights and obligations. According to Case 26/62 *Van Gend en Loos* v. *Nederlandse Administratie der Belastingen* [1963] ECR 1 (→ 4.4), the Treaty implies 'more than mutual obligations of States, also their nationals are subjects of this new legal order'.

A further, more technical justification for 'direct effect' stems from the procedural devices available under the TFEU. Article 267 TFEU (ex Article 234 TEC), which enables national courts to refer questions concerning the validity and interpretation of EU law to the ECJ (→ 5.14–18), somehow presupposes the direct relevance of EU law in private party suits before national courts. Direct effect thus makes **'decentralised law enforcement'** possible, and thereby adds to the traditional international control of Treaty compliance by actions brought against Member States by the Commission or by other Member States according to Articles 258 and 259 TFEU (ex Articles 226 and 227 TEC) (→ *5.11, 5.12*).

4.4 Can Treaty provisions have direct effect?

The most important 'objective' requirement for 'direct effect' seems to be that the norm in question has to be sufficiently 'clear, precise and unconditional' (→ *4.1*). In its case law the ECJ has accorded **direct effect** to a number of **TEC (now TFEU) provisions** and clarified the meaning of the direct applicability of regulations and decisions.

The first case establishing that Treaty provisions may have direct effect was the famous *Van Gend* Case, Case 26/62 *Van Gend en Loos* v. *Nederlandse Administratie der Belastingen* [1963] ECR 1. It involved a Dutch importer who claimed that he was charged an increased import duty on products from Germany contrary to then Article 12 TEC (now Article 30 TFEU) (→ *7.2*). The Court interpreted the obligation under this Article not to impose any new or higher import duties as a 'clear and unconditional … negative obligation … ideally adapted to produce direct effects in the legal relationships between Member States and their subjects'. Going beyond the wording of Article 12 TEC, the Court also found that this Article applied and explained one of the 'essential provisions' of the Treaty, that is, the prohibition of customs duties and charges having equivalent effect. It considered this to be relevant with regard to the **general scheme** of the EC Treaty. Lastly, with regard to the **'spirit'** of the Treaty, the ECJ noted that its **objective** to establish a Common Market (→ *7.1*) 'implies that this Treaty is more than an agreement which merely creates mutual obligations between the contracting states'. Rather, the Court held that 'the Community constitutes a new **legal order of international law** for the benefit of which the states have limited their sovereign rights, albeit within limited fields, and the **subjects** of which **comprise** not only Member States but also their **nationals**'. Thus, the Court concluded that 'according to the spirit, the general scheme and the wording of the Treaty, Article 12 must be interpreted as producing **direct effects** and creating **individual rights** which national courts must protect'.

4.5 Are there any limits to the potential direct effect of Treaty provisions?

In subsequent cases also **'positive obligations'** were clearly held to produce **'direct effect'**. The required standard of 'clear, precise and unconditional' has been interpreted rather liberally in a number of far-reaching decisions by the ECJ. For instance, in Case 2/74 *Reyners* v. *Belgium* [1974] ECR 631, involving a clear discrimination on the basis of nationality, the Court declared that ex Article 52 TEC (now Article 49 TFEU) had direct effect and could be relied upon by an individual so discriminated against (→ *8.12, 8.13*). This was remarkable because Article 52 TEC, at that time, provided for the abolition of restrictions on the **freedom of establishment** of Community nationals in states other than that of their nationality 'within the framework of the provisions set out below'. The relevant 'framework' included a general programme and a number of directives which, contrary to the intentions of the Treaty, had not been adopted after the transitional period as planned. Still, the Court held that 'after the expiry of the transitory period the directives provided for by the chapter on the right of establishment have become superfluous with regard to implementing the rule on nationality, since this is henceforth sanctioned by the Treaty itself with direct effect'.

In Case 43/75 *Defrenne* v. *Sabena* [1976] ECR 455, which can be regarded as an outstanding example of **teleological interpretation** guided by the *effet utile* of Union law, the Court considered the principle of **equal pay** to be **directly effective** (→ *5.10, 10.18*). This was remarkable since the text of what was then Article 119 TEC (now the amended Article 157 TFEU) clearly was not very precise.

Former Article 119(1) TEC provided as follows: 'Each Member State shall during the first stage ensure and subsequently maintain the application of the principle that men and women should receive equal pay for equal work.' Nevertheless, the ECJ found that the plaintiff could rely upon this provision against her employer before Belgian courts.

The limits as to the **objective requirements** of clarity and precision (→ *4.1*) can be seen in Case 126/86 *Zaera* v. *Instituto Nacional de la Seguridad Social* [1987] ECR 3697, a case in which a Spanish national wanted to rely on former Article 2 TEC in order to challenge a Spanish social security incompatibility provision prohibiting him from becoming a civil servant while receiving a retirement pension. Article 2 TEC provided, among other things, that 'the Community shall have as its task ... an accelerated raising of the standard of living'. In rejecting the claim, the ECJ reasoned that the accelerated raising of the standard of living was one of the aims of the EC, which 'owing to its general terms and its systematic dependence on the establishment of the Common Market and progressive approximation of economic policies, cannot impose legal obligations on Member States or confer rights on individuals'.

? 4.6 What are the pre-conditions for a norm of secondary Union law to have direct effect?

Although **regulations** are by definition 'directly applicable in all Member States' they may, in **exceptional** cases, require **implementing measures** by the Member States if their provisions are not sufficiently clear and precise or, more likely, if they expressly provide for such implementing measures. In Case 50/76 *Amsterdam Bulb BV* [1977] ECR 137, the ECJ has warned Member States, however, that with regard to directly applicable regulations they may not 'adopt any measure which would conceal the Community nature and

effects of any legal provision from the person to whom it applies';
for instance, by enacting implementing legislation in a somewhat
different form.

The Treaty does not say anything about the direct applicability
of **decisions**. Article 288 TFEU (ex Article 249 TEC) merely states:
'A decision shall be binding in its entirety. A decision which specifies those to whom it is addressed shall be binding only on them.'
The question that arose in litigation before German courts was
whether individuals could rely upon Council decisions addressed to
the Member States which related to the VAT directive. In a preliminary ruling ($\rightarrow$ 5.14), Case 9/70 *Franz Grad* v. *Finanzamt Traunstein*
[1970] ECR 838, the ECJ reasoned that in cases where:

> "the Community authorities by means of a decision have
> imposed an obligation on a Member State or all the
> Member States to act in a certain way, the effectiveness
> (*l'effet utile*) of such a measure would be weakened if the
> nationals of that State could not invoke it in the courts and
> the national courts would not take it into consideration as
> part of Community law."

? 4.7 Are directives 'directly effective'?

As a matter of principle, **directives** are **not directly applicable** or
effective. Article 288 TFEU (ex Article 249 TEC) provides that they
'shall be binding, as to the result to be achieved, upon each Member
State to which it is addressed, but shall leave to the national authorities the choice of form and methods' ($\rightarrow$ 3.1). As a primary tool for
legal **harmonisation** they are intended to lead to an 'approximation
of the law', not to absolute unification, as do regulations. By leaving the choice of implementation to the Member States, directives
are a **means of federalism**. Serious problems do arise, however,

if Member States refuse or fail to implement properly. The effectiveness of Union law would clearly suffer under such conditions. Thus, inspired by its *effet utile* approach, the ECJ has developed a jurisprudence according to which even provisions of directives may exceptionally be considered directly effective.

The leading case is Case 41/74 *Van Duyn* v. *Home Office* [1974] ECR 1337, in which a Dutch national was refused entry into the UK because she intended to work for the Church of Scientology, which was officially regarded as 'socially harmful'. The ECJ held that she could rely on a provision of Directive 64/221, which required that public policy measures had to be based on the personal conduct of the individual concerned ($\rightarrow$ *8.9*).

Direct effect may work both as a **'shield'** and a **'sword'**. In the *Ratti* Case, Case 148/78 *Ministerio Pubblico* v. *Ratti* [1979] ECR 1629, it protected an Italian national who had complied with the labelling provisions of two directives which had not been implemented in time by the Italian legislator against criminal prosecution under the more stringent Italian rules. The Court held that 'a Member State which has not adopted the implementing measures required by the directive in the prescribed periods may not rely, as against individuals, on its own failure to perform the obligations which the directive entails'. It thereby provided an important policy rationale for the direct effect of directives, the **estoppel** reasoning, that is, Member States should be precluded from relying on their own failure to implement directives correctly.

In Case 8/81 *Becker* v. *Finanzamt Münster-Innenstadt* [1982] ECR 53, direct effect was used as a 'sword' by allowing a German taxpayer to calculate her tax returns in accordance with unimplemented provisions of Community directives.

The present law on direct effect of directives may be restated as follows: wherever **provisions** of a **directive** are **unconditional and sufficiently precise** and **in the absence of implementing measures** adopted **within the prescribed period**, they can be **directly relied**

upon, even against any national provision which is incompatible with the directive. This latter aspect is discussed below under the heading of **supremacy** (→ *4.10, 4.11*) of EU law.

? 4.8 What is 'horizontal' direct effect?

The cases starting with *Van Duyn* (→ *4.7*) concerned individuals who were able to rely upon directives vis-à-vis Member States which had failed to implement them (so-called **vertical direct effect**). At some stage the question arose as to whether such direct effect could also take place vis-à-vis private individuals, that is, **horizontally**.

Clearly, this would enhance the effectiveness of Union law (*effet utile*). However, since the leading case of *Marshall*, Case 152/84 *Marshall* v. *Southampton and South-West Hampshire Area Health Authority (Teaching)* [1986] ECR 723 (→ *10.24*), the ECJ has consistently **refused** to permit a **horizontal direct effect** for **directives** as a matter of principle. Based on the wording of Article 288 TFEU (ex Article 249 TEC), the Court has argued that a directive was binding only upon 'each Member State to which it is addressed. It follows that such a directive may not of itself impose obligations on an individual and that a provision of a directive may not be relied upon as such against such a person.' The advocate-general's opinion (→ *5.2*) added two further concerns militating against 'horizontal' direct effect. First, it would have eliminated the **difference** between **regulations and directives**; and second, since directives were not published in the Official Journal, which was the case until the entry into force of the Maastricht Treaty (→ *1.8*), the private party against which it might be relied upon may not even have had notice of it. One may add that 'horizontal' direct effect would be difficult to reconcile with another main justification for direct effect next to the estoppel argument (→ *4.7*), the rationale of punishing a defaulting

Member State. Why should private parties be blamed for the failure of states to implement directives?

In order to mitigate the limiting result of denying 'horizontal' direct effect, the ECJ has developed a number of judicial techniques **expanding** the effect of **direct effect**.

Starting with the *Marshall* Case, the Court has relied on a **broad concept** of the **state** which includes the **state** in its **'private capacity'** as an employer. Summarising its own case law, the ECJ noted in Case C-188/89 *Foster* v. *British Gas* [1990] ECR I-3313, that directives could be relied upon against tax authorities, local or regional authorities, constitutionally independent authorities responsible for the maintenance of public order and safety and public authorities providing public health services. It then concluded:

> "It follows from the foregoing that a body, whatever its legal form, which has been made responsible, pursuant to a measure adopted by the State, for providing a public service under the control of the State and has for that purpose special powers beyond those which result from the normal rules applicable in relations between individuals, is included in any event among the bodies against which the provisions of a directive capable of having direct effect may be relied upon."

An alternative avenue was opened up by the Court's development of an **'indirect (horizontal) effect'** of directives. According to this **interpretation maxim**, national law has to be interpreted **in the light of directives**. It was expressly used in Case 106/89 *Marleasing SA* v. *La Comercial* [1990] ECR I-4135, in which the plaintiff company sought a declaratory judgment invalidating the contract of incorporation of another Spanish company that had been procured by misrepresentation and fraud to the detriment of its creditors, one of whom was Marleasing. Spanish law provided for such a remedy, whereas the defendant claimed that the exhaustive list of a non-implemented Council directive, which did not include such a remedy for misrepresentation and fraud, would exclude Marleasing's claim. In a preliminary ruling the ECJ denied horizontal direct effect, but held that:

> "a national court called upon to interpret [national law] is required to do so, as far as possible in the light of the wording and the purpose of the Directive in order to achieve a result pursued by the latter and thereby comply with the third paragraph of Article [288 TFEU]."

More recently, the Court demanded some modified 'indirect (horizontal) effect' of directives even before the expiry of the implementation period. In Case C-214/04 *Adeneler and others* v. *ELOG* [2006] ECR I-6057, the ECJ stated that 'from the date upon which a directive has entered into force, the courts of the Member States must refrain as far as possible from interpreting domestic law in a manner which might seriously compromise, after the period for transposition has expired, attainment of the objective pursued by that directive.'

The Court has set some limits to the principle of 'indirect effect' of directives, although some cases blur the line between mere 'indirect effect' and 'horizontal' direct effect. In Case 80/86 *Kolpinghuis Nijmegen* [1987] ECR 3969, the Court held that 'a directive cannot, of itself and independently of a law adopted for its implementation, have the effect of determining or aggravating the liability in criminal law of persons who act in contravention of the provision of that directive'.

Horizontal direct effect is, however, recognised for **Treaty provisions** (→ *4.4, 4.5, 8.5*). This was confirmed in Case 43/75 *Defrenne* v. *Sabena* [1976] ECR 455, for Article 119 TEC (now Article 157 TFEU) (→ *4.5, 10.18*). It is also clear for the Treaty rules on competition in Articles 101 and 102 TFEU (ex Articles 81 and 82 TEC) (→ *ch. 9*). In Case C-281/93 *Angonese* [2000] ECR I-4134, it was also found to apply to Article 39 TEC (now Article 45 TFEU) concerning the free movement of workers (→ *8.5*).

4.9 Are there any remedies if directives are not 'directly effective'?

In the *Francovich* **case**, Joined Cases C-6/90 and C-9/90 *Francovich and Bonifaci* v. *Italian Republic* [1991] ECR I-5357, the ECJ held that the principle of **responsibility** of the state for **damages** caused to individuals by the state's **violations** of **Union law** is '**inherent in the Treaty system**' and can be based on then Article 5 EEC Treaty (ex Article 10 TEC; now Article 4(3) TEU). Under Article 4(3) TEU they are required to take all appropriate measures, whether general or particular, to ensure fulfilment of the obligations arising out of the Treaties or resulting from the acts of the institutions of the Union, and consequently to nullify the unlawful consequences of a breach of Union law. The plaintiffs had instituted proceedings seeking damages from the Italian state for failure to implement Directive 80/987 on the protection of employees in the event of the insolvency of the employer (→ *10.15*). Their employer had become insolvent and since there were no Italian implementing measures the plaintiffs did not receive any wage payments guaranteed under the directive. The Court held that the directive was **not directly effective** because the obligor under the system of salary protection in case of insolvency was **not clearly determined**. However, the Court enunciated the **principle of state liability** for failure to implement a directive for which it basically set three conditions:

(1) the result prescribed by the directive involves the **grant of rights to individuals**;

(2) the **content** of these rights is **identifiable**; and

(3) there is a **causal link** between the violation of EU law, the non-implementation of the directive, and the damage suffered by individuals.

The Court added that the jurisdiction and procedure for such damage claims are left to the law of the Member States which has to provide **an effective remedy**.

In Joined Cases C-24/93 and C-48/93 *Brasserie du Pêcheur/ Factortame III* [1996] ECR I-1029, the first being a follow-up to the *German Beer* Case (→ *7.8*), the ECJ clarified a number of conceptual issues concerning state liability. It held that compensation was also available in case of breaches of directly effective EU law, such as the free movement of goods (→ *ch. 7*) or the freedom of establishment (→ *ch. 8*). It further held that state liability could be derived not only from Article 4(3) TEU, but was also a 'general principle familiar to the legal systems of the member states that an unlawful act or omission gives rise to an obligation to make good the damage caused' – a general principle which also found its expression in Article 340 TFEU providing for the **non-contractual liability** of the **Community/Union** (→ *10.5*). On the basis of an analogy to the requirements for Community liability under that Treaty Article, the Court slightly modified the requirements set out in the *Francovich* Case for the non-implementation of directives to the following more broadly applicable rule:

> "Community law confers a right to reparation where three conditions are met: the **rule of law infringed** must be intended to **confer rights on individuals**; the **breach** must be **sufficiently serious**; and there must be a direct **causal link** between the breach of the obligation resting on the State and the damage sustained by the injured party."

In Case C-224/01 *Köbler* v. *Austria* [2003] ECR I-10239, the ECJ held that the *Francovich* principle also applied to acts of the **judiciary**, such as a breach of the Article 267(3) TFEU (ex Article 234(3) TEC) obligation to make a reference to the ECJ (→ *5.16, 5.18*). In Case C-173/03 *Traghetti del Mediterraneo* v. *Italy* [2006] ECR I-5177, the ECJ rejected a requirement of intentional fault in the case of state liability for national court decisions. Rather, it held that '**State liability** for damage caused to individuals by reason of an infringement of Community law attributable to a **national court** adjudicating at last instance could be incurred in the exceptional case where that court **manifestly infringed** the applicable law.'

4.10 Explain the significance of the case of *Costa* v. *ENEL*

Mr Costa, shareholder of an electricity company which was nationalised by Italy, was billed for electricity by the national electricity company ENEL. Since he refused to pay his bill he was sued by ENEL. In the national court proceedings, Mr Costa raised as a defence that the nationalisation was contrary to EC law. Just as is the case with Union law now, Community law did not prohibit expropriations because it expressly left issues concerning property ownership outside the scope of the TEC (Article 345 TFEU). Nevertheless, the ECJ in Case 6/64 *Flaminio Costa* v. *ENEL* [1964] ECR 585, held that then Article 37 TEC (now Article 37 TFEU), prohibiting the introduction of any new state monopolies of a commercial character, was directly effective and prohibited the Italian nationalisation measures. The matter was, however, a little more complicated since the Italian nationalisation legislation was adopted after the conclusion of the EC Treaty, and according to Italian constitutional law the norm later in time (*lex posterior*) would prevail over the earlier one. Reiterating its reasoning in the *Van Gend* Case (→ *4.4*), the ECJ nevertheless insisted that Community law stands for an **autonomous legal order** which by itself required not only direct effect but also – in case of conflict between a directly applicable Community norm and a norm of the national legal order – the **'supremacy'** or **'primacy'** of EC law. According to the Court:

> "the integration into the laws of each Member State of provisions which derive from the Community, and more generally the terms and the spirit of the Treaty, make it impossible for the States, as a corollary, to accord

precedence to a unilateral and subsequent measure over a
legal system accepted by them on a basis of reciprocity.'"

It is clear that the *effet utile* (→ *3.2, 4.3, 4.7*) has found victory
again: the **supremacy** of EU law over national law enhances the
legal uniformity and effectiveness of EU law.

In Article I-6, the **Draft Constitution Treaty** contained a provision aimed at codifying this principle by stating that the constitution
as well as secondary law 'shall have **primacy** over the law of the
Member States'. The drafters of the Lisbon Treaty could no longer
agree on such a bold statement. Thus, they hid their endorsement of
the *Costa* jurisprudence in Declaration 17 to the Treaty of Lisbon,
which provides more cryptically:

> "The Conference recalls that, in accordance with well
> settled case law of the Court of Justice of the European
> Union, the Treaties and the law adopted by the Union
> on the basis of the Treaties have primacy over the law of
> Member States, under the conditions laid down by the
> said case law. The Conference has also decided to attach
> as an Annex to this Final Act the Opinion of the Council
> Legal Service on the primacy of EC law as set out in
> 11197/07 (JUR 260): 'Opinion of the Council Legal
> Service of 22 June 2007. It results from the case-law of the
> Court of Justice that **primacy** of EC law is a **cornerstone**
> **principle** of Community law. According to the Court, this
> principle is inherent to the specific nature of the European
> Community. At the time of the first judgment of this
> established case law (*Costa/ENEL*, 15 July 1964, Case
> 6/6411) there was no mention of primacy in the treaty. It is
> still the case today. The fact that the principle of primacy
> will not be included in the future treaty shall not in any
> way change the existence of the principle and the existing
> case-law of the Court of Justice.'"

In later cases, such as Case 11/79 *Internationale Handelsgesellschaft*
[1970] ECR 1125, the ECJ clarified the meaning of the *Costa*

judgment and held that the supremacy of EU law also applied vis-à-vis national constitutional law (→ *6.2, 6.8, 6.9*).

4.11 What are the *Simmenthal* Cases?

The impact of a conflict between national constitutional law and Community law came to a head in the *Simmenthal* Case, where it was a rather unimportant piece of secondary Community law that collided with Italian constitutional law.

The first *Simmenthal* Case, Case 35/76 *Simmenthal SpA* v. *Ministero dello Finanze* [1976] ECR 1871, was a preliminary ruling in 1976 in which the ECJ held that Italian **charges** for veterinary and health inspections of imported beef were effectively **equivalent to customs duties** and thus contrary to the free movement of goods (→ *7.2*).

Simmenthal II, Case 106/77 *Amministrazione delle Finanze dello Stato* v. *Simmenthal SpA* [1978] ECR 629, was a follow-up preliminary ruling concerning an Italian court ordering the fiscal authorities to **repay the illegal charges** to the importer. In these proceedings the Italian Ministry of Finance argued that according to Italian law only the Italian Constitutional Court could invalidate an Italian law (on which the charges were based) conflicting with higher norms (the EEC Treaty). The Italian court again referred the case to the ECJ, asking whether the national law must be immediately disregarded or not. The ECJ reiterated the principle of **primacy** of EC law and deduced from it the rule that 'every national court must, in a case within its jurisdiction, apply Community law in its entirety and protect rights which the latter confers upon individuals and must set aside any provision of national law which may conflict with it, whether prior or subsequent to the Community rule'. Thus, in the view of the ECJ it was 'not necessary to request or await the prior setting aside of such provision by legislative or other constitutional means'.

4.12 May international agreements produce direct effect?

The question of the direct effect of **international agreements** (→ *11.3*) relates not only to their status within the legal order of the Member States but also to the Union legal order, in particular whether they may be invoked before the ECJ.

With regard to **free trade agreements** (→ *7.1*, *11.3*) concluded by the Community with third countries, the ECJ held in the *Kupferberg* Case, Case 104/81 *Hauptzollamt Mainz* v. *Kupferberg* [1982] ECR 3641, that certain provisions of the EC–Portugal Free Trade Agreement (before Portugal joined the Community) did have **direct effect**, because they were sufficiently precise, unconditional and their direct application was within the purpose of the agreement. This ruling immediately followed a diametrically opposed outcome in the *Polydor* Case, Case 270/80 *Polydor Ltd & RSO Records Inc.* v. *Harlequin Record Shops Ltd and others* [1982] ECR 329, wherein the ECJ had held that another provision of the same free trade agreement – though identically worded to a directly applicable TEC provision – should not be given direct effect since the free trade agreement and the TEC had different aims and purposes.

The ECJ has meanwhile given direct effect to a number of provisions contained in **association and cooperation agreements** (→ *11.3*, *11.14*), and more recently also to the provisions on freedom of establishment of some **Europe agreements** (→ *1.7*, *11.16*) with Eastern European countries. In Case C-192/89 *Sevince* v. *Staatssecretaris Van Justitie* [1990] ECR I-3461, even the secondary legislation of such agreements, such as **decisions** adopted by

Association Councils (→ *11.14*), has been regarded as amenable to **direct effect**.

4.13 May an individual claim that EU legislation is in violation of GATT/WTO principles?

Contrary to its case law on free trade agreements and despite quite a lot of criticism, the ECJ has consistently **refused** to consider **GATT** provisions **directly applicable**.

The leading case is Case 21–24/72 *International Fruit Company* v. *Produktschap voor Groenten en Fruit* [1972] ECR 1219 (→ *11.13*), in which an apple importer's import licence was rejected by Dutch customs authorities on the basis of EC regulations which were arguably in violation of Article XI GATT. The ECJ rejected the direct effect of this provision, holding that the GATT did not confer rights on citizens of the Community on which they could rely before the courts. The Court invoked the **'great flexibility'** of the GATT's provisions, the possibility of **derogation** from its obligations, the option of measures in exceptional difficulties and the peculiar **GATT conflict settlement provisions**, such as unilateral suspension rights, as reasons preventing the direct effect of the GATT.

This negative attitude towards the GATT was reaffirmed in one of the many *Banana* cases before the ECJ. In Case 280/93 *Germany* v. *Commission* [1994] ECR I-4873, the Court held that 'GATT rules are not unconditional ... an obligation to recognize them as rules of international law which are directly applicable in the domestic legal systems of the contracting parties cannot be based on the spirit, general scheme or terms of GATT'. One of the main reasons why the GATT provisions were considered not to be unconditional was that the GATT did contain numerous exceptions, had only a rather weak dispute settlement system and always provided the opportunity for 'losing' parties to offer compensation instead of complying with the recommendations of a GATT panel ruling. With the new dispute settlement provisions of the WTO after the Uruguay Round, which also implied a 'juridification' of the trade diplomacy of the GATT, many observers expected a change of attitude on the part of the ECJ. This expectation was, however, disappointed in Case C-149/96 *Portugal* v. *Council* [1999] ECR I-8395, in which the ECJ found that 'WTO agreements are not in principle among the rules in the light of which the Court is to review the legality of measures adopted by the Community institutions'. The Court reasoned that even under the 1994 WTO Dispute Settlement Understanding the parties still had broad opportunities for negotiations. Probably most important, the Court noted that the lack of reciprocity with regard to the willingness to directly apply GATT law might lead to serious imbalances which would deprive the Community of the possibility of negotiating trade compensation instead of complying with the strict terms of the WTO agreements.

In practice, the **denial of direct effect** has been somewhat **mitigated** in two types of situations in which the Court has held that GATT provisions may be invoked in order to claim an incompatibility of EC legislation. In accordance with ECJ case law, the Court may thus review the GATT legality of Community acts (a) if the Community **intended to implement** a particular GATT obligation (Case C-69/89 *Nakajima* v. *Council* [1991] ECR 2069); or (b) if the Community act **expressly referred to** specific GATT provisions (Case 70/87 *Fediol* v. *Commission* [1989] ECR 1781).

5 Judicial control within the Union

To a considerable degree EU law has been shaped by the **European Court of Justice** (ECJ). The Court has rightly been called a **'motor of integration'** because, in the years of Euroscepticism and political standstill on the question of 'deepening' integration, it has largely created the *'acquis communautaire'*. Its case law, in particular in the field of the **four freedoms**, has made a significant contribution to the harmonisation and mutual recognition of national standards which, in turn, was essential for the creation of a true **internal market**.

The Court was able to attain this crucial role as a **'quasi-law-maker'** because of its broad jurisdictional powers. In fact, the ECJ acts as **'constitutional court'** of the EU exercising **'judicial review'** over both the EU and its Member States. According to the ECJ's own reasoning in Case 294/83 *Les Verts* v. *Parliament* [1986] ECR 1356, the Community is:

> "based on the rule of law, inasmuch as neither its Member States nor its institutions can avoid a review of whether measures adopted by them are in conformity with the basic constitutional charter, the Treaty. The Treaty established the Court as the judicial body responsible for ensuring that both the Member States and the Community institutions comply with the law."

The ECJ, composed of judges from all Member States, exercises this judicial control mainly through **'annulment actions'** directed against acts of the EU institutions, **'infringement actions'** directed

against Member States and **'preliminary rulings'** providing guidance to national courts for the interpretation of EU law.

The following section will demonstrate that the ECJ's jurisdictional
powers go far beyond the usual dispute settlement mechanisms provided for in international organisations, by explaining in some detail
the Court's powers of judicial control after a brief overview of its
institutional structure. The Treaty of Lisbon has clarified that the ECJ
(now referred to as **'Court of Justice'**) is part of the broader judicial
architecture of the EU. Article 19 TEU states that 'the Court of Justice
of the European Union shall include the Court of Justice, the General
Court and specialised courts'. The **General Court** is the former Court
of First Instance and the most important specialised court currently
existing is the **European Union Civil Service Tribunal**.

5.1 Who sits on the European Court of Justice?

According to Article 253 TFEU (ex Article 223 TEC), the '**Judges**
and **Advocates-General** of the Court of Justice shall be chosen
from persons whose **independence** is beyond doubt and who pos-
sess the qualifications required for appointment to the **highest judicial offices** in their respective countries or who are **jurisconsults of
recognised competence**'. The ECJ, seated in **Luxembourg**, is currently composed of **twenty-seven judges** (one 'nominated' by each
Member State) and **eight advocates-general**. They are appointed by
common accord of the governments of the Member States after having consulted a panel (composed of former EU and senior national
judges) that gives its opinion on the suitability of the person to perform the function of an ECJ judge. They serve for a renewable term
of six years. A **registrar**, who is among other things responsible for
the Court's **administration** and for the **publication** of its decisions,
is elected by the judges. Judges and advocates-general each have
three 'legal secretaries' who perform the tasks of law clerks.

Today, the Court sits in plenary session (as a **'full court'**) only very rarely in cases of 'exceptional importance' or in a number of impeachment-like procedures aimed at depriving senior Union officials of their office. Equally rare are cases decided by a so-called **Grand Chamber** of thirteen judges, which will be convened on the request of a Member State or a Union institution as a party to legal proceedings. Normally, the Court will hear cases in **chambers** of **three** or **five judges**.

Though all Union languages are used in legal proceedings before the Court, its **working language** remains **French**. The ECJ is in permanent session and has delivered several thousand decisions since 1954.

5.2 What is the task of an Advocate-General?

According to Article 252 TFEU (ex Article 222 TEC), it is for the **advocates-general**, 'acting with complete **impartiality** and **independence**, to make, in open court, **reasoned submissions**'. The position of an advocate-general was inspired by the 'commissaire du gouvernement' of the French Conseil d'Etat. It could be viewed as an institutionalised *'amicus curiae'* (literally a 'friend of the court'), whose opinions, although not binding, are in most cases followed by the Court and published as annexes to ECJ judgments. The usually much more extensive and detailed analysis of their opinions helps to understand sometimes rather short Court decisions.

5.3 Describe the scope of jurisdiction of the General Court and the Civil Service Tribunal

As provided for in the 1986 SEA, a **Court of First Instance** was established by a Council Decision in 1988 and started functioning in 1989. With the entry into force of the Treaty of Lisbon, it was renamed **'General Court'**. It currently consists of twenty-seven judges, but the TEU provides that there could be more than one judge per Member State. The General Court usually sits in chambers of three or five judges, though its rules of procedure provide that 'whenever the legal difficulty or the importance of the case or special circumstances so justify' it may decide as a Grand Chamber or as a full court. Since 1999 even single judges may decide routine cases.

One of the main purposes of setting up the General Court was to reduce the case-load of the ECJ. This concern shaped the scope of the General Court's jurisdiction. Originally, the Court of First Instance was competent for **staff** and **competition** law cases (→ *9.15*), as well as for cases brought by individuals under the ECSC Treaty. Its jurisdiction was broadened by a number of amendments to now include basically **all direct actions by private parties**. Preliminary rulings are still excluded from the General Court's jurisdiction, although there is a provision in the TFEU that would allow the transfer of this jurisdiction to the General Court (→ *5.14*). When it became evident that the case-load for the two courts remained at very high levels, another 'outsourcing' of judicial tasks was decided upon. On the basis of a provision in the Nice Treaty, the Council decided in 2004 to establish a **European Union Civil Service Tribunal** consisting of seven judges competent to hear **staff disputes** between the then Communities and their employees.

Appeals against a General Court decision are possible within two months **on questions of law**. The ECJ may then give **final judgment** itself or **refer** the **matter back** to the General Court.

5.4 What are the main types of procedures before the Court of Justice?

Although the Court's task is broadly defined as to ensure that 'the law is observed' in the interpretation and application of the Treaty, the principle of **enumerated powers** (→ *3.2*), valid for all Community institutions, also implies that the ECJ has jurisdiction only for the specific types of procedures mentioned in the Treaty. The three most important procedures are:

(1) **actions for annulment** according to Article 263 TFEU (ex Article 230 TEC) (→ *5.5–10*) (which is complemented by the complaint of failure to act according to Article 265 TFEU (ex Article 232 TEC) in cases where there is no Union act in place);

(2) **infringement proceedings** against Member States according to Articles 258, 259 and 260 TFEU (ex Articles 226, 227 and 228 TEC) (→ *5.11–13*); and

(3) **preliminary references** according to Article 267 TFEU (ex Article 234 TEC) (→ *5.14–18*).

5.5 What kind of 'acts' may be reviewed under an Article 263 TFEU action for annulment?

According to Article 263 TFEU, the ECJ 'shall **review** the **legality** of **legislative acts**, of **acts** of the Council, of the Commission and of the European Central Bank, other than recommendations and opinions, and of acts of the European Parliament and of the European Council **intended to produce legal effects** *vis-à-vis* **third parties'**. This typically covers **regulations, directives** and **decisions** (→ *ch. 3*). With the Treaty of Lisbon, not only acts of the European Council were explicitly added but also acts of 'bodies, offices or agencies of the Union intended to produce legal effects *vis-à-vis* third parties' are now subject to annulment proceedings.

The ECJ clarified early on that the precise form of the acts is immaterial. In Case 60/81 *IBM* v. *Commission* [1981] ECR 2639, it held that 'any measure the legal effects of which are binding on, and capable of affecting the interests of, the applicant by bringing about a distinct change in his legal position is an act ... under Article [230 TEC; now Article 263 TFEU]'. In that case, a Commission letter which only informed IBM that competition law proceedings ($\rightarrow$ *ch. 9*) had been instituted against it was held not to be open to challenge under Article 230 TEC (now Article 263 TFEU).

In the so-called *ERTA* Case, Case 22/70 *Commission* v. *Council* [1971] ECR 263, the ECJ held that 'an action for annulment must be available in the case of all measures adopted by the institutions, whatever their nature or form, which are intended to have legal effect'. The Court found that a Council **'resolution'**, adopting a negotiating procedure, 'had definitive legal effects both on relations between the Community and the Member States and on the relationship between the institutions' and was thus **reviewable**.

? 5.6 Can an individual also bring annulment actions?

Member States, the **Commission**, the **Council** and – since the Nice Treaty – also the **Parliament**, the so-called **privileged applicants**, have an unconditional **right** to ask the Court to **review the legality** of Union acts. The Court of Auditors, the European Central Bank and the Committee of the Regions can do so for the protection of their prerogatives.

Natural or **legal persons**, however, have to prove their **special legal interest** in order to have **standing** or, as lawyers tend to say, *locus standi*, to seek judicial review. In the terms of the TFEU, they have standing in three types of cases:

1) An **'act addressed to that person'** – as is regularly the case in **competition** law decisions ($\rightarrow$ *ch. 9*).
2) An act 'which is of **direct and individual concern** to them' – such as disguised decisions in the form of anti-dumping regulations

($\rightarrow$ *ch. 11*) or in various exceptional cases true regulations where the *Plaumann* test ($\rightarrow$ *below*) applies.

3) '[A] regulatory act which is of direct concern to them and does not entail implementing measures.' Hence whereas the individual has to show direct concern, it does not need to prove individual concern.

These standing requirements enshrined in Article 263(4) TFEU (ex Article 230(4) TEC) have given rise to a considerable body of case law by the ECJ, which has not always been very encouraging for individual applicants.

According to the ECJ in the *International Fruit* Case, Case 41–44/70 *NV International Fruit Company* v. *Commission* [1971] ECR 411, **direct concern** requires that the act in question 'directly affects the legal position of the parties concerned'. The effects on the legal position of the individual have to directly result from the act in question without it leaving 'to the national authorities and undertakings concerned such a margin of discretion with regard to the manner of its implementation [...] that the Decision cannot be regarded as being of direct and individual concern' (Case 222/83 *Municipality of Differdange* v. *Commission* [1984] ECR 2889).

With regard to the meaning of **individual concern**, the early *Plaumann* test is the leading authority. In fact, by laying down rather **restrictive** criteria in the *Plaumann* Case, Case 25/62 *Plaumann & Co.* v. *Commission* [1963] ECR 95, from which the Court has not since distanced itself, the ECJ has considerably reduced the number of review cases brought by individual plaintiffs. In that case the Court held that:

> "persons other than those to whom a decision is addressed may only claim to be individually concerned if that decision affects them by reason of certain attributes which are peculiar to them or by reason of circumstances in which they are differentiated from all other persons and by virtue of these factors distinguishes them individually just as in the case of the person addressed."

One of the **rare cases** where this standard was met was the *Töpfer* Case, Cases 106 and 107/63 *Alfred Töpfer and Getreide-Import Gesellschaft* v. *Commission* [1965] ECR 405. In that case, a Commission decision addressed to Germany authorising it to reject import licences as a safeguard measure was considered to be of individual concern to importers, because the only persons affected by the said measures were the importers who had already applied for a licence. The number and identity of these importers had already become fixed and ascertainable before the date when the contested decision was made.

The right to seek the annulment of acts which are of direct and individual concern also covers individual challenges to decisions addressed to other persons. This occurs most frequently in disputes concerning **state aid** (→ *9.33*). Thus, Commission decisions which deny Member States the right to grant subsidies are regularly challenged by the potential recipients of such aid.

Under the *Plaumann* test individual challenges to regulations are almost always excluded. An exception can be seen in Case C-309/89 *Codorniu SA* v. *Council* [1994] ECR I-1853. There, the Court accepted that the Spanish sparkling wine producer and trademark owner of 'Gran Crémant' could challenge a Council regulation reserving the term 'crémant' to French and Luxembourg sparkling wines, because this regulation was of individual concern to the applicant.

In practice, the most frequent cases of successful individual challenges to regulations are found in the area of anti-dumping law (→ *11.5*). **Anti-dumping duties** are regularly imposed in the form of regulations, although they do in fact have individual addressees, as was recognised in Case C-358/89 *Extramet Industrie SA* v. *Council* [1991] ECR I-2501. Such so-called **disguised decisions** are commonly challenged before the ECJ, and now also before the General Court.

The ECJ's restrictive stance on the *locus standi* of individuals in challenges of regulations has remained controversial even to the point that the two Union courts have split in their views, and one advocate-general has sharply criticised the existing case law in Case C-50/00P *Unión de Pequeños Agricultores* v. *Council* [2002] ECR I-6677. In Case T-177/01 *Jégo-Quéré* v. *Commission* [2002] ECR II-2365, the CFI adopted a more liberal approach which, on appeal, was promptly overruled by the ECJ in Case C-263/02P *Commission* v. *Jégo-Quéré* [2004] ECR I-3425.

With the entrance into force of the Treaty of Lisbon, the standing rules are liberalised insofar as **'regulatory acts'** are concerned, which do not entail 'implementing measures', as in such cases the individual is no longer required to show 'individual' but only 'direct' concern (Article 263(4) TFEU). However, the Treaty of Lisbon does not define regulatory acts. The only legal acts explicitly provided for include legislative acts, delegated acts and implementing acts (Article 288 to 291 TFEU) ($\rightarrow$ *3.1*). Therefore, much will depend on the courts' interpretation of the meaning of 'regulatory acts' and 'implementing measures' though it seems that the two types of 'non-legislative acts', **delegated acts** and **implementing acts**, should fall under this notion.

5.7 What is a 'plea of illegality'?

A **plea of illegality** is not a distinctive form of action. Instead, Article 277 TFEU (ex Article 241 TEC) allows an **indirect challenge** to an act of general application even after the two-month time-limit for annulment actions has expired. In Cases 31 and 33/62 *Milchwerke Heinz Wohrmann & Sohn and Alfons Lütticke GmbH* v. *Commission* [1962] ECR 501, the ECJ stated that Article 277 TFEU cannot be used before national courts, but only before the ECJ itself. It further clarified that Article 277 TFEU does not permit a direct challenge under Article 263 TFEU once the time-limit has expired because 'the sole object of [now Article 277 TFEU] is thus to protect an interested party against the application of an illegal regulation, without thereby in any way calling in issue the regulation itself which can no longer be challenged because of the expiry of the time limit laid down in [now Article 263 TFEU]'.

Typically, a plea of illegality may be used to assert the illegality of a regulation on which a challenged decision is based as in Case 92/78 *Simmenthal SpA* v. *Commission* [1979] ECR 777, where the ECJ held that Article 277 TFEU 'enables the applicant to challenge indirectly during the proceedings, with a view to obtaining the annulment of the contested decisions, the validity of the measures laid down by Regulation which form the legal basis of the latter'.

According to Case 66/80, *International Chemical Corporation* v. *Amministrazione delle Finanze dello Stato* [1981] ECR 1191, a successful plea of illegality in the course of a preliminary reference does **not** lead to **formal annulment** but constitutes 'sufficient reason for any other national court to regard that act as void'.

? 5.8 For what reasons may the ECJ invalidate Union acts?

Article 263 TFEU (ex Article 230 TEC) specifies four **grounds of invalidity**, which are also valid for purposes of preliminary rulings according to Article 267 TFEU (ex Article 234 TEC) (→ *5.14*) and under a plea of illegality pursuant to Article 277 TFEU (ex Article 241 TEC) (→ *5.7*):

(1) lack of competence;
(2) infringement of an essential procedural requirement;
(3) infringement of the Treaties or any rule of law relating to their application; and
(4) misuse of powers.

Lack of competence and **infringements of the Treaties** are relatively straightforward grounds for annulment. **Lack of competence** is usually invoked when it is alleged that EU institutions have violated the principle of **enumerated powers** ($\rightarrow$ *3.2*) enshrined in Article 13(2) TEU (ex Article 7(1) TEC) by exceeding the powers transferred to them. Lawyers refer to such acts that are 'beyond the powers' of an organ as *'ultra vires'* acts. Any **inconsistency** of **Union legislation** with the **provisions of the Treaties** may be raised in an annulment action alleging **infringement** of the **Treaties**. The somewhat more mysterious formulation of infringements of 'any rule of law relating to [the Treaties'] application' has been broadly interpreted by the ECJ to cover not only implementing law, but also **international agreements** ($\rightarrow$ *11.3*) as well as **fundamental rights** ($\rightarrow$ *6.6*), and other general principles of Union law.

The annulment ground of **misuse of powers**, stemming from the French administrative law concept of 'détournément de pouvoir', has only rarely been successfully invoked before the Union courts. Basically, it occurs when Union institutions **use** their **powers** to **obtain an objective** for which the powers were **not intended**. The infringement of an essential procedural safeguard, however, has been made more precise in a considerable body of ECJ case law.

5.9 Give examples of infringements of essential procedural safeguards

For example, in Case 138/79 *Roquettes Frères SA* v. *Council* [1980] ECR 3333, the Court used its power of **judicial review** to strengthen considerably the constitutional position of the European Parliament in the **law-making process**. It annulled a Council regulation which had been adopted without proper regard to the **consultation** procedure provided for under the pertinent Treaty provision ($\rightarrow$ *3.10*). In the Court's view 'due consultation of the Parliament in the cases

provided for by the Treaty therefore constitutes an essential formal-
ity disregard of which means that the measure concerned is void'.

In the so-called *Branntwein* (German for *Brandy*) Case, Case
24/62 *Germany* v. *Commission* [1963] ECR 63, the Court found
a breach of the **duty to provide reasons** (→ *3.5*). In its view, a
Commission decision approving a lower rate of import of wine
failed to state reasons as required by Article 296 TFEU (ex Article
253 TEC) by merely saying that 'on the basis of existing information' wine production in the Community was amply sufficient. In a
later case, Case C-76/01P *Eurocoton and others* v. *Council* [2003]
ECR I-10091, the ECJ clarified that:

> "the statement of reasons required by Article [253 TEC;
> now Article 296 TFEU] must be appropriate to the act
> at issue and must disclose in a clear and unequivocal
> fashion the reasoning followed by the institution which
> adopted the measure in question in such way as to enable
> the persons concerned to ascertain the reasons for the
> measure and to enable the competent Community Court to
> exercise its power of review."

In Case 17/74 *Transocean Marine Paint* v. *Commission* [1974]
ECR 1063, it was the requirement to **provide a hearing** (→ *6.4*)
which was violated in the eyes of the ECJ. The Court demanded
that 'a person whose interests are perceptibly affected by a decision
taken by a public authority must be given the opportunity to make
his point of view known'. Thus, a Commission decision granting a
renewal of competition law exemptions according to Article 81(3)
TEC (now Article 101(3) TFEU) (→ *9.12*) under new conditions
upon which the addressee could not comment was invalidated. The
right to a **fair hearing** was equally recognised in anti-dumping procedures (→ *11.2*) in Case C-49/88 *Al-Jubail* v. *Council* [1991] ECR
I-3187, and in customs law (→ *11.2*) in Case C-269 *Technische
Universität München* v. *Hauptzollamt München-Mitte* [1991] ECR
I-5469.

The importance of the right to a fair hearing and the obligation to provide reasons was reaffirmed in the *Kadi* case (→ *3.4, 10.29, 11.21*) concerning the EU implementation of UN Security Council targeted sanctions. The applicant, who was listed in a regulation as a suspected terrorist and whose assets were frozen, successfully complained that his **due process** rights were infringed because he initially had no possibility to challenge his listing. In Joined Cases C-402/05 P and C-415/05 P *Kadi and Al Barakaat* v. *Council and Commission* [2008] ECR I-6351, the ECJ held that the EU 'principle of effective judicial protection' (→ *6.4*) required that EU institutions had to communicate the ground for the listing in order to enable the affected persons to bring an annulment action. The Court further reasoned that:

> "Observance of that obligation to communicate the grounds is necessary both to enable the persons to whom restrictive measures are addressed to defend their rights in the best possible conditions and to decide, with full knowledge of the relevant facts, whether there is any point in their applying to the Community judicature … and to put the latter fully in a position in which it may carry out the review of the lawfulness of the Community measure in question which is its duty under the EC Treaty."

5.10 Do the judgments and rulings of the ECJ have retroactive effect?

In principle, **judgments** and rulings of the ECJ have **retroactive effect** because they are merely **declaratory** statements of what has always been the correct interpretation of the law even before formal annulment. However, Article 264(2) TFEU (ex Article 231(2) TEC) allows the Court to qualify the extent of the nullity.

In case of serious financial implications, the Court has also held that its preliminary rulings (→ *5.14–18*) may have only prospective effect. In the follow-up to the famous **'equal pay'** case of *Defrenne*, Case 43/75 *Defrenne* v. *Sabena (Defrenne II)* [1976] ECR 455 ($\rightarrow$ *4.5, 10.18*), the ECJ ruled that for 'important considerations of legal certainty', the 'direct effect of Article 119 cannot be relied on in order to support claims concerning pay periods prior to the date of this judgment'. The Court's interpretation of the equal pay principle of then Article 119 TEC (now Article 157 TFEU) ($\rightarrow$ *10.18*), as being directly applicable Community law from the end of the transitional period, could have driven many employers into bankruptcy.

Independent of any such qualification by the Court, Article 266(1) TFEU (ex Article 233(1) TEC) provides that any **institution** 'whose act has been declared void … shall be **required** to take the necessary measures **to comply** with the judgment of the Court'.

? 5.11 What are the stages leading to an Article 258 TFEU procedure?

Article 258 TFEU allows the Commission, as guardian of the Treaties, to take action if it 'considers that a Member State has failed to fulfil an obligation under the Treaties'. The peculiar sequencing of an **enforcement action** against Member States is the result of the multiple purposes it pursues. It is intended to give the **Commission** considerable **supervisory** power ($\rightarrow$ *2.11*), to offer **individuals indirect access** for their complaints (although the Commission is under no duty to act upon private complaints) and to provide room for **diplomatic settlement**. **Infringement proceedings** involve four distinct stages:

(1) in the pre-contentious stage, the Commission and the Member State concerned merely engage in **negotiations** which may informally resolve the matter;

(2) if this is not the case, the 'letter from Brussels' will formally **notify** the Member State of the specific infringement allegations.

This Commission **'letter of notice'** requires a reasonable time (usually two months) for a reply;

(3) if negotiations are still unsuccessful, the administrative stage will move on to the judicial stage. The Commission will issue a **'reasoned opinion'** (Article 258(1) TFEU), which clearly spells out the grounds for the alleged infringement and calls for remedial action within a specified time period; and

(4) if the Member State does not comply with the Commission's opinion, the latter may **institute proceedings** before the ECJ.

In Case C-350/02 *Commission* v. *The Netherlands* [2004] ECR I-6213, the ECJ has clarified that 'the purpose of the pre-litigation procedure is to give the Member State concerned an opportunity, on the one hand, to comply with its obligations under Community law and, on the other, to avail itself of its right to defend itself against the charges formulated by the Commission'. From the latter aspect the Court derived that 'the subject-matter of proceedings under [Article 258 TFEU] is delimited by the pre-litigation procedure'. Thus, the Court is prevented to examine a ground of complaint that was not contained in the reasoned opinion.

5.12 What is the legal effect of an Article 258 TFEU judgment?

The result of a successful infringement action is a **declaratory judgment**. However, according to Article 260(1) TFEU (ex Article 228(1) TEC), Member States are required to take the **necessary measures** to **comply** with the judgment of the Court. Next to remedial steps, such as the abolition of national law found in violation of EU law, national authorities are no longer permitted to apply domestic rules violating EU law as a result of the **supremacy/primacy** of EU law (→ *4.10, 4.11*).

In addition, the Maastricht Treaty Amendment (→ *1.8*) introduced in Article 260(2) TFEU (ex Article 228(2) TEC) the possibility of awarding a **'lump sum** or **penalty payment'** in cases of **non-compliance** by Member States. In Case C-387/97 *Commission v. Greece* [2000] ECR I-5047, the first case decided under the new provision, the Court basically accepted the Commission's guidelines and awarded penalty payments of €20,000 per day of non-compliance with the initial judgment. It accepted that the 'basic criteria which must be taken into account in order to ensure that penalty payments have coercive force … are, in principle, the **duration** of the infringement, its degree of **seriousness** and the **ability** of the Member State **to pay**'. In Case C-304/02 *Commission v. France* [2005] ECR I-6263, the ECJ imposed both a lump sum and a penalty payment arguing, in an exemplary fashion of **teleological** reasoning, that 'in the light of the objective pursued by Article 228 EC [now Article 258 TFEU], the conjunction "or" in Article 228(2) EC [now Article 258(2) TFEU] must be understood as being used in a cumulative sense'.

? 5.13 Can the violation of Union law by a Member State be easily justified?

Member States have been rather ingenious in developing **defences** of their EU law infringements. The ECJ, however, has not been very receptive to the arguments brought forward in this context.

Noting that Member States are free to challenge Union acts under the **annulment procedure** (→ *5.5–10*) the Court held in Case 226/87 *Commission v. Greece* [1988] ECR 3611, that 'a Member State cannot therefore plead the unlawfulness of a decision addressed to it as a defence in an action for a declaration that it has failed to fulfil its obligations arising out of its failure to implement that decision'. Thus, **Member States** are under a **duty to comply** with EU law

until annulled by the ECJ. The only exceptions may be found in particularly serious and manifest defects of Union measures that might qualify as non-existent acts that need not be followed.

In Joined Cases 90 and 91/63 *Commission* v. *Luxembourg and Belgium* [1964] ECR 1217, the Court held that the '*tu quoque*' excuse under international law, allowing suspension or withdrawal of treaty performance as a consequence of another party's failure to perform, 'cannot be recognised under Community law'. In the Court's view, even where an institution failed to carry out its obligations, 'the basic concept of the Treaty requires that Member States shall not fail to carry out their obligations and shall not take the law into their own hands'. Similarly, in Case C-146/89 *Commission* v. *United Kingdom* [1991] ECR 3533, the Court has consistently held that 'under the legal order established by the Treaty, the implementation of Community law by Member States cannot be made subject to a condition of reciprocity'.

It is clear from the ECJ's case law that a Member State may **not** plead **constitutional**, **administrative** or **institutional difficulties** in complying with EU law. In Case 77/69 *Commission* v. *Belgium* [1970] ECR 237, the Court refused to regard the dissolution of a national parliament as *force majeure* preventing the adoption of implementing legislation. It equally rejected the Belgian **separation of powers** argument stating unequivocally that 'liability of a Member State … arises whatever the agency of the State whose action or inaction is the cause of the failure to fulfil its obligations, even in the case of a constitutionally independent institution'. In another case against Belgium, Case 301/81 *Commission* v. *Belgium* [1983] ECR 467, the ECJ went so far as to assert that 'only … an objective finding of a failure' to implement a directive on credit institutions was relevant for the infringement action. In Case C-129/00 *Commission* v. *Italy* [2003] ECR I-14637, the ECJ held that even the **judgments** of a Member State's highest court may entail that Member's responsibility.

? 5.14 What is a preliminary reference?

The preliminary ruling procedure is an important part of the ECJ's jurisdiction and has been of paramount importance in the development of EU law itself and its relationship to national law. According to **Article 267 TFEU** (ex Article 234 TEC), the ECJ:

> "shall have jurisdiction to give **preliminary rulings** concerning:
> (a) the **interpretation** of the **Treaties**;
> (b) the **validity and interpretation** of **acts of the institutions**, bodies, offices or agencies of the Union;
> Where such a question is raised before **any court or tribunal** of a **Member State**, that court or tribunal may, if it considers that a decision on the question is **necessary** to enable it to give judgment, **request** the **Court** to give a **ruling** thereon."

Already the Nice Treaty (→ *1.8*) provided for the possibility of also submitting certain preliminary references to the General Court (→ *5.3*), which might further help the ECJ to reduce its case-load in the future.

In practice, requests for the **interpretation** of Union acts, that is, regulations, directives, decisions, recommendations with legal effects and international agreements (→ *ch. 3*), are the most frequent uses of the preliminary reference procedure made by national courts.

? 5.15 May national courts invalidate secondary EU law?

In Case 314/85 *Firma Foto Frost* v. *Hauptzollamt Lübeck-Ost* [1987] ECR 4199, the Court affirmed that 'requests for preliminary rulings, like actions for annulment, constitute means for reviewing the legality of acts of the Community institutions'. When a German court asked whether it could declare a Commission decision in the field of external trade invalid, the **ECJ** rejected this idea insisting on its own **exclusive right** of **invalidating** Community law. The Court reasoned that it was one of the main purposes of Article 234 TEC (now Article 267 TFEU):

> "to ensure that Community law is applied uniformly by national law. That requirement of uniformity is particularly imperative when the validity of a Community act is in question. Divergences between courts in the Member States as to the validity of Community acts would be liable to place in jeopardy the very unity of the Community legal order and detract from the fundamental requirements of legal certainty."

5.16 What is a 'tribunal' for the purposes of Article 267 TFEU and when is it obliged to ask for a preliminary ruling?

In Case 246/80 *Broekmeulen* v. *Huisarts Registratie Commissie* [1981] ECR 2311, the Dutch Appeals Committee for General Medicine was recognised as a **'tribunal'** because it operated with the **consent** and **cooperation** of **public authorities**, used **adversarial procedures** and delivered **final decisions**. In addition to these characteristics, general establishment by law, permanency, compulsory jurisdiction, *inter partes* procedure, independence and applying rules of law, are seen as criteria to be evaluated when determining whether a decision-making body qualifies as a 'court or tribunal' enabled to ask for a preliminary ruling. The **status** (public authority) and **function** (independent judicial tasks) seem to be the guiding principles for the ECJ. After *Broekmeulen* other professional, including disciplinary, bodies, tax and immigration adjudicators, as well as review bodies for public contracts have been held to qualify as 'tribunals' in the sense of Article 267 TFEU (ex Article 234 TEC). Though 'tribunal' is a wide term, it does **not** include **arbitral tribunals**. In Case 102/81 *Nordsee Deutsche Hochseefischerei* [1982] ECR 1095, the ECJ qualified commercial arbitration as a form of private and not state dispute settlement.

According to Article 267(2) TFEU 'any court or tribunal of a Member State' may request a preliminary ruling. However, pursuant to Article 267(3) TFEU, tribunals 'against whose decisions there is no judicial remedy under national law' **have to** make a **request** for a preliminary ruling. Since the ECJ favours the **'concrete'** over the 'abstract' theory, this is not necessarily the highest court but the court having the **final say** in the **special case**, as was confirmed in Case C-99/00 *Lyckeskog* [2002] ECR I-4839.

However, the obligation to make a preliminary reference is in practice limited by the so-called **'*acte clair*'** doctrine, which provides a certain amount of discretion to national courts as to whether they consider a ruling 'necessary' for their ensuing judgment (→ *5.18*).

? 5.17 Does the ECJ decide on all requests for preliminary rulings?

The ECJ does not have to rule on all requests. Rather, it has always insisted on its discretion to reserve the preliminary ruling procedure to **'genuine disputes'**.

Case 104/79 *Foglia* v. *Novello* [1980] ECR 745, is one of the first cases where the ECJ limited access to the sometimes overly successful Article 267 TFEU procedure. Foglia sold wine to Novello stipulating that Novello should not pay for any taxes charged in violation of EC law. Although Foglia had a similar clause in his carriage contract with his general transporter, he reimbursed the transporter for French taxes, which were believed to be contrary to EC law, and passed these charges on to Novello in his invoice. When Novello refused to pay, Foglia sued in Italian courts. The ECJ declared a request for a preliminary ruling **inadmissible** because Article 267 TFEU required a 'genuine dispute' and not a **hypothetical case**.

When the Italian court made a second request in Case 244/80 *Foglia v. Novello (No. 2)* [1981] ECR 3045, speculating on the consistency of the ECJ's first ruling under the principle that it was for the national courts to assess the necessity for a reference, the Court reaffirmed its earlier decision stressing that it would **not** render **'advisory opinions'**.

The *Foglia* cases have been very controversial since they may be interpreted as giving the Court a wide-ranging **discretion** to pick and choose those cases it wishes to hear. Still, the Court has reaffirmed in Case C-341/01 *Plato Plastik v. Caropack* [2004] ECR I-4883, that it:

> "has **no jurisdiction** to give a preliminary ruling on a question submitted by a national court where it is quite obvious that the interpretation or assessment of the validity of a Community rule sought by that court bears **no relation to the facts or purpose** of the main action, where the problem is **hypothetical** or where the Court does **not** have before it the **factual or legal material** necessary to enable it to give a useful answer to the questions submitted to it."

5.18 When is a ruling on a preliminary question 'necessary' to enable a national court to give judgment?

Next to the *Foglia* requirement of a 'genuine dispute' (→ *5.17*), the only other effective safety valve ensuring that the ECJ may limit the case-load of references brought to it is the acceptance of the ***acte clair* doctrine** (→ *5.16*), originally devised by national courts which were hesitant to make references.

In *Bulmer* v. *Bollinger* [1974] 2 WLR 202, Lord Denning of the English Court of Appeal laid down the following guidelines as to whether a decision is **'necessary'**: (a) the point must be **conclusive**; (b) **previous rulings** are relevant and, as a rule, they should be followed by national courts, and only if they think that a previous ruling may have been wrong should they re-submit the point to the ECJ; and (c) if a point is **'reasonably clear and free from doubt'** it constitutes an '*acte clair*' and in such a situation 'there is **no need** to interpret the Treaty but only to apply it'.

The *acte clair* doctrine was accepted by the ECJ in Case 283/81 *CILFIT* v. *Ministero della Sanita* [1982] ECR 3415, where the Court accepted that the 'correct application of Community law may be **so obvious** as to leave **no scope for any reasonable doubt**'. The Court cautioned, however, that only if the matter was 'equally obvious to the courts of other Member States' and to the ECJ itself, may a national court 'refrain from submitting a question to the Court of Justice'.

6 Protecting fundamental rights within the EU

The **initial Community Treaties** establishing the ECSC, the EEC and EURATOM did **not** contain **any fundamental rights** provisions at all. The 1953 Draft Treaty embodying the Statute of a European Political Community envisaged human rights protection as a major task and proposed to incorporate the **European Convention on Human Rights** (ECHR), a treaty concluded by many European states in 1950 under the auspices of the **Council of Europe** and enforced by the **European Court of Human Rights** (ECtHR) in Strasbourg. After the plans for a European Defence Community were buried by the French National Assembly in 1954, this idea also became **obsolete**. With the resurgence of the **'functionalist approach'**, culminating in the 1957 Rome Treaties, the view prevailed that the economic integration now pursued did **not warrant** the inclusion of **human rights** guarantees.

With the growth of the activities of the European Union, however, the likelihood of **infringement** of fundamental rights also **increased**. Clearly, the extension of Union law into many fields beyond the core aspects of the four freedoms was not a wholly unintended **'spill-over effect'** of economic integration. This tendency was reinforced by the specific development of EU law, in particular of **direct effect** and **primacy** in such landmark cases as *Van Gend en Loos* and *Costa* v. *ENEL*. Both direct effect and primacy increase the probability that it is EU law itself and not any national implementation that may infringe human rights.

Again, it was the **ECJ** which played a crucial role in **developing** a **fundamental rights protection** within the Union. The Court found that fundamental rights constituted an integral part of the **general principles of law** which were binding upon the Union, and it identified a number of specific basic rights through a comparative exercise looking at the **constitutions** of the Member States and **drawing inspiration** from the **ECHR**. It was only after the Maastricht Treaty amendments that this approach was codified and integrated into the text of the TEU.

The **Lisbon Treaty** significantly strengthened the role of fundamental rights in the EU legal order. The EU is founded on the respect for human dignity and human rights, values, which the Union shall uphold and promote also in its relations with the wider world. For Member States, which seriously and persistently breach human rights, the Treaties envisage a sanctions mechanism. Article 6 TEU contains three formal sources of EU human rights law. According to Article 6(1) TEU, the Charter of Fundamental Rights of the European Union (CFR), proclaimed in 2000, 'shall have the same legal value as the Treaties'. Article 6(2) TEU envisages accession of the Union to the ECHR. Pursuant to Article 6(3) TEU, fundamental rights, as they result from the ECHR and 'the constitutional traditions common to the Member States, shall constitute general principles of the Union's law'. Article 19 TFEU furthermore empowers the Union to 'take appropriate action to combat discrimination'.

EU human rights are binding on the institutions, bodies, offices and agencies of the Union in all their activities as well as on the Member States whenever 'they are implementing Union law' (Article 51 CFR). The extent to which Member States are bound by EU human rights continues to be a controversial topic.

This chapter will explain the gradual development of the ECJ's **jurisprudence** on the protection of fundamental rights against potential infringements by acts of the Union institutions and analyses recent developments of EU fundamental rights law.

? 6.1 What were the initial responses of the ECJ to calls for a human rights protection?

The **initial reaction** of the **ECJ** to human rights arguments was not very promising. In Case 1/58 *Stork* v. *High Authority* [1959] ECR 17, Joined Cases 36, 37, 38 and 40/59 *Geitling* v. *High Authority* [1960] ECR 423, and Case 40/64 *Sgarlata* v. *High Authority* [1965] ECR 215, the Court denied the possibility of examining alleged infringements of national constitutional law by the adoption of Community acts. It also **denied** the existence of any **general principles** in Community law **protecting** vested **rights**, as well as the possibility that fundamental principles common to the legal systems of all the Member States could override an express Treaty provision.

Only pressure by courts in some Member States, particularly the Italian and German constitutional courts (→ *6.9–11*), as a reaction to the ECJ's **primacy** doctrine (→ *4.10, 4.11*) which would encroach upon national human rights protection, ultimately led to a change in the ECJ's jurisprudence.

? 6.2 What was the role of the ECJ in developing fundamental rights protection and where did the Court find fundamental rights in EU law?

In the absence of a clear Treaty mandate to scrutinise the compliance of the institutions of the Community in the area of fundamental rights, the ECJ used its powers of **judicial review** (→ *5.8*) of Community acts in order to check whether they conformed to legal principles which it gradually interpreted in an ever more expansive way.

One of the first cases reflecting such a new approach was Case 29/69 *Stauder* v. *Stadt Ulm* [1969] ECR 419. In order to reduce the Community's butter surplus a Commission decision authorised

Member States to make butter available to social assistance recipients at lower cost. Persons claiming the benefit had to present certain coupons to retailers. The German text of the decision provided for the identification of the recipient. Stauder, a war victim, considered the identification requirement to be contrary to his constitutionally guaranteed right to privacy. A German administrative court asked the ECJ for a preliminary ruling on this matter. In *Stauder*, the **ECJ** for the first time **acknowledged** the relevance of **fundamental rights** for the Community. The Court held that 'the provision in question must be interpreted as not requiring – although it does not prohibit – the identification of beneficiaries by name'; it thus 'contains nothing capable of prejudicing the **fundamental human rights** enshrined in the **general principles of Community law** and protected by the Court'.

The ECJ further elaborated on this approach in Case 11/70 *Internationale Handelsgesellschaft* v. *Einfuhr- und Vorratstelle für Getreide und Futtermittel* [1970] ECR 1125. After reasoning why Community legislation cannot be tested against fundamental rights of the constitutions of the Member States, the Court held that there were analogous guarantees **inherent** in the Community legal order:

> " "respect for **fundamental rights** forms an **integral part** of the **general principles of law** protected by the Court of Justice. The protection of such rights, whilst inspired by the **constitutional traditions** common to the Member States, must be ensured within the framework of the structure and objectives of the Community. " "

In Case 4/73 *Nold* v. *Commission* [1974] ECR 491, the ECJ broadened the sources of inspiration when it came to ascertaining specific fundamental rights as forming general principles of law. In addition to the 'constitutional traditions common to the Member States', the Court also found that 'international **treaties** for the **protection of human rights** on which the Member States have collaborated or of which they are signatories, can supply guidelines which should be followed within the framework of Community law'. In the particular case, a new Community decision required that the German national coal producer, Ruhrkohle, would sell only to large wholesalers on two-year contracts. Nold, a small wholesaler, who under the previous system purchased directly from Ruhrkohle, considered this to be a violation of his right to property and his freedom to pursue economic activities. Nold sued the Commission directly under the annulment procedure (→ *5.6*). Though the Court reaffirmed its position that 'fundamental rights form an integral part of the general principles of law, the observance of which it ensures', it found no violation of such rights in this particular case. It justified this by holding that rights of ownership do not protect 'mere commercial opportunities'.

Similarly, in Case 44/79 *Hauer* v. *Land Rheinland-Pfalz* [1979] ECR 3727, the ECJ recognised the right to own **property** as one of the general principles of Union law to be respected by Union legislation. However, after a careful analysis of various national constitutional provisions restricting the use of real property for various public interests, it found that a Council regulation prohibiting the planting of vines in certain areas did not violate this right.

? 6.3 Does the ECJ recognise the same rights as the European Court of Human Rights?

In practice, the ECJ is not only guided by international human rights instruments like the ECHR, but also by the specific interpretation given to its articles by the ECtHR. Nevertheless, sometimes the **interpretation** of ECHR rights adopted by the **ECJ** may **differ** from that of the **ECtHR** in Strasbourg.

This happened with regard to the **right to privacy**, which the ECJ interpreted rather restrictively. In Case 136/79 *National Panasonic* v. *Commission* [1980] ECR 2033, the Court upheld the legality of Commission investigations on commercial premises. Similarly in Joined Cases 97–99/87 *Dow Chemical Ibérica and others* v. *Commission* [1989] ECR 3165, the ECJ held that Article 8 ECHR, according to which 'everyone has the right to respect for his private and family life, his home and his correspondence' was **limited to private dwellings** of private persons, and 'may not therefore be extended to business premises'.

This contrasts with the broader interpretation given to Article 8 ECHR by the ECtHR in cases like *Niemetz* v. *Germany* (1993) 16 EHRR 97, where the court in Strasbourg held that the right to privacy also **encompassed business premises** where this was necessary to protect the individual against arbitrary interference by public authorities.

Generally, in the EU legal order, the ECHR is perceived as a 'floor' rather than a 'ceiling', which means that the ECJ can go beyond the rights protected under the ECHR. This idea is enshrined in Article 52(3) CFR which outlines that whenever the Charter contains rights which correspond to rights guaranteed by the ECHR, 'the meaning and scope of those rights shall be the same as those laid down by the said Convention'. However, this 'shall not prevent Union law providing more extensive protection'. The ECJ has already granted protection, which may not necessarily be protected to the same extent under the ECHR, for example in Case C-465/07 *Elgafaji* v. *Staatssecretaris van Justitie* [2009] ECR I-921, concerning refugee rights and the freedom from torture.

? 6.4 Which human rights have been accepted in the jurisprudence of the ECJ?

Over the years the ECJ and the General Court have recognised a considerable number of fundamental rights, not only of an economic nature, which include:

(1) **freedom** to practise one's **religion**: Case 130/75 *Prais* v. *Council* [1976] ECR 1589;

(2) **respect** for **family** and **private life**: Case 165/82 *Commission* v. *United Kingdom* [1983] ECR 3431, Case C-249/86 *Commission* v. *Germany* [1989] ECR 1263;

(3) **protection** of **personal data**: Joined Cases C-456/00, C-138/01 and C-139/01 *Rechnungshof* v. *Österreichischer Rundfunk* [2003] ECR I-4919;

(4) **freedom of expression**: Case 100/88 *Oyowe and Traore* v. *Commission* [1989] ECR 4285, Case 34/79 *R.* v. *Henn and Darby* [1979] ECR 3975 (→ *7.9*), Case 260/89 *Elleniki Radiophonia Tiléorassi (ERT)* v. *Dimtiki (DEP)* [1991] ECR I-2925 (→ *6.13*), Case C-274/99P *Connolly* v. *Commission* [2001] ECR I-1611;

(5) the **right** to form **trade unions**: Case 175/73 *Union Syndicale* v. *Council* [1974] ECR 917;

(6) the **right** to an effective **judicial remedy**: Case 222/84 *Johnston* v. *RUC* [1986] ECR 1651, Joined Cases C-402 and 415/05 *P Yassin Abdullah Kadi and Al Barakaat International Foundation* v. *Council and Commission* [2008] ECR I-6351 (→ *3.4, 5.9*);

(7) the **right to be heard**: Case 17/74 *Transocean Marine Paint* v. *Commission* [1974] ECR 1063 (→ *5.9*);

(8) protection against **self-incrimination**: Case 374/87 *Orkem* v. *Commission* [1989] ECR 3283;

(9) the right to own **property**: Case 44/79 Hauer v. Land Rheinland-Pfalz [1979] ECR 3727 (→ 6.2), Joined Cases C-402 and 415/05 P Yassin Abdullah Kadi and Al Barakaat International Foundation v. Council and Commission [2008] ECR I-6351 (→ 3.4, 10.29);

(10) the right to freely **pursue trade** and professional activities: Case 230/78 *SpA Eridania Zuccherifici nazionali and others* v. *Minister of Agriculture and Forestry* [1979] ECR 2749;

(11) **equality** (equal pay): Case 43/75 *Defrenne* v. *Sabena* [1976] ECR 455 (→ *4.5, 5.10, 10.18*);

(12) **freedom from torture**: Case C-465/07 *Elgafaji* v. *Staatssecretaris van Justitie* [2009] ECR I-921 (→ *6.3*).

? 6.5 Which other general principles of law has the ECJ identified?

In addition to the fundamental rights identified by the ECJ as general principles of Union law, which largely correspond to human rights guarantees found in many national constitutions as well as in international agreements, the Court has also elaborated on a number of **general principles** which are more akin to **principles of administrative law**, such as proportionality, equal treatment, legal certainty and legitimate expectations.

In Case 122/78 *Buitoni SA* v. *Fonds d'Orientation et de Régularisation des Marchés Agricoles* [1979] ECR 677, the ECJ scrutinised a Commission regulation providing for the forfeiture of security deposits for the importation of agricultural goods if import formalities had not been completed in time. Here the Court found, however, that, particularly when the imports themselves were made timely, the system was 'excessively severe in relation to the objectives of administrative efficiency' and, thus, not in line with the requirements of **proportionality**, a principle already recognised in Case 11/70 *Internationale Handelsgesellschaft* v. *Einfuhr- und Vorratstelle für Getreide und Futtermittel* [1970] ECR 1125 (→ *6.8*).

In the so-called *Skimmed Milk* Case, Case 114/76 *Bela-Mühle Josef Bergmann KG* v. *Grows-Farm GmbH & Co. KG* [1977] ECR 1211, the Court combined **proportionality** and **equal treatment** as major grounds for invalidating a Community act in the field of agriculture. The challenged regulation aimed at the reduction of a milk surplus in the Community by requiring animal feed producers to use skimmed milk as a protein ingredient instead of cheaper alternatives. *Bela-Mühle* refused to pay its supplier the resulting price increase, maintaining that the regulation was invalid. The ECJ found an imposition of a financial burden not only on milk producers, but also on producers in other agricultural sectors in the form of the compulsory purchase and the price-fixing at a threefold level. It held that the 'obligation to purchase at such a disproportionate price constituted a discriminatory distribution of the burden of costs between the various agricultural sectors'.

The related principles of **legal certainty** and **legitimate expectations** have also figured prominently in the ECJ's jurisprudence. In Case 98/78 *Firma A. Racke* v. *Hauptzollamt Mainz* [1979] ECR 69, the Court found that 'in general the principle of legal certainty precludes a Community measure from taking effect from a point in time before its publication …', thus, affirming also the principle of **non-retroactivity**.

The first *Mulder* Case (→ *10.5*), Case 120/86 *Mulder* v. *Minister van Landbouw en Visserij* [1988] ECR 2321, illustrates how the disappointment of **legitimate expectations** may lead to the annulment of a Community act. The ECJ invalidated a 1984 Council regulation under which a Dutch farmer had agreed not to market milk for a five-year period, and was refused permission to resume production after that period because quotas were issued on the basis of production levels of the previous years. The Court considered this to be a violation of the producer's legitimate expectations, because

> "[W]here such a producer, as in the present case, has been encouraged by a Community measure to suspend marketing for a limited period in the general interest and against payment of a premium he may legitimately expect not to be subject, upon the expiry of his undertaking, to restrictions which specifically affect him precisely because he availed himself of the possibilities offered by the Community provisions."

6.6 How does the Court protect fundamental rights as a matter of procedure?

Since the Treaty provisions on the jurisdiction of the ECJ do not provide for a special fundamental rights complaint, the Court had to find a way to extend its powers over such cases. As a result of the principle of enumerated powers, which binds all European institutions (→ *3.2, 5.8*), the ECJ can act only within the scope of powers conferred to it. Human rights scrutiny is not expressly mentioned in the jurisdictional provisions of the Treaty. The Court does, however, interpret its express **mandate** broadly and regards human rights protection as forming part of its general task under Article 19 TEU (ex Article 220 TEC), namely to '**ensure** that in the interpretation and application of the Treaties **the law is observed**'.

More specifically, it considers fundamental rights violations of Union acts as constituting grounds for **annulment** under Article 263(2) TFEU (ex Article 230(2) TEC), being an 'infringement of the Treaties or of any rule of law relating to their application' (→ *5.8*). The general principles of Union law, of which fundamental rights form an integral part, are regarded as rules of law relating to the Treaties' application. In a similar vein, the ECJ has shown its willingness to test the validity of Union acts in preliminary references (→ *5.14*).

6.7 Is the EU bound to respect the ECHR?

For a long time, the Community was not formally bound by the ECHR. **Only** its **Member States** were **Contracting Parties** of the Convention. In the early 1990s, the Commission proposed that the Community should formally accede to the ECHR. But in 1996 the ECJ delivered its Advisory Opinion 2/94 on the *Accession of*

the Community to the European Convention on Human Rights
[1996] ECR I-1759, according to which an accession was not
possible on the basis of then existing Community law. Although
the Court couched its ruling in terms of lack of Community competence ($\rightarrow$ *3.2*), many observers felt that the underlying reason
may have been the Court's reluctance to accept a superior court
as final arbiter in fundamental rights matters.

Like in the Draft Constitution Treaty this obstacle was overcome
by the express authorisation contained in Article 6(2) TEU, through
the Lisbon Treaty, providing that the Union 'shall accede' to the
ECHR. However, the accession of the EU to the ECHR does not lie
within the powers of the EU alone, as also the Council of Europe has
to provide for the possibility of accession. With the entry into force
of Protocol No. 14 to the ECHR on 1 June 2010, Article 59(2) ECHR
was introduced, establishing that 'the European Union may accede
to this Convention'. Nevertheless, accession is not yet completed.
Several details of the required agreement between the EU and the
Council of Europe concerning the accession are still open. Among
them, the particular mechanism of how and by whom a measure
allegedly related to EU law is to be defended before the ECtHR as
well as what a mechanism to grant the ECJ the possibility to remedy
an alleged violation could look like are controversially discussed.

Hence, at the end of 2011, the Union is not yet formally bound by
the ECHR. Only the Member States are Contracting Parties of the
Convention.

As far as the substance is concerned, however, the Court's approach
towards fundamental rights protection was already endorsed by a 1977
Joint Declaration of the Parliament, the Council and the Commission,
[1977] OJ C103/1, in which the institutions formally committed themselves to ensuring **respect** for **fundamental rights** in the **exercise of
their powers**. It equally found its expression in the preamble to the
SEA which spoke of the willingness 'to promote democracy on the
basis of the fundamental rights recognized in the constitutions and

laws of the Member States, in the Convention for the Protection of Human Rights and Fundamental Freedoms and the European Social Charter, notably freedom, equality and social justice'.

Today, the ECJ's **jurisprudence** is encapsulated or, as lawyers would say, **codified** in Article 6(3) TEU which provides as follows:

> ''**Fundamental rights**, as guaranteed by the **European Convention for the Protection of Human Rights and Fundamental Freedoms** and as they **result** from the **constitutional traditions** common to the **Member States**, shall constitute **general principles** of the Union's law.''

Furthermore, Article 52(3) CFR makes the ECHR the 'minimum standard' of EU human rights law, whenever a right enshrined in the CFR corresponds to a right guaranteed by the ECHR ($\rightarrow$ *6.3*).

6.8 Why is the *Internationale Handelsgesellschaft* Case so important?

In Case 11/70 *Internationale Handelsgesellschaft* v. *Einfuhr- und Vorratsstelle für Getreide und Futtermittel* [1970] ECR 1125, the ECJ held that the Community's forfeiture scheme of an export licensing system did not violate general principles of law. It was a rather technical case; however, it is of particular importance for the development of fundamental rights protection in the EU as a prelude to the German *Solange I* Case discussed below ($\rightarrow$ *6.9*).

The facts of the case are as follows: under a 1967 Council regulation, export licences for certain agricultural products were conditional upon prior payment of a deposit, which was to be forfeited if the export was not made. This forfeiture provision was challenged before a German administrative court, which thought that the system violated principles of the German Basic Law (that is, the German Constitution), *inter alia*, the freedom of disposition and proportionality, and that EC law must yield before these principles. Still, the German court referred the question to the ECJ.

The ECJ affirmed the **primacy** of EC law even **vis-à-vis national constitutional law** (→ *4.10*):

> "The law stemming from the Treaty, an independent source of law, cannot because of its very nature be overridden by rules of national law, however framed, without being deprived of its character as Community law and without the legal basis of the Community itself being called into question. Therefore the validity of a Community measure or its effect within a Member State cannot be affected by allegations that it runs counter to either fundamental rights as formulated by the constitution of that state or the principles of a national constitutional structure."

It did, however, hold that **'analogous guarantees inherent in Community law'** must be respected. Nevertheless, according to the ECJ, the forfeiture deposit system was 'necessary and appropriate to enable the competent authorities to determine in the most effective manner their interventions on the market of cereals'. Hence, even though the Court held that fundamental rights form an integral part of EU law, in the specific case, it did not detect a violation. Internationale Handelsgesellschaft further pursued its cause in the German Constitutional Court, which then resulted in the so-called *Solange I* decision (→ *6.9*), where the German Constitutional Court ruled that the fundamental rights of the German Constitution would prevail as long as the Community did not provide for an adequate protection. This challenge to the primacy of EU law was only reversed by the German Constitutional Court in its *Solange II* decision (→ *6.10*). These developments show how deeply the development of fundamental rights in the EU legal order was connected to the doctrine of primacy (→ *4.10*).

In *Internationale Handelsgesellschaft*, the ECJ also formulated important principles of **proportionality** in the Union legal order

($\rightarrow$ *6.5*): that is, Union action must be relevant and necessary to the attainment of a Union objective, and the aggregate burden upon affected persons must be no greater than that which is needed for the attainment of that objective.

6.9 What was the *Solange I* Case?

Both *Solange* (literally: 'as long as') **decisions** were rendered by the **German Federal Constitutional Court**. *Solange I*, as *Internationale Handelsgesellschaft* v. *Einfuhr- und Vorratsstelle für Getreide und Futtermittel* [1974] 2 CMLR 540, is usually referred to, relates to the *Internationale Handelsgesellschaft* Case of the ECJ ($\rightarrow$ *6.8*). After the ECJ's decision the applicant referred to the German Constitutional Court, asking basically the same question and contending that the scheme contravened fundamental human rights provisions of the **German Constitution**, that is, the Bonn Basic Law.

The Constitutional Court held that Article 24 of the Basic Law ('The Federation may by legislation transfer sovereign powers to intergovernmental institutions') was **inherently limiting** ('Integrationsschranke'), insofar as it nullified any primary or secondary Community law which would 'destroy the identity of the valid constitution of the Federal Republic of Germany'. Since '**fundamental rights** [were] an **inalienable** essential **feature** of the valid **Constitution** of the Federal Republic of Germany' the limitation of Article 24 of the Basic Law applied. As a result, Community law not complying with German fundamental rights guarantees could not be applied by German authorities. **'As long as'** the **EC** had **no adequate human rights** catalogue, the Constitutional Court would have **jurisdiction** to rule on the compatibility with the Basic Law and, thus, the applicability in Germany of a Community law norm.

On the merits, however, it was held that the contested system did not violate German fundamental rights guarantees.

6.10 Why was there a *Solange II* Case?

Wünsche Handelsgesellschaft [1987] 3 CMLR 225, the so-called *Solange II* decision of the German Federal Constitutional Court, was rendered in 1986. A German importer, having been denied licences under a Community system, claimed a violation of his right to a fair hearing. The Constitutional Court essentially affirmed its previous jurisprudence concerning Article 24 of the Basic Law. It reaffirmed that there were inherent limitations to the transfer of sovereign powers, but it altered its view on the human rights guarantees provided by the Community. It held that they were 'essentially comparable' or 'substantially similar' to those under the German Constitution. The German Court thereby **recognised** that in the time between the two *Solange* decisions the **ECJ** had **developed** an established **case law protecting fundamental rights**.

Thus, the Court concluded that **'as long as'** the EC 'generally ensured an effective protection of fundamental rights as against the sovereign powers of the Communities' that were 'substantially similar' to that of the German Constitution – safeguarding the essential content of fundamental rights – the Federal Constitutional Court 'will **no longer exercise its jurisdiction**' to decide upon the applicability of secondary EC law as the basis for acts of German organs within Germany. As a result the complaint was inadmissible.

In the judicial challenge to the ratification of the **Lisbon Treaty** the German Constitutional Court reaffirmed its *Solange* jurisprudence in 2 BvE 2/08 *Gauweiler* v. *Treaty of Lisbon*, 30 June 2008:

> "The Federal Constitutional Court has suspended its general competence, which it had originally assumed, to

> review the application of European Community law in
> Germany against the standard of the fundamental rights
> of the German constitution, in reliance on the Court
> of Justice of the European Communities performing
> this function accordingly. In view of the position of
> the Community institutions, which is derived from
> international treaties however, the Federal Constitutional
> Court could recognise the final character of the decisions
> of the Court of Justice only 'in principle'."

Thus, the highest German Court still **retains** certain **supervisory powers** which may in extreme cases lead to a declaration of
inapplicability of EU law in Germany. Nevertheless, the court
asserted that it did not contradict the objective of openness towards
European law 'if exceptionally, and under special and narrow conditions, the Federal Constitutional Court declares European Union law
inapplicable in Germany'.

6.11 Were other national courts also reluctant to accept full supremacy of EU law?

The German Constitutional Court was not alone in its scepticism
towards an unbound **supremacy** of EU law. In a ruling similar to the
Solange I decision, the Italian Constitutional Court held in *Frontini*
v. *Ministero delle Finanze* [1974] 2 CMLR 372, that:

> "by Article 11 of the Constitution limitations of
> sovereignty are allowed solely for the purpose of the ends
> indicated therein, and it should therefore be excluded
> that such limitations of sovereignty, concretely laid out in
> the Rome Treaty, signed by countries whose systems are
> based on the principle of the rule of law and guarantee
> the essential liberties of citizens, can nevertheless give
> the organs of the EEC an unacceptable power to violate
> the fundamental principles of our constitutional order

or the inalienable rights of man. And it is obvious that if
ever Article [288 TFEU] had to be given such an aberrant
interpretation, in such a case the guarantee would always
be assured that this Court would control the continuing
compatibility of the Treaty with the above mentioned
fundamental principles.??

? 6.12 Discuss the importance of the *Wachauf* Case and subsequent cases addressing the relationship between Union and Member State measures

The fundamental rights jurisprudence of the ECJ was primarily concerned with challenges directed against Community (now Union)
acts. Since Union law is often implemented by national authorities,
sooner or later the question had to arise as to whether and to what
extent **Member States** are bound to **respect fundamental rights**
when **implementing** and applying Union law.

Case 5/88 *Wachauf* v. *Germany* [1989] ECR 2609 is the leading
case affirmatively answering this question. According to the *Wachauf*
Case, human rights 'requirements are also binding on the Member
States when they implement Community rules'. The case concerned
a German farmer who was threatened with losing Community compensation for the discontinuance of milk production ($\rightarrow$ *10.5*) as
a result of the specifics of German implementing legislation of a
Community regulation ($\rightarrow$ *4.6*). In a preliminary ruling the ECJ:

> ""observed that Community rules which, upon the expiry
> of the lease, had the effect of depriving the lessee,
> without compensation, of the fruits of his labour and
> of his investments in the tenanted holding would be
> incompatible with the requirements of the protection of
> fundamental rights in the Community legal order. Since

> those requirements are also binding on the Member States
> when they implement Community rules, the Member
> States must, as far as possible, apply those rules in
> accordance with those requirements."

This case law of the Court relating to the scope of application of EU fundamental rights is reflected in Article 51(1) CFR which states that '[t]he provisions of this Charter are addressed to the institutions, bodies, offices and agencies of the Union with due regard for the principle of subsidiarity and to the Member States only when they are implementing Union law'.

However, according to Joined Cases 60 and 61/84 *Cinéthèque* v. *Fédération Nationale des Cinémas Français* [1985] ECR 2605, the ECJ 'has no power to examine the compatibility with the European Convention of national legislation which concerns ... an area which falls within the jurisdiction of the national legislator'. This latter holding was affirmed in Case 12/86 *Demirel* v. *Stadt Schwäbisch Gmünd* [1987] ECR 3719, where 'national rules at issue did not have to implement a provision of Community law. In those circumstances, the Court does not have jurisdiction to determine whether national rules such as those at issue are compatible with the principles enshrined in Article 8 of the ECHR'. This clearly underlines the position that the ECJ's jurisdiction over fundamental rights cases is, in principle, limited to those with a strong Union connection.

The Court has, however, found another limited possibility of fundamental rights review of Member State action in cases of **derogations** from **fundamental freedoms**. In Case 260/89 *Elleniki Radiophonia Tiléorassi (ERT)* v. *Dimtiki (DEP)* [1991] ECR I-2925, it held that:

> "where a Member State relies on [Treaty provisions]
> in order to justify rules which are likely to obstruct
> the exercise of the freedom to provide services, such

justification, provided for by Community law, must be interpreted in the light of the general principles of law and in particular of fundamental rights. Thus, the national rules in question can fall under the exceptions provided for by the combined provisions of Articles [52 and 62 TFEU] only if they are compatible with the fundamental rights the observance of which is ensured by the Court.''

In Case C-112/00 *Schmidberger* v. *Austria* [2003] ECR I-5659, the ECJ stated that the protection of **fundamental rights** '**justified** a **restriction** of the obligations imposed by Union law, even under a **fundamental freedom** guaranteed by the Treaty such as the free movement of goods' ($\rightarrow$ 7.7). In the particular case, it found that the permission given to hold a demonstration against the environmental danger stemming from trans-Alpine road traffic, which implied the temporary closure of transit roads between Italy and Austria did not violate the free movement of goods. The ECJ held that the measures taken to ensure the freedom of expression and assembly were limited, necessary and proportionate.

The *Schmidberger* reasoning was extended to the freedom to provide services in Case C-36/02 *Omega Spielhallen- und Automatenaufstellungs-GmbH* v. *Oberbürgermeisterin der Bundesstadt Bonn* [2004] ECR I-9609. In that case the ECJ accepted the prohibition of a particularly drastic paintball type game in Germany on the ground that it violated the German constitutional law guarantee of **human dignity**, which the Court also regarded as a general principle of EU law. According to the ECJ, 'by prohibiting only the variant of the laser game the object of which is to fire on human targets and thus "play at killing" people, the contested order did not go beyond what is necessary in order to attain the objective pursued by the competent national authorities'. It thus concluded that the prohibition could not be regarded as a measure unjustifiably undermining the freedom to provide services.

6.13 Does Union law provide for 'sanctions' against Member States for human rights violations?

In general, the **human rights** performance of **EU Member States** is a matter of compliance with the **ECHR** and is supervised by the **ECtHR in Strasbourg**. The EU's fundamental rights policy, on the other hand, is aimed at **acts** of **EU institutions** ($\rightarrow$ *6.2*) and only exceptionally addresses the actions of Member States, as in the case of implementing measures ($\rightarrow$ *6.12*).

The Amsterdam Treaty inserted, however, a very broad fundamental rights commitment into the EU Treaty, which was further expanded by the Lisbon Treaty. According to Article 2 TEU (ex Article 6(1) TEU):

> "The **Union** is **founded** on the **values** of respect for human dignity, freedom, democracy, equality, the rule of law and respect for **human rights**, including the rights of persons belonging to minorities. These values are common to the Member States in a society in which pluralism, non-discrimination, tolerance, justice, solidarity and equality between women and men prevail."

The Amsterdam Treaty also introduced a political **supervisory procedure**. Article 7(2) TEU now provides that:

> "the European Council, acting by unanimity on a proposal by one-third of the Member States or by the Commission and after obtaining the consent of the European Parliament, may determine the existence of a **serious and persistent breach** by a **Member State** of the values referred to in Article 2, after inviting the Member State in question to submit its observations."

If such a determination were made, the Council, acting by a qualified majority, could decide to **suspend** certain **rights** of the Member States, deriving from the application of the Treaties, including voting rights. In so doing, it would take into account the possible consequences of such a suspension on the rights and obligations of natural and legal persons. To date, however, no such action has been taken and it remains doubtful whether this suspension power will ever be invoked because of its highly disruptive potential.

Evidence of serious and persistent breaches of fundamental rights may be collected by the **European Union Agency for Fundamental Rights** which was established in 2007 and has wide ranging tasks in the field of fundamental rights promotion.

? 6.14 What is the Charter of Fundamental Rights of the EU?

In 1999, the Cologne European Council decided to commission the drafting of a **Charter of Fundamental Rights for the EU** in order to 'make their overriding importance and relevance more visible to the Union's citizens'. This task was carried out by a **'Convention'**, an ad hoc body composed of representatives of various constituent bodies, such as the European institutions, national parliaments and the heads of state or government of the Member States. In a relatively transparent and participatory procedure, this Convention **drafted** the text of the **Charter**. The CFR basically contains the rights found in the ECHR, as well as in other more recent human rights instruments and in national constitutions. They are grouped into six chapters, entitled as follows: I. – dignity; II. – freedoms; III. – equality; IV. – solidarity; V. – citizen's rights; and VI. – justice. While the traditional civil and political rights are mostly found in Chapter II, some of the more controversial social and economic guarantees are contained in Chapter III.

The Fundamental Rights Charter was **'solemnly proclaimed'** by the Commission, the Council and the Parliament and approved by the Member States at the **Nice European Council** in December 2000. Clearly this fell short of being legally binding.

The ECJ's advocates-general as well as the General Court have been quick, however, to rely on the Charter's **persuasive authority**, while the ECJ itself has remained more cautious. Only in 2006, in Case C-540/03 *European Parliament* v. *Council* [2006] ECR I-5769 and in Case C-131/03P *Reynolds Tobacco* v. *Commission* [2006] ECR I-7795, did the ECJ start to refer approvingly to the CFR as a reaffirmation of the existing case law.

With the entry into force of the **Lisbon Treaty**, the CFR, which was amended and proclaimed a second time in December 2007, became a **legally binding document**, 'which shall have the same legal value as the Treaties' (Article 6(1) TEU). In the recent Case *Test Achats*, Case C-236/09 *Association Belge des Consommateurs Test-Achats ASBL and Others* v. *Conseil des Ministres*, 1 March 2011, the ECJ for the first time quashed parts of a Directive by relying on the Charter. The case was brought by a Belgian consumers' association and concerned the legality of gender as a risk factor in insurance contracts. Directive 2004/113 prohibited all discrimination based on sex in the access to and supply of goods and services. Thus, the Directive, in principle prohibited the widely used practice of reliance on gender as a factor in the calculation of premiums and benefits in relation to insurance contracts. However, by way of derogation, Article 5(2) of the Directive allowed the Member States to make exemptions to the rule of unisex premiums and benefits as long as the risk assessment was 'based on relevant and accurate actuarial and statistical data'. The ECJ held that Article 5(2) was invalid as it contravened the aim of the Directive and was inconsistent with Articles 21 and 23 of the CFR, dealing with non-discrimination and equality between men and women respectively.

7 The free movement of goods

Gradually establishing the free movement of goods, one of the **four freedoms** of the internal market, was one of the centre-pieces of early market integration in the EEC. This was pursued by **internal and external measures**. Already Article 9(1) of the original 1957 EEC Treaty (now Article 28(1) TFEU, ex Article 23(1) TEC) provided for the gradual establishment of a **customs union** between the Member States and a **common customs tariff** vis-à-vis third countries.

Internally, a customs union requires the elimination of **customs duties** and **'charges having equivalent effect'** (Article 30 TFEU, ex Article 25 TEC) as well as of discriminatory or protectionist **internal taxes** (Article 110 TFEU, ex Article 90 TEC), plus the elimination of **quantitative restrictions** on imports and exports and **'measures having equivalent effect'** (Article 34 and 35 TFEU, ex Articles 28 and 29 TEC).

Externally, the **Common Customs Tariff** is fixed by EU legislation in the form of Council regulations, which have been regularly updated since 1968. The Common Customs Tariff forms part of the Community's exclusive powers in the field of the **Common Commercial Policy**.

However, the establishment of a true internal market for goods freely circulating within the entire area of the EU was not only a 'legislative' task, pursued by rule-making through treaty norms as well as secondary **legislation** in the form of harmonisation directives and regulations. To a large extent, the common market is the 'product' of the ECJ. The Court has pushed forward market integration in a line of landmark cases, such as **Dassonville** and **Cassis de Dijon**, in which it broadly interpreted the Treaty notion of 'measures having equivalent effect', and deduced a duty of 'mutual recognition' of goods lawfully produced and marketed in any of the Member States of the EU. The combined effect of these and subsequent ECJ cases has been a considerable **limitation** of the **power of Member States** to maintain rules which could exclude the goods of other Member States from their national markets. However, the Court has not been insensitive to criticism from the national level and proved in cases such as **Keck** that it was willing to restore, at least to some extent, the autonomous **rule-making power** of **Member States**.

This chapter provides an overview of the TFEU rules on the free movement of goods, as well as the ECJ's relevant case law in its historical evolution. It thereby illustrates that EU law is to a considerable extent judicially made and reflective of the inherent tension between market integration and the preservation of national peculiarities. It, thus, also mirrors the broader constitutional question as to whether the **appropriate level of regulation** is on the European or on the Member State level.

7.1 Explain the difference between a free trade agreement, a customs union, a common market and an economic and monetary union

These are all different forms of regional economic integration organisations which, if formed by GATT/WTO members, have to fulfil certain conditions under Article XXIV of the GATT, such as covering substantially all trade and not increasing the total burden to external trade.

In a **free trade agreement** the participating states agree to **eliminate all customs duties** among themselves. However, they retain their **autonomous external trade policy** towards third countries, particularly their own customs duties. This necessitates a (rather costly) system determining where imports originate in order to apply the correct customs rate for the particular country of destination for the imported goods. Rules of origin help in making this assessment.

A **customs union** makes the additional step of adopting one **common external customs tariff**.

The **internal market** also comprises other **factors of production**, in the terminology of the EU other 'freedoms', namely the **free movement of persons, services and capital**. According to Article 26 TFEU (ex Article 14 TEC), 'the internal market shall comprise an area without internal frontiers in which the free movement of goods, persons, services and capital is ensured in accordance with the provisions of the Treaties'.

A **common market**, although not defined in the TFEU, is usually considered to refer to the **internal market** plus other **common policies**, such as competition, agriculture, or the environment.

Finally, in an **economic and monetary union** economic policy becomes 'communitarised' and a **single currency** is adopted.

7.2 What is a charge equivalent to a customs duty?

While it is relatively clear what a **customs duty** is and while the Member States – in a relatively disciplined fashion and even ahead of schedule – complied with the requirement to gradually eliminate them over a twelve-year period, the question of what exactly constituted a **charge equivalent to a customs duty** repeatedly troubled the ECJ. Obviously, it was too tempting for states to influence trade by these alternative tools, requiring, for instance, export levies in order to collect statistical data, art export charges to prevent the sale of national cultural treasures and the like. Today, **Article 30 TFEU** (ex Article 25 TEC) unequivocally provides:

> "**Customs duties** on imports and exports and **charges having equivalent effect** shall be **prohibited** between Member States. This prohibition shall also apply to customs duties of a fiscal nature."

It did not take the ECJ very long to adopt a strict test laying down a very **broad definition** of what is prohibited as a charge equivalent to a customs duty. In Case 24/68 *Commission* v. *Italy* [1969] ECR 193, the ECJ held that:

> "**any pecuniary charge**, however small and whatever its designation and mode of application, which is **imposed unilaterally** on domestic or foreign goods **by reason of** the fact that they **cross a frontier**; and which is not a customs duty in the strict sense, constitutes a charge having equivalent effect within the meaning of Articles 9 and 12 of the Treaty, **even if** it is **not** imposed for the **benefit** of the State, is **not discriminatory** or **protective** in effect or if the product on which the charge is imposed is **not** in **competition** with any domestic product."

This standard was relied upon in Cases 2 and 3/69 *Sociaal Fonds voor de Diamantarbeiders* v. *SA Ch. Brachfeld & Sons* [1969] ECR 211, where the Court held that the payment of 0.33 per cent of the value of imported uncut diamonds as contribution to a social benefit fund was an unlawful charge having equivalent effect.

In the *First Art Treasures* Case, Case 7/68 *Commission* v. *Italy* [1968] ECR 428, the ECJ had already determined that the qualification as a charge having equivalent effect depended only upon the **effect of the charge**, **not** on its **purpose**. In that case, the Court was of the opinion that the purpose of an Italian art export charge, which was, arguably, non-fiscal, and rather aimed at the protection of national art heritage, was irrelevant. Instead, its effect (a pecuniary burden levied on the crossing of a border) made it *per se* unlawful.

In the same case the Court made the important incidental finding that art treasures are also goods covered by the Treaty provisions on the free movement of goods, since they can be valued in money and are capable of forming the subject of commercial transactions.

The irrelevance of the non-fiscal purpose of a charge due upon goods crossing an intra-Community border was reaffirmed in Case 87/75 *Bresciani* v. *Amministrazione delle Finanze* [1976] ECR 129, where the Court also prohibited charges for veterinary and public health inspections, which implied that these have to be borne by society at large ($\rightarrow$ *4.11*).

The only exception applies in situations where Union law itself requires such inspections. In Case 18/87 *Commission* v. *Germany* [1988] ECR 5427, the Court held that veterinary inspection costs did not constitute unlawful charges having equivalent effect if they reflected the actual cost, the inspection was obligatory and pre-scribed by Community law and ultimately promoted the free move-ment of goods.

? 7.3 Outline the facts and significance of the *Dassonville* judgment

In **Directive 70/50**, which was applicable during the transitional period leading to the establishment of a Common Market, the Commission had already listed a number of measures by which states discriminated against imported goods and which were to be considered contrary to **Article 34 TFEU** (ex Article 28 TEC), pro-viding that '**quantitative restrictions** on imports and all **measures having equivalent effect** shall be **prohibited** between Member States'. The measures listed included minimum or maximum prices for imported products, less favourable payment conditions for imports, special conditions with regard to size, packaging, compos-ition, identification for imported goods and others. The directive only reluctantly referred to rules that were not discriminatory on their face. While the extension to such 'indistinctly applicable rules' was clearly expressed in the *Cassis* Case (→ *7.5*), the *Dassonville* Case had already laid the groundwork for this development.

Case 8/74 *Procureur du Roi* v. *Dassonville* [1974] ECR 837 is still the leading case providing a workable definition of **'measures having equivalent effect'** according to Article 34 TFEU. In this judgment the Court held that:

> "**All trading rules** enacted by Member States which are **capable** of **hindering**, directly or indirectly, actually or potentially, **intra-Community trade** are to be considered as measures having an effect equivalent to quantitative restrictions."

In this particular case, a Belgian importer was fined for violating Belgian law which required whisky importers to provide a certificate of authenticity from the country of origin (Scotland) and not only from the country of direct import (France). The ECJ considered that this constituted an unreasonable hindrance to intra-Community trade.

? 7.4 Are there measures other than state laws, regulations or administrative practices that may violate Article 34 TFEU?

Although the *Dassonville* formula speaks of 'trading rules enacted by Member States' it was quickly recognised that these should not be limited to statutes or other formal law. ECJ practice clearly also covers **regulatory measures** and **administrative practices**. However, the Court went beyond even that in the so-called *Buy Irish* Case, Case 249/87 *Commission* v. *Ireland* [1982] ECR 4005, where it qualified a **publicity campaign** promoting 'guaranteed Irish products' of the Irish Goods Council, a private company, as a measure having equivalent effect. In the Court's eyes it was crucial that the promoting agency **received public funding** and that there was state **influence on its management** in order to consider its activities as national practice. The ECJ sweepingly declared that 'even measures adopted by the government of a Member State which do not have binding effect may be capable of influencing the conduct of traders and consumers in that State and thus of frustrating the aims of the Community'.

In the so-called *Spanish Strawberries* Case, Case C-265/95 *Commission* v. *France* [1997] ECR I-6959, the ECJ stunned many observers by holding France responsible for the damage done by angry French farmers blockading roads against agricultural imports from Spain. The Court held that France had violated Articles 28 and 10 TEC (now Articles 34 TFEU and Article 4(3) TEU) by **not taking sufficient measures** to **prevent** the farmers from disrupting agricultural imports.

7.5 What is the *Cassis* principle?

The *Cassis* **Case**, short for its – to most non-German speakers unpronounceable – official name Case 120/78 *REWE Zentral AG* v. *Bundesmonopolverwaltung für Branntwein* [1979] ECR 649, is one of the cornerstones of the EU's free movement law. There are two main lessons to be drawn from that case, which involved the French blackcurrant liqueur, *Cassis de Dijon* (together with champagne – a crucial ingredient for *Kir Royal*).

First, *Cassis* states the principle of **mutual recognition** which was re-formulated in a 1980 policy communication of the Commission in the following words:

> "Any **product lawfully produced** and **marketed** in one **Member State** must, in principle, be **admitted** to the market of **any other Member State**."

Second, *Cassis* stands for a broadening of the permissible **grounds to derogate** from the **free movement obligations**. This is, of course, conditional upon the fact that Union law has not developed appropriate rules in the area concerned, which in effect means that there is no harmonisation by secondary Union law. In such situations Member States may enact **'reasonable'** and **'proportionate'** regulations to ensure that the public is not harmed. The court held that:

> "obstacles to movement within the Community resulting from disparities between the national laws relating to the marketing of the products in question must be accepted insofar as those provisions may be recognized as being necessary in order to satisfy **mandatory requirements** relating in particular to the effectiveness of fiscal supervision, the protection of public health, the fairness of commercial transactions and the defence of the consumer."

In this particular case, the ECJ held that a German minimum alcoholic content rule for beverages was not a reasonable measure. The Germans had unsuccessfully argued that public health and consumer protection considerations could justify the prohibition of marketing French fruit liqueur containing less alcohol than comparable German liqueurs on the grounds that this could eventually lead Germans to increased alcohol consumption and mislead them as to the liqueur's alcohol content.

? 7.6 For what reasons may the principle of free movement of goods be restricted?

After *Cassis*, the law has become relatively clear on this matter. On the one hand, there are the **Treaty provisions** expressly derogating from the general prohibition of quantitative restrictions and measures having equivalent effect. They are stated in **Article 36 TFEU** (ex Article 30 TEC):

" "The provisions of Articles 34 and 35 shall not preclude
prohibitions or restrictions on imports, exports or goods
in transit justified on grounds of **public morality, public
policy or public security**; the protection of **health
and life** of humans, animals or plants; the protection
of **national treasures possessing artistic, historic or
archaeological value**; or the protection of **industrial and
commercial property**. Such prohibitions or restrictions
shall not, however, constitute a means of **arbitrary
discrimination** or a **disguised restriction** on trade
between Member States.""

On the other hand, there are the **'mandatory requirements'** of
Cassis 'relating in particular to the **effectiveness of fiscal supervision**, the **protection of public health**, the **fairness of commercial
transactions** and the **defence of the consumer**' which – if applied
in a non-discriminatory and reasonable fashion – may equally justify a derogation from the free movement obligations 'in the absence
of common rules' (→ *7.5*).

Subsequent cases have added further 'mandatory requirements' in
the sense of *Cassis*, such as **environmental protection** in Case 302/86
Commission v. *Denmark* [1988] ECR 4607 (→ *10.11*), **pluralism of
the press** in Case C-368/95 *Vereinigte Familiapress* v. *Heinrich Bauer
Verlag* [1997] ECR I-3689, the **health and safety of workers** in Case
155/80 *Oebel* [1981] ECR 1993, and the **promotion of culture** and
fostering certain forms of art in Cases 60 and 61/84 *Cinéthèque* v.
Fédération Nationale des Cinémas Français [1985] ECR 2605.

7.7 Is there also a role for fundamental rights?

The ECJ has also taken into account potential clashes between the
protection of fundamental rights by Member States (→ *ch. 6*) and
the demands of the unrestricted free movement of goods. In Case

C-112/00 *Schmidberger* v. *Austria* [2003] ECR I-5659, the Court held that the protection of **fundamental rights** 'justified a **restriction** of the obligations imposed by Community law, even under a fundamental freedom guaranteed by the Treaty such as the free **movement of goods**' (→ *6.12, 8.19*). The case concerned a blockade of the trans-Alpine traffic routes in Austria by demonstrators expressing their concern over the environmental impact of unrestricted road traffic. The demonstrations were officially permitted by the Austrian authorities. This made the ensuing constraint on intra-Community trade clearly attributable to the Austrian government under the *Spanish Strawberries* Case doctrine (→ *7.4*). However, the ECJ found a justification of the measures in the freedom of expression and assembly. Since the permissions to hold the demonstration were limited, necessary and proportionate there was no violation of the free movement of goods.

? 7.8 Is the so-called German purity law of 1516 which requires beer to be manufactured only from malted barley, hops, yeast and water consistent with EU law?

The *German Beer* Case, Case 178/84 *Commission* v. *Germany* [1987] ECR 1227, exemplifies the *Cassis* rule on mandatory requirements at work (→ *7.5*). Pursuant to the German Beer Duty Act 1952, which was in turn based on a venerable statute of the early sixteenth century, only products manufactured according to the **'purity law'**, that is, without any artificial additives, could be marketed under the term 'beer'. According to the ECJ, this clearly constituted a **measure having equivalent** effect which, openly defying the principle of mutual recognition as enunciated in *Cassis*, was inconsistent with EU law.

The Court went on to address the justifications raised by the German government. The consumer protection argument, according to which German beer consumers had to be protected because they associated 'beer' exclusively with purely produced beverages, was rejected by the ECJ as disproportionate. In the Court's eyes, labelling requirements would have been sufficient to inform consumers about the content of a product.

In addition to the purity law, the German Foodstuffs Act 1974 prohibited the marketing of beer containing additives. The Court, in principle, upheld the right of Member States – in the absence of harmonisation – to decide what degree of protection of the health and life of humans they intended to assure. Such a public health justification was, however, subject to a rule of proportionality. The Court could not be persuaded that there was indeed a long-term risk to public health from additives, and found that the absence of any provisions permitting additives meeting a technological need rendered the German legislation disproportionate.

? 7.9 Is a Member State entitled to forbid the importation of 'indecent and obscene articles' from other Member States?

In its first reference for a preliminary ruling from the ECJ, the House of Lords wanted to know whether a total ban on the importation of Danish sex films into the UK could be justified under Article 36 TFEU (ex Article 30 TEC). In Case 34/79 *R.* v. *Henn and Darby* [1979] ECR 3795, the ECJ held that not only 'limitations' but also a **total import ban** constituted a **'quantitative restriction'**, but that such a restriction was **justified** 'on the grounds of **public morality**' because 'it is for each Member State to determine in accordance with its own scale of values and in the form selected by it the requirements of public morality in its territory'.

What remained problematic with this ruling was the fact that different standards applied within the UK insofar as that there was no

absolute ban on the possession of the items in question. This latter aspect was crucial to the different outcome in a similar, subsequent case. In Case 121/85 *Conegate Ltd* v. *Customs and Excise
Commissioners* [1986] ECR 1007, involving the seizure of inflat-
able erotic dolls imported from Germany to the UK, the ECJ held
that 'a Member State may not rely on grounds of public morality to
prohibit the importation of goods from other Member States when
its legislation contains no prohibition on the manufacture or marketing of the same goods on its territory'. In other words, this import
ban was considered to constitute an arbitrary discrimination or pro-
tectionism contrary to Article 36, 2nd sentence TFEU in view of the
absence of comparably strict rules against similar domestic articles
(→ *7.6*).

7.10 Are national retail sales restrictions on Sundays, which lead to a demonstrable reduction of imports from other Member States, compatible with EU law?

After *Dassonville* and *Cassis*, the ECJ seemed to be willing to extend
the prohibition of Article 34 TFEU (ex Article 28 TEC) to virtually
any (even non-discriminatory) rules which affected trade in some
negative way.

The so-called *Sunday trading* **cases** provide a good example of
the potential scope of 'measures having equivalent effect' in which
it was repeatedly argued that national laws prohibiting retail sales on
Sundays and public holidays reduced the total sales volume, including the sale of imported goods from other Member States. In Case
145/88 *Torfaen Borough Council* v. *B & Q plc* [1989] ECR 3851,
the Court, with apparent uneasiness, accepted this premise but held
in rather cryptic language that:

> "Article [34 TFEU] must be interpreted as meaning that the prohibition which it lays down does not apply to national rules prohibiting retailers from opening their premises on Sunday where the restrictive effect on Community trade which may result therefrom does not exceed the effects intrinsic to rules of this kind."

It reached this conclusion by finding a justification in the *Cassis* sense, holding that:

> "[Sunday trading rules] reflect certain political and economic choices insofar as their purpose is so arranged as to accord with national or regional socio-cultural characteristics, and that, in the present state of Community law, is a matter for Member States."

To arrive at this Community law blessing the Court relied on its earlier decision in Case 155/80 *Oebel* [1981] ECR 1993, where it had held that 'national rules governing hours of work, delivery and sale for bakers constitute a legitimate part of economic and social policy consistent with the objectives of public interest pursued by the Treaty'.

Following the *Torfaen* approach, a Sunday closing requirement was upheld as **proportionate** and lawful in Joined Cases C-306/88, 304/90 and 169/91 *Council of the City of Stoke-on-Trent* v. *B & Q plc* [1992] ECR I-6457, and in Case C-312/89 *Union Département des Syndicats CGT de l'Aisne* v. *Conforama* [1991] ECR I-997, where a French Labour Code requirement providing for Sunday as a day of rest for employees was upheld as protecting an imperative social interest.

7.11 What was new in the *Keck* Case?

Although the *Sunday trading* cases and others have demonstrated the ECJ's willingness to accept certain justifications for national rules regulating the marketing of goods, the implicit message that these rules were, in principle, considered to constitute measures prohibited by Article 34 TFEU (ex Article 28 TEC) did not make the Member States very happy.

For them relief came in the form of an important case which was transferred from chamber to plenary proceedings, and which is generally considered as having partly **overruled** *Dassonville* and *Cassis*. In a preliminary ruling in Joined Cases C-267 and 268/91 *Criminal Proceedings against Keck and Mithouard* [1993] ECR I-6097, the Court held that **'selling arrangements'**, or better **'marketing modalities'**, which are applied **indiscriminately** to all traders were **not** to be regarded as **'measures having equivalent effect'** in the sense of *Dassonville*. Keck and Mithouard were prosecuted in French courts for re-selling goods at a loss which was contrary to a French law. The ECJ recognised the correlation to the *Sunday trading* cases invoked by Keck and Mithouard in order to characterise the prohibition on resale at a loss as an unlawful measure having equivalent effect. It found that such legislation might restrict the volume of sales and hence the volume of sales of products from other Member States. It hastened to add, however, that it remained unclear 'whether such a possibility is sufficient to characterize the legislation in question as a measure having equivalent effect'. In this respect the Court came to a negative answer:

> "However, contrary to what has previously been decided, the application to products from other Member States of national provisions restricting or prohibiting certain selling arrangements is not such as to hinder directly or indirectly, actually or potentially, trade between Member States within the meaning of the *Dassonville* judgment, provided that those provisions apply to all affected traders operating within the national territory and provided that they affect in the same manner, in law and in fact, the marketing of domestic products and of those from other Member States."

"Where those conditions are fulfilled, the application of such rules to the sale of products from another Member State meeting the requirements laid down by that State is not by nature such as to prevent their access to the market or to impede access any more than it impedes the access of domestic products. Such rules therefore fall outside the scope of Article [34] of the Treaty."

Thus, it did not come as a surprise that in the post-*Keck* phase, in Joined Cases C-69 and 258/93 *Punto Casa* v. *Sindaco del Comune di Capena* [1994] ECR I-2355, Italian **Sunday closing rules** were held to fall outside the scope of Article 34 TFEU. Other **'selling arrangements'** that were covered by the new *Keck* rule concerned an **advertising prohibition** of a pharmacists' association in Case C-292/92 *Hünermund* v. *Landesapotheker Baden-Württemberg* [1993] ECR I-6787, **shop opening hours** in Joined Cases C-401 and 402/92 *Criminal Proceedings against Tankstation 't Heukske vof and J.B.E. Boermans* [1994] ECR I-2199 and **restrictions on places** where tobacco could be **sold** in Case C-387/93 *Banchero* [1995] ECR I-4663.

Subsequent cases have also shown that the **distinction** between **'product requirements'** and **'selling arrangements'** is not always easy to draw. Some marketing restrictions, in particular for consumer protection reasons, are so closely related to the products in question that they have been considered under Article 34 TFEU (ex Article 28 TEC). In Case C-470/93 *Verein gegen Unwesen in Handel und Gewerbe Köln* v. *Mars* [1995] ECR I-1923, the ECJ held that German Unfair Competition Law rules which prohibited the sale of ice cream bars with a logo on them saying '+10%' was held to hinder intra-Community trade because it 'may compel the importer to adjust the presentation of his product according to the place where they are to be marketed and consequently to incur additional packaging and advertising costs'. Similarly, in Case C-315/92 *Verband Sozialer Wettbewerb* v. *Clinique Laboratories* [1994] ECR I-317, it was the dual burden of regulation both in the state of production as well as the state of sale which made the German ban on the use of the word 'clinique' for cosmetics an unlawful measure under Article 34 TFEU (ex Article 28 TEC).

The line between 'product requirements' and 'selling arrangements' was further blurred by Case C-189/95 *Criminal Proceedings against Franzén* [1997] ECR I-5909, in which the ECJ held that the Swedish licensing system for wholesalers importing alcoholic beverages, apparently a 'selling arrangement', was contrary to Article 34 TFEU (ex Article 28 TEC). According to the Court, the highly restrictive system 'constitutes an obstacle to the importation of alcoholic beverages from other Member States in that it imposes additional costs on such beverages, such as intermediary costs, payment of charges and fees or the grant of a licence, and costs rising from the obligation to maintain storage capacity in Sweden'.

Another 'Scandinavian' preliminary ruling equally narrowed down the impact of the *Keck* exception by holding that non-discriminatory product use regulations may constitute an impermissible hindrance to market access. In Case C-142/05 *Aklagaren* v. *Mickelsson and Roos* [2009] ECR I-4273, the ECJ held that a Swedish regulation limiting the use of personal watercraft to designated waterways affected the access of such products to the Swedish market. Although it applied to imported as well as to domestic products, it was likely to reduce the interest of Swedish consumers to buy such goods coming from other Member States. The Court found, however, that the measure could be justified for environmental reasons (→ *10.11*).

? 7.12 What is the role of the tax provision of Article 110 TFEU in the context of free movement of goods?

Article 110 TFEU (ex Article 90 TEC) provides:

> "No Member State shall impose, directly or indirectly, on the products of other Member States any internal taxation

of any kind in excess of that imposed directly or indirectly on similar domestic products.

"Furthermore, no Member State shall impose on the products of other Member States any internal taxation of such a nature as to afford indirect protection to other products."

This prohibition of **discriminatory** or **protective internal taxation** complements the Treaty's provisions on the elimination of customs duties and charges having equivalent effect in order to ensure undistorted free movement of goods within the EU's internal market. While Article 30 TFEU (ex Article 25 TEC) prohibits duties or charges collected as a result of goods crossing a border ($\rightarrow$ 7.2), Article 110 TFEU (ex Article 90 TEC) outlaws internal fiscal discrimination once goods have entered a particular Member State.

In its case law as exemplified in Case 45/75 *REWE* v. *Hauptzollamt Landau/Pfalz* [1976] ECR 181, the ECJ has clarified that similarity in the sense of Article 110 TFEU does not require identity but rather refers to goods which 'have similar characteristics and meet the same needs from the point of view of the consumer'. Applied to the unavoidable field of alcoholic products, the Court struck down a number of national tax regimes providing for different tax rates for different kinds of spirits. For instance, in Case 168/78 *Commission* v. *France* [1980] ECR 347, the Court found that a 'characteristic of [the French tax] system is in fact that an essential part of domestic production ... spirits obtained from wine and fruit, come within the most favourable tax category whereas at least two types of product, almost all of which are imported from other Member States, are subject to higher taxation'. As the Cases 169/78 *Commission* v. *Italy* [1980] ECR 409, and 171/78 *Commission* v. *Denmark* [1980] ECR 447 demonstrate, France was not the only Member State engaging in such a practice.

The ECJ clarified that Article 110(1) TFEU prohibits both **direct** and **indirect discrimination**. In Case 112/84 *Humblot* v. *Directeur des Services Fiscaux* [1985] ECR 1367, the Court had to assess the legality of a French car tax system which depended upon the power rating of the cars. It held that 'although the system embodies no formal distinction based on the origin of the products it manifestly exhibits discriminatory or protective features contrary to Article [110], since the power rating determining liability to the special tax has been fixed at a level such that only imported cars, in particular from other Member States, are subject to the special tax whereas all cars of domestic manufacture are liable to the distinctly more advantageous differential tax'. The ECJ made clear, however, that differential car tax rates may be compatible with Article 110 TFEU if they serve, for instance, **environmental purposes**. In Case C-132/88 *Commission* v. *Greece* [1990] ECR I-1567, the Court held that this objective justification can be upheld even where imported cars only fall into the highest tax category.

In Case 170/78 *Commission* v. *United Kingdom* [1983] ECR 2265, the Court had to deal with a tax regime that imposed an excise tax on wine that was roughly five times higher than that for beer. Though the Court did not consider the two alcoholic products to be sufficiently similar in order to consider the UK practice under Article 110(1) TFEU, it found a violation of Article 110(2) TFEU because the 'United Kingdom's tax system has the effect of subjecting wine imported from other Member States to an additional burden so as to afford protection to domestic beer production'.

The precise distinction between Article 110(1), prohibiting discriminatory taxation of 'similar' goods, and Article 110(2) TFEU, prohibiting 'protective' taxation against imported goods which may compete with domestic goods, is not always easy to draw. Thus, in the abovementioned Case 168/78 *Commission* v. *France* [1980] ECR 347, the ECJ found that the French alcohol tax system, imposing rather high taxes on grain-based spirits, such as rum, gin, whisky and vodka, while providing for rather low taxes for fruit-based spirits, such as Armagnac, calvados and cognac, also had a protective effect contrary to Article 110(2) TFEU.

8 The free movement of persons

In addition to the effective implementation of the **free movement of goods**, characteristic of a customs union, the Community has always aimed at guaranteeing the **free movement of persons** in order to create a true internal market. This 'internal market' is defined in Article 26(2) TFEU (ex Article 14(2) TEC) as 'an area without internal borders in which the free movement of goods, persons, services and capital is ensured'. The history of the EU is the history of the gradual implementation of these so-called **four freedoms** which follows a similar regulatory pattern, that is, **ensuring non-discrimination** and **eliminating intra-EU restrictions** by Member States.

This chapter will provide an overview on the EU rules on the free movement of natural and legal persons, that is, individuals and companies. They originate in three sets of Treaty provisions: **the free movement of 'workers'**; the **freedom of establishment**; and the **freedom to provide services**. The resulting, rather narrow economic rights have been broadened through the case law of the ECJ and secondary EU legislation, which has almost led to a **general right of free movement**. The Luxembourg Court did so by broadly interpreting the entitlements contained in Treaty provisions and by gradually restricting the powers of Member States to limit these rights.

? 8.1 Is there a general right to free movement for all EU citizens?

Article 20 TFEU (ex Article 17(1) TEC) establishes a citizenship of the Union, a concept which has already been introduced by the Maastricht Treaty. Union citizenship **derives** from and **complements** the **nationality** of the **Member States**.

Although Article 21(1) TFEU (ex Article 18(1) TEC) broadly stipulates that '[e]very **citizen of the Union** shall have the **right to move and reside freely within the territory of the Member States**', one should not overlook the *caveat* that any such right is '**subject to** the **limitations** and conditions laid down in the Treaties and by the measures adopted to give them effect'. In reality, therefore, the right of free movement and residence remains dependent upon availing oneself of economic rights either as a worker or as a self-employed person or other EU entitlements.

The precise conditions of the **free movement rights of workers** are laid down in **Article 45 TFEU** (ex Article 39 TEC) as follows:

(1) **Freedom of movement for workers** shall be secured within the Union.

(2) Such freedom of movement shall entail the **abolition** of any **discrimination** based on nationality between workers of the Member States as regards employment, remuneration and other conditions of work and employment.

(3) It shall entail the right, subject to limitations justified on grounds of public policy, public security or public health:

(a) to **accept offers of employment** actually made;

(b) to **move freely within the territory** of Member States **for this purpose**;

(c) to **stay** in a Member State **for the purpose of employment** in accordance with the provisions governing the employment of nationals of that State laid down by law, regulation or administrative action;

(d) to **remain** in the territory of a Member State **after having been employed** in that State, subject to conditions which shall be embodied in regulations to be drawn up by the Commission.

(4) The provisions of this Article shall **not** apply to employment in the **public service**.

In addition, the Union has adopted a wide range of **secondary legislation** based on Article 46 TFEU (ex Article 40 TEC), which provides that the Council shall 'acting in accordance with the ordinary legislative procedure and after consulting the Economic and Social Committee, issue directives or make regulations setting out the measures required to bring about freedom of movement for workers, as defined in Article 45 …' ($\rightarrow$ *3.9*). The most important early legislative acts were: Directive 64/221 on public policy, security and health derogations ($\rightarrow$ *8.9*); Directive 68/360 on entry and residence requirements of workers and their families; Regulation 1612/68, which contains several core rights of workers and their family members ($\rightarrow$ *8.4, 8.6–8*); and Regulation 1251/70 on the right to remain in another Member State after employment.

Rights of residence of persons **other than workers** or self-employed persons have been accepted by the Member States only reluctantly. In the 1990s a number of directives conferred such rights on persons who had ceased to work (Directive 90/365), students exercising the right to vocational training (Directive 90/366, replaced by Directive 93/96) and others, such as the so-called 'Playboy' Directive 90/364 which gave free movement rights also to persons not participating in any economic activity as long as they could afford their expenses. According to all these directives, however, **residence rights** were **dependent** upon the **availability of adequate resources** so as not to become a burden on the social assistance schemes of the Member States and sickness insurance coverage.

Most of these acts have been replaced by **Directive 2004/38 on the Rights of Citizens of the Union and their Family Members**

to Move and Reside Freely within the Territory of the Member States, which had to be implemented by April 2006 (→ *8.6–9*). This directive harmonised the existing, rather fragmented, law, although Article 14(1) retained the basic idea that residence rights of EU citizens 'must not become an unreasonable burden on the public finances of the host Member State', as the ECJ had expressed in Case C-413/99 *Baumbast* v. *Secretary of State for the Home Department* [2002] ECR I-7091.

> **? 8.2 Who is a 'worker' benefiting from the free movement rights enshrined in the Treaty and secondary EU law?**

In general, the ECJ adopted a rather **expansive interpretation** of who qualifies as a **'worker'**.

In Case 58/81 *Levin* v. *Staatssecretaris van Justitie* [1982] ECR 1035, the ECJ held that **part-time workers** could also benefit from free movement rights as long as they pursued **'effective and genuine economic activities'**. The only exclusion was work 'on such a small scale as to be regarded as purely marginal and ancillary'.

In Case 66/85 *Lawrie-Blum* v. *Land Baden Württemberg* [1986] ECR 2121, the Court considered that a trainee teacher also qualified as a worker under Article 45 TFEU (ex Article 39 TEC) (→ *8.1*). It suggested the following test: 'The essential feature of an employment relationship, however, is that for a certain time a person **performs services** for and **under the direction** of another person in return for which he receives **remuneration**.' In Case 196/87 *Steymann* v. *Staatssecretaris van Justitie* [1988] ECR 6159, the ECJ held that even 'unpaid work' for a religious community (Bhaghwan) was 'work', since remuneration existed in the form of the religious community's obligation to provide for the material needs of its members. In Case C-456/02 *Trojani* v. *CPAS* [2004] ECR I-7573, the Court confirmed that 'activities cannot be regarded as real and genuine economic activity if they constitute merely a means of rehabilitation or reintegration for the persons concerned'. It cautioned, however, that services performed by a former drug addict in the course of a reintegration programme could constitute 'work' if they were 'capable of being regarded as forming part of the normal labour market'.

Although not fully qualifying as workers, the ECJ has expansively interpreted the Treaty provisions for the benefit of **job-seekers**. In the *Antonissen* Case, Case C-292/89 *R. v. Immigration Appeal Tribunal, ex parte Antonissen* [1991] ECR I-745, the Court considered that former Article 39(3) TEC (now Article 45(3) TFEU) 'must be interpreted as enumerating, in a non-exhaustive way, certain rights benefiting nationals of Member States in the context of the free movement of workers and that that freedom also entails the right for nationals of Member States to move freely within the territory of the Member States and to stay there for the purposes of seeking employment'. However, states still retain the power to expel those who remain unsuccessful for a longer period of time.

? 8.3 Discuss the scope of the non-discrimination obligation contained in Article 45(2) TFEU

It is clear that Article 45(2) TFEU prohibits any **direct discrimination** on the basis of **nationality**, which may be justified only under the **'public service'** exception of Article 45(4) TFEU discussed below (→ *8.10*).

Most of the practical issues arose, however, in the context of various forms of **indirect discrimination**. In this context the ECJ has traditionally been rather suspicious about various national rules that can be fulfilled more easily by nationals than non-nationals, such as **residence** or **requirements** relating to the **place of education**. Two other forms of indirect discrimination were found by the ECJ in the cases discussed below.

In Case 13/69 *Württembergische Milchverwertung-Südmilch-AG* v. *Ugliola* [1970] ECR 363, the ECJ held that German legislation, which provided that only military service in the Bundeswehr, the German army, counted as surrogate employment time for seniority, pension and job security purposes was 'indirectly introducing discrimination in favour of their own nationals alone', since service in the Bundeswehr would be satisfied by a greater number of Germans than other Community nationals. In a reverse nationality constellation, in Case C-419/92 *Scholz* v. *Universitaria di Cagliari* [1994] ECR I-505, the Court held that a job recruitment system for canteen workers, awarding points for previous employment in the Italian public sector, constituted indirect discrimination against a German worker.

? 8.4 Are language requirements for certain jobs forms of indirect discrimination contrary to EU law?

While **language requirements** are a typical form of indirect discrimination they may still be justifiable for certain jobs. Thus, Article 3(1) of Regulation 1612/68 permits the imposition of 'conditions relating to **linguistic knowledge** required **by reason of the nature of the post to be filled**'.

In Case 379/87 *Groener* v. *Minister for Education* [1989] ECR 3967, the ECJ upheld as non-discriminatory an Irish language test which was a condition of employment for a teaching post, even though Irish was not the language of instruction. The Court reasoned that the Treaty did not prohibit the protection and promotion of the national language if the measures are proportionate. It has been rightly suggested that this outcome was influenced by the high political importance attached to the protection of cultural diversity and identity in the Union, and the judgment may be seen as an example of the Court reacting to strong political pressure from Member States in certain fields.

In Joined Cases C-259, 331–332/91 *Allué, Coonan and others* v. *Università degli studi di Venezia and Parma* [1993] ECR 4309, however, the ECJ found an indirect discrimination on the basis of language unjustifiable. The Court was of the opinion that different employment contracts for foreign-language assistants and other university personnel in Italy mainly disadvantaged non-Italians. In this context, it reiterated that:

> ❝the principle of equal treatment, of which Article [45(2)] of the Treaty is one embodiment, prohibits not only overt discrimination based on nationality but all covert forms of discrimination which, by applying other distinguishing criteria, in fact achieve the same result.❞

⁇ 8.5 Are private parties bound by the non-discrimination obligation of Article 45(2) TFEU?

This is an issue similar to the question raised in the context of free movement of goods law, asking what constitutes a 'measure' in the sense of Article 34 TFEU (ex Article 28 TEC) and how far activities of private parties could fall under its prohibition, which was discussed in cases such as *Buy Irish*, Case 249/87 *Commission* v. *Ireland* [1982] ECR 4005 and *Spanish Strawberries*, Case C-265/95 *Commission* v. *France* [1997] ECR I-6959 (→ *7.4*).

With regard to the free movement of persons, it is discussed as the **'horizontal effect'** of Article 45(2) TFEU, that is, whether free movement obligations may be invoked only against a Member State ('vertically') or also against **private parties** ('horizontally') (→ *4.8*). Thanks to cyclists, football and basketball players and other professional athletes, the ECJ has successively struck down as discriminatory (on the basis of nationality) the regulations of sporting associations.

In the early leading case involving Belgian speed cyclists, in Case 36/74 *Walrave & Koch* [1974] ECR 1405, the Court broadly stated that:

> "Prohibition of such discrimination does not only apply to the action of public authorities but extends likewise to rules of any other nature aimed at regulating in a collective manner gainful employment and the provision of services ...
>
> "Since, moreover, working conditions in the various Member States are governed sometimes by means of provisions laid down by law or regulations and sometimes by agreements and other acts concluded or adopted by private persons, to limit the prohibitions in question to acts of a public authority would risk creating inequality in their application."

In the famous *Bosman* Case, Case C-415/93 *Union Royal Belge des Sociétés de Football Association* v. *Bosman* [1995] ECR I-4921, the ECJ found fault with the transfer system of European national and transnational football associations. It held that transfer rules which regularly involved rather large sums of money being paid to clubs in order to engage a player as constituting:

> "an obstacle to freedom of movement for workers prohibited in principle by [Article 45] of the Treaty. It could only be otherwise if those rules pursued a legitimate aim compatible with the Treaty and were justified by pressing reasons of public interest. But even if that were so, application of those rules would still have to be such as to ensure achievement of the aim in question and not go beyond what is necessary for that purpose."

This latter rule of reason clearly echoes the Court's reasoning in *Cassis*, Case 120/78 *REWE Zentral AG* v. *Bundesmonopolverwaltung für Branntwein* [1979] ECR 649 (→ *7.5*). At the same time, the Court rejected the suggestion to regard the transfer rules as comparable to 'selling arrangements' in the sense of *Keck*, Joined Cases C-267 and 268/91 *Criminal Proceedings against Keck and Mithouard* [1993] ECR I-6097, which would thus fall outside the scope of the free movement provisions (→ *7.11*).

The *Bosman* decision was followed in Case C-176/96 *Jyri Lehtonen and Others* v. *Fédération Royale Belge des Sociétés de Basket-ball ASBL (FRBSB)* [2000] ECR I-2681, where the Court held that rules preventing professional basketball players from taking part in competitions if they had been transferred after a certain date may constitute an obstacle to free movement of workers.

All these cases involved employers or employers' associations which had some general regulatory powers. The open question as to whether the **horizontal effect** of Article 45(2) TFEU also applied to individual employers was resolved affirmatively by the ECJ in Case C-281/89 *Angonese* v. *Cassa di Risparmio di Bolzano SpA* [2000] ECR I-4139, wherein the Court said that 'the prohibition of discrimination on grounds of nationality laid down in [Article 45] … must be regarded as **applying to private persons** as well'. As a consequence, it held the requirement of possessing a special certificate of bilingualism in order to compete for a post with a private Italian bank to be contrary to the non-discrimination rule of Article 45 TFEU, since such certificates were issued by authorities only in northern Italy.

? 8.6 How did the ECJ interpret the crucial notion of 'social advantages' contained in the EU's free movement of workers legislation?

The Treaty not only prohibits discrimination and other obstacles to the free movement of workers, it also confers **positive rights** on EU **workers**. Many of these rights are spelled out in more detail in **secondary legislation**, the centre-piece of which has been Regulation 1612/68 on the free movement of workers within the Union. Part I contained the most important provisions relating to eligibility for employment (Articles 1–6), equality of treatment within employment (Articles 7–9) and on workers' families (Articles 10–12), which are now governed by Directive 2004/38.

Article 7 Regulation 1612/68 **extended** the **non-discrimination** obligation of Article 45(2) TFEU, which is literally limited to 'conditions of work and employment', **to social and tax issues** and to **vocational training**. In particular, the ECJ's **teleological interpretation** (*effet utile*) of Article 7(2) Regulation 1612/68, which provides that Union workers 'shall enjoy the same social and tax advantages as national workers', has broadened considerably the rights of Union workers.

The Court rejected attempts to limit the notion of social and tax benefits to those directly connected to the employment relation itself, although it insisted that the advantages had to be **connected** to the claimants' **'objective status'** as **workers**.

In Case 32/75 *Cristini (Fiorini)* v. *SNCF* [1975] ECR 1085, the ECJ held that, 'in view of the equality of treatment which the provision seeks to achieve, the substantive area of application must be delineated so as to include all social and tax advantages, whether or not attached to the contract of employment, such as reduction in fares for large families'. Thus, the refusal by the French state railway to issue such a reduced fare card to the Italian widow of an Italian worker in France was unlawful. In Case 65/81 *Reina* v. *Landeskreditbank Baden-Württemberg* [1982] ECR 33, the ECJ even qualified interest-free childbirth loans granted under German legislation to German nationals as 'social advantages' wherein no discrimination was admissible.

A certain limit to the expansive interpretation of Article 7(2) Regulation 1612/68 was drawn in Case 207/78 *Ministère Public* v.

Even [1979] ECR 2019, in which a French national complained that a special retirement pension benefit given exclusively to Belgian Second World War veterans unlawfully discriminated against him in the field of social advantages. The ECJ, however, considered that the essential objective of the benefit in question was to give Belgian nationals 'an advantage by reason of the hardships suffered for that country', and that such a benefit 'cannot therefore be considered as an advantage granted to a national worker by reason primarily of his status of worker or resident on the national territory and for that reason does not fulfil the essential characteristics of the "social advantages" referred to in Article 7(2) of Regulation no 1612/68'. A similar logic was applied in Case C-386/02 *Baldinger* v. *Pensionsversicherungsanstalt der Arbeiter* [2004] ECR I-1417, with regard to an Austrian system of compensation payments for prisoners of war. In the Court's view, such payments, which were made to Austrian citizens only, were not linked to the recipients' status as workers but instead granted 'in testimony of national gratitude for the hardships they endured and is thus paid as a quid pro quo for the services they rendered to their country'.

Article 7(2) Regulation 1612/68 is limited to workers; it does not cover those who are self-employed. The ECJ, however, inferred social advantages of self-employed Union nationals and their families directly from Article 49 TFEU (ex Article 43 TEC), providing for the freedom of establishment (→ *8.12*). Thus, in Case C-111/91 *Commission* v. *Luxembourg* [1993] ECR I-817, a residence requirement for the entitlement to certain child allowances was considered to constitute an unjustifiable indirect discrimination contrary to both Article 7(2) Regulation 1612/68 and Article 49 TFEU. With regard to social advantages, the distinction between workers and self-employed has become a moot point as a result of Article 24(1) Directive 2004/38, which provides that all EU citizens residing in another Member State shall enjoy equal treatment.

? 8.7 How are the rights of the family members of workers protected?

The free movement of workers would hardly be effective if it were narrowly confined to the workers themselves, in particular, if it did not include a **right to be joined by** the **family** members of those workers.

While family members are not even mentioned in the TFEU, they are expressly covered by Regulation 1612/68. Most importantly, Article 10 provides:

(1) The following shall, irrespective of their nationality, have the right to install themselves with a worker who is a national of one Member State and who is employed in the territory of another Member State:

    (a) his spouse and their descendants who are under the age of 21 years or are dependants;

    (b) dependent relatives in the ascending line of the worker and his spouse.

(2) Member States shall facilitate the admission of any member of the family not coming within the provisions of paragraph 1 if dependent on the worker referred to above or living under his roof in the country whence he comes.

(3) For the purposes of paragraphs 1 and 2, the worker must have available for his family housing considered as normal for national workers in the region where he is employed; this provision, however, must not give rise to discrimination between national workers and workers from the other Member States.

In spite of the ECJ's rather **broad approach** to the rights of **family members**, **continuing family links** remain **important**, especially for third country nationals. In Case 267/83 *Diatta* v. *Land Berlin* [1985] ECR 567, the Court held that a Senegalese national, who was already separated from her French husband and wanted to divorce him, still had a right of residence in Germany since her marital relationship had not yet been terminated. In the Court's view:

""Article 10 of the Regulation does not require that the member of the family in question must live permanently with the worker, but, as is clear from Article 10(3), only that the accommodation which the worker has available must be such as may be considered normal for the purpose of accommodating his family. A requirement that the family must live under the same roof permanently cannot be implied.""

In addition, Article 11 gave spouses and under-aged children of workers – even if they are not Union nationals – an independent right to employment in the host state.

Articles 10 and 11 Regulation 1612/68 have been repealed by Directive 2004/38, which now governs the entry and residence rights of all EU citizens. Article 2(2)(b) extends the definition of 'family members' to include not only spouses, descendants and certain ascendant relatives, but also partners in 'registered partnerships' if recognised as equivalent to marriage by the legislation of the host Member State. Directive 2004/38 is also a typical piece of EU legislation in that it partially codifies rulings of the ECJ. A clear example is Article 13 of the directive entitled 'Retention of the right of residence by family members in the event of divorce, annulment of marriage or termination of registered partnership'. However, the Court's rather liberal approach may have been cut back by the legislator who, in Article 16(2) of the new directive, for example, provided that family members must have resided 'with the Union citizen' for five years in order to be eligible for permanent residence rights or that rights may be withdrawn in cases of abuse of rights 'such as marriages of convenience'.

8.8 Does EU law confer rights to education?

Though **education** is, of course, crucial for getting good jobs, it was not part of the Union's express competences until the Maastricht

Treaty. Nevertheless, some **educational rights** were already included in **Union legislation** and could be derived from **general Union principles** by the ECJ. For example, Article 12 Regulation 1612/68 provided that:

> "The children of a national of a Member State who is or has been employed in the territory of another Member State shall be admitted to that State's general educational, apprenticeship and vocational training courses under the same conditions as the nationals of that State, if such children are residing in its territory.
>
> "Member States shall encourage all efforts to enable such children to attend these courses under the best possible conditions."

In a rather controversial ruling in Case 9/74 *Casagrande* v. *Landeshauptstadt München* [1974] ECR 733, the ECJ held that a Bavarian student grant was an issue of 'admittance to education' in the sense of Article 12, Regulation 1612/68 where no discrimination is allowed. Less controversial – because clearly in line with the text of Article 12 – was the Court's ruling in Case C-7/94 *Gaal* [1996] ECR I-1031, in which the educational rights of non-dependent children over 21 were confirmed. This resulted from the fact that Article 12 had a broader coverage than Article 10 of the Regulation (→ 8.7).

Interestingly, the educational rights of workers themselves were narrower under Regulation 1612/68. Its Article 7(3) provided that they should have equal access only to 'training in vocational schools and retraining centres'. Thus, the ECJ held in cases such as Case 39/86 *Lair* v. *Universität Hannover* [1981] ECR 3161 and Case 197/86 *Brown* v. *Secretary of State for Scotland* [1988] ECR 3205, that EC law did not provide general equal treatment with regard to access to and financial and other support for studying at universities, since both education and social policy were, in principle, matters within the competence of the Member States. In the *Lair* Case, the Court clarified that 'the concept of a vocational school is a more limited one and refers exclusively to institutions which provide only instruction either alternating with or closely linked to an occupational activity'.

Also the TFEU's **general non-discrimination clause** in **Article 18 TFEU** (ex Article 12 TEC) was used by the ECJ to further educational rights. This was particularly important for persons who could not claim the same rights as workers or as their dependants. In the famous *Gravier* Case, Case 293/83 *Gravier* v. *City of Liège* [1985] ECR 593, the Court held that a Belgian enrolment fee which was requested from a French student (but not from Belgian students) was contrary to Article 12 TEC (now Article 18 TFEU). With its typical teleological reasoning the ECJ found the required connection of access to education with Community law in the potential effect of education on subsequent ability to find work. Thus, the case fell within the scope of the Treaty. The ECJ held that:

> "Access to vocational training is in particular likely to promote free movement of persons throughout the Community, by enabling them to obtain a qualification in the Member State where they intend to work …"

In Case 24/86 *Blaizot* v. *University of Liège* [1988] ECR 378, the Court clarified that the Treaty-based non-discrimination right was not limited to actual job-related training, but that 'vocational training' could include university education unless it was pursued only to improve one's general knowledge.

? 8.9 Outline the major exceptions to the principle of free movement of workers as reflected in the case law of the ECJ

The **public policy**, **public security** and **public health** exceptions provided for in Article 45(3) TFEU (→ *8.1*) have been made more precise by Directive 64/221, now Articles 27–33 of Directive 2004/38, and have been **interpreted restrictively** by the ECJ. These directives prohibit the invocation of such grounds as 'to service economic ends' and restrict them to grounds '**based** exclusively **on the personal conduct** of the individual concerned' (Article 27(1) Directive 2004/38).

The latter concept was the subject of litigation in the well-known *Van Duyn* Case, Case 41/74 *Van Duyn* v. *Home Office* [1974] ECR 1337 (→ *4.7*), where UK immigration authorities refused entry and residence to a Dutch national who wanted to work for the Church of Scientology which was considered 'socially harmful' by the UK. In a rather deferential ruling – not in line with the Court's otherwise restrictive approach – the ECJ found that, although membership of an organisation alone did not constitute 'personal conduct', active participation and identification with it would do so. The Court further held that even though there was no prohibition on UK nationals working for the Church of Scientology, 'the particular circumstances justifying recourse to the concept of public policy may vary from one country to another and from one period to another, and [that] it is therefore necessary in this matter to allow the competent national authorities an area of discretion within the limits imposed by the Treaty'.

This discretion was limited in Cases 115 and 116/81 *Adoui and Cornuaille* [1982] ECR 1665, where two sex workers, 'suspect from the point of view of morals', were threatened with deportation from Belgium. Although the ECJ confirmed that Community law did not provide a 'uniform scale of values as regards the assessment of conduct which may be considered as contrary to public policy', it held that:

> "conduct may not be considered as being of a sufficiently serious nature to justify restrictions on the admission to or residence within the territory of a Member State of a national of another Member State in a case where the former Member State does not adopt, with respect to the same conduct on the part of its own nationals repressive measures or other genuine and effective measures intended to combat such conduct."

In Case 36/75 *Rutili* v. *Ministre de l'Intérieur* [1975] ECR 1219, the Court considered a French restriction imposed upon an Italian national to reside in certain parts of France only contrary to Article 45(3) TFEU because the latter merely permitted for whole territory restrictions. Partial prohibitions were legal only if non-discriminatory according to Article 18 TFEU. The Court also reaffirmed that the 'personal conduct' prerequisite under Directive 64/221 required that the 'conduct constitutes a genuine and sufficiently serious threat to public policy'.

In Case 67/74 *Bonsignore* [1975] ECR 297, the ECJ considered a German deportation order concerning an Italian national who had fatally shot his brother to be of a 'general preventive nature'. It was thus not based 'exclusively on the personal conduct of the individual concerned' and was, therefore, contrary to EC law. The Court came to a similar conclusion in Case C-348/96 *Criminal proceedings against Donatella Calfa* [1999] ECR I-11. It held that the criminal penalty of expulsion for life from the territory of one Member State of nationals of another Member State who had been found guilty of committing offences under its drug laws constituted an obstacle to the freedom to provide services and to the other fundamental freedoms guaranteed by the Treaty, which cannot be justified on grounds of public policy.

Article 29 of Directive 2004/38 ensures that public health reasons may be invoked only by Member States with regard to diseases with epidemic potential as defined by the World Health Organization.

? 8.10 Are all employees in the public service sector exempted from the rights contained in Article 45 TFEU?

With regard to the public service exception provided for in Article 45(4) TFEU (→ *8.1*) the ECJ has consistently pursued a restrictive line of interpretation.

In Case 152/73 *Sotgiu* v. *Deutsche Bundespost* [1974] ECR 153, the Court held unequivocally that **'public service'** was a **Community notion** not open to interpretation by the Member States. It further held that Member States may restrict **admission** of foreign nationals **only** to certain activities in the public service sector, but that Article 39(4) TEC (now Article 45(4) TFEU) 'cannot justify discriminatory measures with regard to remuneration or other conditions of employment against workers once they have been admitted to the public service'.

Without giving a clear definition, the Court has consistently used a **restrictive** Union law **meaning**, which basically requires 'participation in the **exercise of powers** conferred by **public law**' and duties designed to safeguard the general interests of the state or of other public authorities. Typical examples of the exercise of **'official authority'** ($\rightarrow$ *8.13*) are the judiciary, the police, defence forces or tax inspectors, as was stated by the advocate-general in Case 307/84 *Commission* v. *France* [1986] ECR 1725, and as they follow *e contrario* from Commission Communication [1988] OJ C72/2, which lists public transport, utility provision, education and research as services which should be open to nationals of other Member States. Judicial examples are provided in the so-called *Belgian Public Service* Cases, Case 149/79 *Commission* v. *Belgium* [1980] ECR 3881 and [1982] ECR 1845, where the ECJ considered that, with the exception of a few posts such as city architects, night watchmen and certain supervisory posts which were regarded as exercising 'official authority', all other employment forms, such as city nurses and railway workers, did not fall under the public service exception.

8.11 Explain the issue of 'reverse discrimination'

'Reverse discrimination' is not a felicitous notion. It basically means that **Union law** does **not apply** to **'wholly internal situations'**. As a result of this non-application, national workers may find themselves in a worse position than other Union nationals.

In Case 175/78 *R.* v. *Saunders* [1979] ECR 1129, the ECJ held that the applicant could not rely on Article 45 TFEU to challenge an order which excluded her from part of her own territory, because there was 'no connecting factor to any situation envisaged by EC law'.

In Cases 35 and 36/82 *Morson and Jhanjan* [1982] ECR 3723, the Court ruled that two Dutch nationals working in the Netherlands could not rely on Article 10 Regulation 1612/68 (→ *8.7*) to enable them to bring their Surinamese parents into the country where they worked since they 'had never exercised the right to freedom of movement within the Community'.

In Case 180/83 *Moser* v. *Land Baden Württemberg* [1984] ECR 2539, a German citizen, who was a member of the Communist Party and was thus disadvantaged in his search for a job, could not invoke Community law vis-à-vis German hiring authorities. The Court held that a potential disadvantage in a future search for employment in another Member State was an insufficient nexus to trigger the application of Article 45 TFEU.

This ruling was reaffirmed in Case C-299/95 *Kremzow* v. *Austria* [1997] ECR I-2629, concerning a former Austrian judge imprisoned in Austria for murdering a lawyer. The ECJ held that even though any deprivation of liberty might impede a person's exercise of his or her free movement rights, the purely hypothetical possibility of doing so did not entail a sufficient connection with Community law.

Reverse discrimination may be **avoided**, however, if one travels abroad in order to exercise Treaty rights. Such a **Union nexus** also helps to avoid reverse discrimination in the context of the right of establishment. Thus, in Case 115/78 *Knoors* [1979] ECR 399, a Dutch plumber with a qualification to practice in Belgium could rely thereon in order to work in the Netherlands. In Case C-370/90 *Singh* [1992] ECR I-4265, an Indian national married to a British national could claim entry and residency rights as a spouse of a Community national in the UK after they had returned from Germany where they both had been working for a number of years. Furthermore, in Case C-18/95 *Terhoeve* [1999] ECR I-345, a Dutchman successfully challenged a discriminatory Dutch social security provision after he had been employed and resided in another Member State.

? 8.12 What does the freedom of establishment guarantee?

While the rights of employees are protected by the free movement of workers, discussed above (→ *8.1–10*), the economic rights of self-employed persons are guaranteed by the TFEU and secondary law rules on the **freedom of establishment** and the **freedom to provide services**. As regards the former, Article 49 TFEU (ex Article 43 TEC) provides that:

> "Within the framework of the provisions set out below, restrictions on the freedom of establishment of nationals of a Member State in the territory of another Member State shall be prohibited. Such prohibition shall also apply to restrictions on the setting-up of agencies, branches or subsidiaries by nationals of any Member State established in the territory of any Member State.
>
> "Freedom of establishment shall include the right to take up and pursue activities as self-employed persons and to set up and manage undertakings, in particular companies or firms within the meaning of the second paragraph of Article 54, under the conditions laid down for its own nationals by the law of the country where such establishment is effected, subject to the provisions of the chapter relating to capital."

Unlike the **provision of services**, which has a more **temporary character** (→ *8.16*), 'establishment' requires a 'stable and

continuous basis' with the host Member State. In Case C-221/89 *R.* v. *Secretary of State for Transport, ex parte Factortame* [1991] ECR I-3905, the ECJ spoke of 'the actual pursuit of an economic activity through a **fixed establishment** in another Member State for an **indefinite period**'. This important judgment further clarified that local ownership requirements for the registration of a ship were contrary to the freedom of establishment.

8.13 Are lawyers excluded from the right of establishment because they exercise 'official authority'?

Similar to the **public service exception** provided for in the context of the free movement of workers ($\rightarrow$ *8.1*, *8.10*), the Treaty provides in Article 51 TFEU (ex Article 45 TEC) that:

> "The provisions of this chapter shall not apply, so far as any given Member State is concerned, to activities which in that State are connected, even occasionally, with the **exercise of official authority**."

In Case 2/74 *Reyners* v. *Belgium* [1974] ECR 63, the ECJ not only affirmed that the **freedom of establishment** in Article 49 TFEU (ex Article 43 TEC) had **direct effect** ($\rightarrow$ *4.5*), it also refused to exempt the legal profession as a whole under the 'official authority' exception, thus rendering a Belgian nationality requirement for lawyers unlawful. The Court found that:

> "Professional activities involving contacts, even regular and organic, with the courts, including even compulsory cooperation in their functioning, do not constitute, as such, connection with the exercise of official authority.
>
> "The most typical activities of the profession of *avocat*, in particular, such as consultation and legal assistance and also representation and the defence of parties in court,

even when the intervention or assistance of the *avocat* is compulsory or is a legal monopoly, cannot be considered as connected with the exercise of official authority. "

? 8.14 Are non-discriminatory regulations for the exercise of the legal profession lawful under EU law?

The text of Article 49 TFEU (ex Article 43 TEC) (→ *8.12*), providing for a right of establishment 'under the conditions laid down for its own nationals', seems to prohibit direct discrimination only. In a number of cases, however, many of which have been instituted by lawyers who certainly had a fair amount of self-interest in these cases, the ECJ interpreted Article 49 TFEU as prohibiting **indirect discrimination** as well.

In Case 71/76 *Thieffry* v. *Conseil de l'Ordre des Avocats à la Cour de Paris* [1977] ECR 765, the ECJ held that any restrictive qualification requirement required a 'practical benefit'. Thus, a French law degree as a prerequisite for admission to the bar, although on its face non-discriminatory, was an 'unjustified restriction' of the right of establishment where a foreign (Belgian) degree had been recognised as equivalent and where a specific professional qualifying certificate (bar exam) had been produced.

Case 107/83 *Ordre des Avocats au Bareau de Paris* v. *Klopp* [1984] ECR 2971, concerned a German lawyer who was refused admission to the Paris bar since French rules disallowed a second establishment of a lawyer outside his or her Paris chambers. The ECJ held that this rule, although non-discriminatory, violated a Union principle according to which the right of establishment 'includes the freedom to set up more than one work place in the Community', which was arguably already contained in the wording of Article 49 TFEU. The Court also rejected possible justifications by holding that there were less restrictive ways of ensuring suffi-cient client and court contacts of lawyers and their obedience to professional rules.

In Case 340/89 *Vlassopoulou* v. *Ministerium für Justiz Baden-Württemberg* [1991] ECR 2357, the ECJ openly addressed the indir-ect discrimination issue. In this case German authorities refused bar admission to a Greek national who had a Greek law degree and prac-tised German law in Germany on the grounds that she did not have the required German exams. The Court held that:

> "Even if applied without any discrimination on the basis of nationality, national requirements concerning qualifications may have the effect of hindering nationals of the other Member States in the exercise of their right of establishment …
>
> "Consequently, a Member State which receives a request to admit a person to a profession to which access, under national law, depends upon the possession of a diploma or a professional qualification must take into consideration the diplomas, certificates and other evidence of qualifications which the person concerned has acquired in order to exercise the same profession in another Member State by making a comparison between the specialized knowledge and abilities certified by those diplomas and the knowledge and qualifications required by the national rules."

The approach taken by the Court largely resembles what had been agreed upon in Directive 89/48 on the mutual recognition of higher education diplomas. This directive provided for a 'general system for the recognition of higher-education diplomas awarded on com-pletion of professional education and training of at least three years' duration'. It required a general **'mutual recognition'** approach (→ 7.5) from which Member States may deviate only in justified situ-ations by requiring either an adaptation period or an aptitude test. This and similar directives have now been replaced by Directive 2005/36 on the recognition of professional qualifications.

In Case C-55/94 *Gebhard* v. *Consiglio dell'ordine degli avvocati e procuratori di Milano* [1995] ECR I-4165, the ECJ most explicitly extended its broad approach against **non-discriminatory rules** developed in the free movement of goods context to the freedom of establishment. The case involved a German lawyer against whom disciplinary measures were taken because he practised law in Italy, although he was not admitted to the Milan Bar and his professional qualifications were not recognised in Italy. The ECJ considered that:

> "national measures liable to hinder or make less attractive the exercise of fundamental freedoms guaranteed by the Treaty must fulfil four conditions: they must be applied in a non-discriminatory manner; they must be justified by imperative requirements in the general interest; they must be suitable for securing the attainment of the objective which they pursue; and they must not go beyond what is necessary in order to attain it."

Much of the case law was codified and 'progressively' developed in the so-called **Lawyers' Establishment Directive**. Directive 98/5/EC (to facilitate practise of the profession of lawyer on a permanent basis in a Member State other than that in which the qualification was obtained) now provides that lawyers already admitted in one Member State may immediately practise in another Member State under the professional title acquired in the former state. After effectively and regularly pursuing an activity involving the law of the host Member State for a period of three years, a lawyer will be entitled to admission to the profession and use of the title of that Member State.

8.15 Does the freedom of establishment also apply to companies?

Article 54 TFEU (ex Article 48 TEC) provides:

> "Companies or firms formed in accordance with the law of a Member State and having their registered office, central

administration or principal place of business within the Union shall, for the purposes of this chapter, be treated in the same way as natural persons who are nationals of Member States.

"'Companies or firms' means companies or firms constituted under civil or commercial law, including cooperative societies, and other legal persons governed by public or private law, save for those which are nonprofit-making."

In Case C-212/97 *Centros* v. *Erhvervs- og Selskabsstyrelsen* [1999] ECR I-1459, the ECJ weakened the position of Member States wishing to restrict the use of liberal incorporation rules in other Member States. It held that:

"the fact that a national of a Member State who wishes to set up a company chooses to form it in the Member State whose rules of company law seem to him the least restrictive and to set up branches in other Member States cannot, in itself, constitute an abuse of the right of establishment. The right to form a company in accordance with the law of a Member State and to set up branches in other Member States is inherent in the exercise, in a single market, of the freedom of establishment guaranteed by the Treaty."

Thus, the Danish authorities could not restrict the right of a company which was incorporated in the UK but did not conduct any business there to set up a branch in Denmark, even though they feared that the incorporation in the UK had just been accomplished in order to circumvent Danish requirements, such as those relating to the payment of a minimum capital for companies. This approach was confirmed by the ECJ in Case C-208/00 *Überseering* v. *NCC* [2002] ECR I-9919, where the Court held that in order to enjoy the rights under Article 49 TFEU a company had only to be validly incorporated in one Member State and to have its central administration somewhere in the Community. Thus, German legislation which provided that a company's legal status was governed by the law where it had its central place of administration could not prevent a company incorporated in the Netherlands and having its administrative seat in Germany from operating there, even though it did not comply with all German prudential requirements aimed at protecting the interests of creditors, shareholders and employees.

? 8.16 What is understood by the freedom to provide services?

While Article 49 permits EU nationals to set up 'permanent' establishments in other Member States (→ *8.12*), the freedom to **provide services** allows them to operate abroad on a more **'temporal'** basis. Article 56(1) TFEU (ex Article 49(1) TEC) provides that:

> "Within the framework of the provisions set out below, restrictions on freedom to provide services within the Union shall be prohibited in respect of nationals of Member States who are established in a Member State other than that of the person for whom the services are intended."

Although the TFEU does not contain a definition of the distinction between establishment and the provision of services, it is clear from the case law of the ECJ that the most important factor is the former's permanent as opposed to the temporary nature of service activities. However, in Case C-55/94 *Gebhard* v. *Consiglio dell'ordine degli avvocati e procuratori di Milano* [1995] ECR I-4165 (→ *8.14*), the ECJ cautioned that:

> "the temporary nature of the activities in question has to be determined in the light, not only of the duration of the provision of the services, but also of its regularity, periodicity or continuity. The fact that the provision of services is temporary does not mean that the provider of services ... may not equip himself with some form of infrastructure in the host Member State (including an

office, chambers or consulting rooms) insofar as such infrastructure is necessary for the purposes of performing the services in question.''

8.17 What was the *Van Binsbergen* Case all about?

In Case 33/74 *Van Binsbergen* v. *Bestuur van de Bedrijsverenigung voor de Metaalnijverheid* [1974] ECR 1299, a Dutch residency requirement for lawyers to be able to provide legal representation services in the Netherlands was ruled to be contrary to Article 56 TFEU (ex Article 49 TEC) (→ *8.16*). The ECJ held not only that this article had direct effect, but also that 'the provisions of that article abolish all discrimination against the person providing the service by reason of his nationality or the fact that he is established in a Member State other than that in which the service is to be provided'. With regard to a possible justification of the residency requirement the Court held that:

"The requirement that persons whose functions are to assist the administration of justice must be permanently established for professional purposes within the jurisdiction of certain courts or tribunals cannot be considered compatible with the provisions of Article [56 and 57 TFEU], where such requirement is objectively justified by the need to ensure observance of professional rules of conduct connected, in particular, with the administration of justice and with respect for professional ethics.''

8.18 Explain the concept of 'passive services'

While Article 56 TFEU (ex Article 49 TEC) expressly guarantees the **'provision'** of services only (→ *8.16*), the ECJ has consistently also held that persons wishing to **receive services** are **protected** by Union law. Cases 286/82 and 26/83 *Luisi and Carbone* [1984] ECR 377 involved two Italians who were fined because when travelling abroad they carried with them foreign currency above the lawful amount under Italian legislation. They wanted to pay for services as tourists and recipients of medical treatment. Thus, the ECJ regarded them as recipients of services and held that 'to go to a State in which the person providing the services is established' is a **'necessary corollary'** of the freedom to provide services and thus covered by Article 56 TFEU. Thereby the Court paid tribute to the fact that in some sectors it is usually the service recipients and not the service providers who have to travel in order to make the provision of services possible.

This notion of protecting **'service recipients'** was considerably broadened in Case 186/87 *Cowan* v. *Le Trésor Public* [1989] ECR 195, which concerned a British tourist as a consumer of services in France. This triggered the application of Article 12 TEC (now Article 18 TFEU) prohibiting discrimination on the basis of nationality. It was thus held that Cowan, who had been mugged in the Paris Metro, could not be lawfully excluded from claiming compensation under French crime victim legislation.

8.19 What kind of restrictions to the rendering of cross-border services has the ECJ allowed?

Through Article 62 TFEU (ex Article 55 TEC), the **public service** exception as well as **public policy**, **public security** and **public health** derogations are also relevant for the provision of services ($\rightarrow$ *8.9, 8.10*). In addition, the Court has recognised **implicit limitations**, similar to those developed under the *Cassis* **rule of reason** ($\rightarrow$ *7.5*).

For instance, in the abovementioned *Van Binsbergen* Case (→ *8.17*) the ECJ, in principle, recognised the need to ensure the **observance of professional** rules, such as 'rules relating to the organization, qualifications, professional ethics, supervision and liability'. In the *German Insurance* Case, Case 205/84 *Commission* v. *Germany* [1986] ECR 3755, the Court acknowledged **consumer protection** considerations as 'imperative reasons relating to the public interest', and in Case C-275/92 *HM Customs and Excise* v. *Schindler* [1994] ECR I-1039, involving the restriction of German lottery ticket sales to the UK, it recognised **social policy grounds**. In Case C-36/02 *Omega* v. *Oberbürgermeisterin der Bundesstadt Bonn* [2004] ECR I-6909, the ECJ acknowledged that the protection of **fundamental rights** was a 'legitimate interest which, in principle, justifies a restriction of the obligations imposed by Community law, even under a fundamental freedom guaranteed by the Treaty such as the freedom to provide services' (→ *6.12, 7.7*).

In a number of cases the Court has made it clear, however, that any **'imperative requirements'** (→ *7.5*) invoked by Member States will be **strictly scrutinised** to ascertain whether they pursue a legitimate aim which is not incompatible with Union law, in a non-discriminatory fashion and in a proportionate manner.

? 8.20 How did Union legislation facilitate the freedom of establishment and the freedom to provide services?

Initially, the Community pursued a policy of sectoral **harmonisation** through a number of directives providing for minimum standards of professional qualifications in sectors such as the medical profession, nursing, pharmacy, architecture and the legal profession. This piecemeal approach was abandoned by the **Mutual Recognition**

Directive 89/48 concerning higher education diplomas which introduced a horizontal 'mutual recognition' approach. The basic philosophy of this approach was simple:

(1) it applied to all professions that required a university training of at least three years;

(2) it stated a basic principle of 'mutual recognition' according to which Member States had to recognise professional qualifications acquired in another Member State; and

(3) if the professional training acquired in another Member State differed substantially from the one required in the state where recognition is sought, the latter state was permitted to require either an adaptation period or an aptitude test.

These principles have been carried over to the new **Directive 2005/36** on the **recognition of professional qualifications**.

In 2006, after years of controversy, Directive 2006/123 on services in the internal market was adopted. This so-called **Services Directive** applies to both the 'exercise of the freedom of establishment for service providers and the free movement of services'. It provides for various administrative simplifications to reduce obstacles to the freedom of establishment and services through a 'one-stop-shop' principle in the form of so-called points of single contact. The draft Directive's most controversial idea, that is, that service providers should be regulated by their country of origin and not by the host country, the so-called **country-of-origin principle**, was not kept in the final version. Instead, a rather complex Article 16 now provides that, in principle, the 'Member State in which the service is provided shall ensure free access to and free exercise of a service activity within its territory'. However, in addition to a list of prohibited restrictions, the Directive lays down a number of mandatory requirements that may justify the restriction of the provision of services, such as public policy, public security, public health, the protection of the environment and rules on employment conditions. If Member States stick to these five grounds, the Directive may, indeed, have a liberalising effect. If the ECJ allows them, however, to invoke the further grounds for derogation recognised in its free movement jurisprudence the overall changes will remain modest.

9 EU competition law

In a technical sense, **EU competition policy** covers what is known in many countries as **cartel law** or, in the United States, **'anti-trust law'**. The latter term was adopted because in the late nineteenth century, when anti-trust law was 'invented', most American cartels were established in the form of trusts. EU competition law rests on the triad of a **cartel ban** contained in Article 101 TFEU (ex Article 81 TEC), a **prohibition on market abuse** in Article 102 TFEU (ex Article 82 TEC) and **merger control legislation**. All three branches of EU competition law are handled by DG IV, now **DG Competition**, as the Directorate-General for Competition supporting the responsible Commissioner for Competition is known.

In a broader sense, other Union law also contributes to the overall aim of creating conditions for **fair competition within the EU's internal market**. These include:

(1) treaty provisions on **free movement** as a framework prohibiting mainly public restrictions on the free circulation of goods and services, such as duties and quantitative restrictions and their equivalent counterparts;

(2) special **competition rules** for **public undertakings** in Article 106 TFEU (ex Article 86 TEC); and

(3) the identification and justification or elimination of **subsidies** provided for in the state aid provisions of Articles 107–109 TFEU (ex Articles 87–89 TEC).

9.1 What are the economic rationales for the EU's emphasis on competition policy?

As the American debate about the wisdom of anti-trust policies demonstrates, there is still controversy over the need to intervene in the free play of market forces in order to maintain fair competition. The EU pursues a strategy of regulating competition based on the assumption that **effective competition** would **allocate resources** in the **most efficient way**, **reduce costs** for **consumers**, **guarantee market access** and openness to new participants and **protect consumers** and **small enterprises against monopolies** (→ *9.12*). Thus, **competition policy** is regarded as a powerful tool for the creation and preservation of a **single market**. In addition, it complements the EU internal market rules, which aim at the elimination of state imposed tariffs, quotas and measures having equivalent effect, by prohibiting the division of the internal market by private parties (→ *7.1*).

9.2 Which anti-competitive activities are prohibited by Article 101(1) TFEU?

Article 101(1) TFEU prohibits:

    ❝as **incompatible** with the internal market: all **agreements** between **undertakings**, **decisions** by associations of undertakings and **concerted practices** which may affect trade between Member States and which have as their object or **effect** the prevention, **restriction or distortion of competition** within the internal market.❞

It continues to list, in a non-exhaustive fashion, **examples of prohibited anti-competitive behaviour**, activities which:

(a) directly or indirectly fix purchase or selling prices or any other trading conditions;

(b) limit or control production, markets, technical development, or investment;

(c) share markets or sources of supply;

(d) apply dissimilar conditions to equivalent transactions with other trading parties, thereby placing them at a competitive disadvantage; and

(e) make the conclusion of contracts subject to acceptance by the other parties of supplementary obligations which, by their nature or according to commercial usage, have no connection with the subject of such contracts.

Article 101(1) TFEU is a very broad **prohibition** covering **classic cartels** through price fixing or market sharing. Its concept of restrictive agreements extends to **informal agreements**, not only on a **horizontal** level (between firms on the same production stage) but also in a **vertical** sense (covering, for example, agreements between producers and distributors or the latter and retailers) ($\rightarrow$ 9.5). As to the notion of an **'agreement'** between undertakings, the Commission and the ECJ have adopted an expansive view, including **oral**, **non-binding**, **gentlemen's agreements** as can be seen in the *Quinine Cartel* Case, Cases 41, 44 and 45/69 *ACF Chemiefarma NV v. Commission* [1970] ECR 661 and in the *Polypropylene* Case, Commission Decision 86/398 [1986] OJ L230/1.

In a number of cases involving vertical agreements, such as Case C-338/00P *Volkswagen AG v. Commission* [2003] ECR I-9189, the Commission and the EU courts have broadly read an 'agreement' into even the unilateral actions of manufacturers trying to dissuade their distributors from exporting goods in order to prevent parallel imports.

Subsequently, however, in the *Bayer* Case, the ECJ adhered to a narrower notion of agreement. In Joined Cases C-2/01P and C-3/01P *Bundesverband der Arzneimittel-Importeure eV and Commission v. Bayer* [2004] ECR I-23, the Court held that:

> "for an agreement within the meaning of [Article 101(1)]
> of the Treaty to be capable of being regarded as having

been concluded by tacit acceptance, it is necessary that the manifestation of the wish of one of the contracting parties to achieve an anti-competitive goal constitute an invitation to the other party, whether express or implied, to fulfil that goal jointly, and that applies all the more where, as in this case, such an agreement is not at first sight in the interests of the other party, namely the wholesalers.''

Thus, the distribution policy of a pharmaceutical firm that limited deliveries to its distributors in low-price Member States in order to prevent harmful parallel imports into high-price Member States by third parties was regarded as 'only the expression of a unilateral policy of one of the contracting parties', which did not form part of the distribution agreement.

'Decisions by associations of undertakings' were involved in the 1980 *FEDETAB* Case, Joined Cases 209–215 and 218/78 *van Landewyck SARL* v. *Commission* [1980] ECR 3125, where FEDETAB, a Belgian trade association of tobacco manufacturers, promulgated 'recommendations' restricting tobacco distribution. FEDETAB sought an Article 101(3) TFEU individual exemption (→ *9.12, 9.15*), claiming consumer benefits through upholding choice and other advantages. The ECJ, however, had doubts about these benefits and rejected the claim, because the 'recommendations' eliminated competition in respect of a substantial part of the products in question since FEDETAB members produced or imported 95 per cent of the products in question.

9.3 What are 'concerted practices'?

The most elusive concept contained in Article 101(1) TFEU is that of **'concerted practices'**. In the so-called *Dyestuffs* Case, Case 48/69 *Imperial Chemical Industries Ltd* v. *Commission* [1972] ECR 619

(→ 9.9), the Court developed a general definition which remains pertinent today. In that case the Commission had fined seventeen dyestuffs producers after three general and uniform price increases between 1964 and 1967. In challenge proceedings before the ECJ, the Court defined 'concerted practices' as:

> "a form of **coordination** between undertakings which, without having reached the stage where an agreement properly so-called has been concluded, **knowingly substitutes** practical **cooperation** between them **for** the risks of **competition**."

It continued to regard **parallel behaviour** as strong **evidence**, although insufficient proof in itself, of 'concerted practices'.

This evaluation of parallel behaviour was crucial for the ECJ's partial annulment of a Commission decision in the so-called *Wood Pulp* Case, Joined Cases 89, 104, 114, 116–17 and 125–9/85 *Ahlström Oy* v. *Commission* [1993] ECR I-1307 (→ 9.9). Therein the Court held that:

> "parallel conduct cannot be regarded as furnishing proof of concertation unless concertation constitutes the only plausible explanation for such conduct. It is necessary to bear in mind that, although [Article 101] of the Treaty prohibits any form of collusion which distorts competition, it does not deprive economic operators of the right to adapt themselves intelligently to the existing and anticipated conduct of their competitors."

? 9.4 What are the legal consequences of a violation of Article 101(1) TFEU?

Where, as a result of an investigation, the Commission finds that an agreement is in violation of Article 101(1) TFEU, it is empowered to **impose fines** of up to 10 per cent of an infringing undertaking's turnover. In its fining policy the Commission has to take into account the gravity and duration of the infringement. Since the mid-1990s the Commission has adopted a leniency policy according to which firms cooperating with the Commission's investigations may receive up to 50 per cent reductions in their fines, while so-called 'whistle-blowers' who inform the Commission about the existence of a cartel may even receive total enforcement 'immunity'.

In addition to giving rise to substantial fines, agreements contrary to Article 101(1) TFEU are automatically **void** and, thus, unenforceable under Article 101(2) TFEU. According to the case law of the ECJ, Article 101(1) TFEU infringements may also lead to **liability** in damages for competitors. In Case C-453/99 *Courage* v. *Crehan* [2001] ECR I-6297, the Court again boosted the *effet utile* of Community law by allowing a damages claim for loss caused by anti-competitive contracts or conduct, which may even be raised by a party to the restrictive agreement. According to the Court:

> "the existence of such a right strengthens the working of the Community competition rules and discourages agreements or practices, which are frequently covert, which are liable to restrict or distort competition."

In Joined Cases C-295/04 to C-298/04 *Manfredi and others* v. *Lloyd Adriatico Assicurazioni Spa and others* [2006] ECR I-6619, the ECJ further refined its view on the level of compensation to be provided by national courts. It held that 'it must be possible to award particular damages, such as exemplary or punitive damages, pursuant to actions founded on the Community competition rules, if such damages may be awarded pursuant to similar actions founded on domestic law'. The Court further considered that, as a result of the principle of effectiveness, 'injured persons must be able to seek compensation not only for actual loss (*damnum emergens*) but also for loss of profit (*lucrum cessans*) plus interest.

? 9.5 What was the anti-competitive behaviour challenged in *Consten* and *Grundig*?

Joined Cases 56 and 58/64 *Établissements Consten S.à.R.L. and Grundig-Verkaufs-GmbH* v. *Commission* [1966] ECR 299, is one of the early leading competition law cases, evidencing that Article 101(1) TFEU prohibits not only the classical 'horizontal' cartels but also certain **'vertical' agreements** (→ *9.2*). It involved a German electronics producer, Grundig, who appointed Consten as sole distributor in France enabling it to exclude Grundig products put on the market in other Member States. For this purpose, Grundig assigned to Consten its French trademark, GINT, in order to exclude parallel imports. When a French competitor of Consten started to import from Germany, which was substantially cheaper, he was sued by Consten for trademark infringement and unfair competition resulting from knowingly violating its contractual terms with Grundig. In this law-suit the French competitor argued that the contract between Grundig and Consten was invalid because it contravened Article 101(1) TFEU (→ *9.4*).

At the same time, the Commission denied Consten's request for an exemption under Article 101(3) TFEU (→ *9.12*), citing the substantially higher prices for Grundig products on the French market. In the ensuing annulment action, the ECJ upheld the Commission's decision and found a violation of Article 101(1) TFEU in the absolute territorial protection and the GINT assignment, not, however, in the exclusive dealing provisions which were severable and remained legally binding. In effect, the Court affirmed the concept of a 'vertical restraint' which led to an isolation of the French market:

> "Competition may be distorted within the meaning of Article [101(1)] not only by agreements which limit it as between the parties but also by agreements which prevent or restrict the competition which might take place between one of them and third parties. For this purpose

it is irrelevant whether the parties to the agreement are or are not on a footing of equality as regards their position and function in the economy.

"A sole distributorship contract may, without involving an abuse of a dominant position, affect trade between the Member States and at the same time have as its object or effect the prevention, restriction or distortion of competition, thus falling under the prohibition of Article [101(1)]."

? 9.6 Why can the determination of what constitutes an 'undertaking' in the sense of Article 101 TFEU be of crucial importance in competition cases?

The Treaty does not define the term **'undertaking'**. However, the Commission and the European courts have broadly understood 'undertakings' to include **any entity** engaged in an **economic/ commercial activity** regardless of its legal status and financing, a definition that comprises trade associations, partnerships, individuals, and state-owned corporations as long as they do not exercise public law powers. For the latter reason, the Court found in the *Eurocontrol* Case, Case C-364/92 *SAT Fluggesellschaft* v. *Eurocontrol* [1994] ECR I-43, that international organisations may escape the qualification as 'undertakings'. It held that Eurocontrol's activities:

"by their nature, their aim and the rules to which they are subject, are connected with the exercise of powers relating to the control and supervision of air space which are typically those of a public authority. They are not of an economic nature justifying the application of the Treaty rules of competition."

In addition to the **exercise of sovereign powers**, the ECJ has exempted activities based on the principle of solidarity from those performed by 'undertakings'. Though the precise test is sometimes unclear it has been particularly relevant in the field of **social security insurance**. For instance, in Case C-218/00 *Cisal di Battistello Venanzio* v. *INAIL* [2002] ECR I-691, the Court found that

> "in participating in this way in the management of one of the traditional branches of social security, in this case insurance against accidents at work and occupational diseases, the INAIL fulfils an exclusively social function. It follows that its activity is not an economic activity for the purpose of competition law and that this body does not therefore constitute an undertaking within the meaning of Articles [101 and 102 TFEU]."

In a number of subsequent judgments the EU courts extended this exemption to the commercial transactions of social security providers as long they were 'integrally connected' with their public service activities. See, e.g., Joined Cases C-264/01, C-306/01, C-354/01 and C-355/01 *AOK Bundesverband and others* v. *Ichthyol-Gesellschaft Cordes, Hermani & Co.* [2004] ECR I-2493; Case T-319/99 *FENIN* v. *Commission* [2003] ECR II-357.

The economic perspective prevailing in EU competition law may also lead to qualify separate legal entities as one 'undertaking', which has implications for the application of both Article 101 and 102 TFEU.

According to the **'single enterprise doctrine'**, which was aptly captured by the ECJ in Case 15/74 *Centrafarm BV et Adriaan de Peijper* v. *Sterling Drug Inc.* [1974] ECR 1147, agreements between legally distinct firms may not fall under the cartel prohibition of Article 101(1) TFEU if they 'form an **economic unit** within which the **subsidiary** has **no real freedom** to determine its course of action on the market'. Similarly, the Court concluded in the *Dyestuffs* Case (→ *9.3*) that:

> "where a subsidiary does not enjoy real autonomy on
> determining its course of action in the market, the
> prohibitions set out in [Article 101(1) TFEU] may be
> considered inapplicable in the relationship between it and
> the parent company with which it forms one economic
> unit."

One should be aware, however, that the inapplicability of Article
101 TFEU may open up the possibility of using Article 102 TFEU if
the single enterprise is found to be in a **dominant position** (→ *9.17*)
which it abuses, as the ECJ reminded us in the so-called *Parker
Pen* Case, Case C-73/95P *Viho Europe* v. *Commission* [1996] ECR
I-5457, where a producer bought all its formerly independent distributors and, thus, avoided scrutiny of its distribution practices
under Article 101 TFEU.

9.7 When does anti-competitive behaviour 'affect trade between Member States'?

The ECJ held in *Consten and Grundig* (→ *9.5*) that restrictive
behaviour may reach Community relevance if it is 'capable of
constituting a threat, either direct or indirect, actual or potential,
to freedom of trade between Member States in a manner which
might harm the attainment of the objectives of a single market
between States': a test closely resembling the *Dassonville* formula, laid down in the leading case on the free movement of
goods, Case 8/74 *Procureur du Roi* v. *Dassonville* [1974] ECR
837 (→ *7.3*).

Thus, purely national cartels fall outside the scope of Article
101(1) TFEU. However, in practice the Court is likely to liberally accept a Union effect. In Case 8/72 *Cementhandelaren* v.
Commission [1972] ECR 977, the ECJ found a Union effect with the
following reasoning:

"An agreement extending over the whole of the territory
of a Member State by its very nature has the effect
of reinforcing the compartmentalization of markets
on a national basis, thereby holding up the economic
interpenetration which the Treaty is designed to bring
about and protecting national production."

However, according to the Court's *de minimis* rule, as explained in
Case 5/69 *Völk* v. *Vervaecke* [1969] ECR 295, an effect on inter-state
trade that is not noticeable 'may escape the prohibition laid down in
[Article 101(1) TFEU]'.

? 9.8 How has the Commission acted in order to clarify the Court's *de minimis* rule?

This judge-made *de minimis* **rule** has been clarified in a series of
Commission Notices since 1970. The 1986 Commission Notice on
Agreements of Minor Importance excluded Commission review if an
agreement represented less than 5 per cent of the market share and
if the aggregate annual turnover did not exceed 300 million ECUs,
the predecessor currency to the Euro. These thresholds have been
repeatedly amended and currently provide for a 10 per cent combined market share of participating undertakings in cases of horizontal agreements and 15 per cent in cases of vertical agreements. They
are laid down in the 2001 Commission Notice on Agreements of
Minor Importance which do not Appreciably Restrict Competition
under Article 81(1) (now Article 101(1) TFEU) (*de minimis*), OJ
2001 C368/13.

   Things are further complicated by the Commission Guidelines
on the Effect on Trade Concept contained in Articles 81 and 82 of
the Treaty (now Articles 101 and 102 TFEU), OJ 2004 C101/81,
which refine the *de minimis* test into the so-called NAAT ('no appreciable affectation of trade') test. According to this test, agreements

are considered outside the scope of EU competition law if the parties' aggregate market share is less than 5 per cent and if, in cases of horizontal agreements, their aggregate turnover does not exceed €40 million or, in cases of vertical agreements, the turnover of the supplier is less than €40 million. It should be kept in mind, however, that if an agreement is considered to be below the threshold of Union law, it may still be governed by national competition rules.

? 9.9 Does the Treaty prohibit anti-competitive behaviour abroad that merely produces effects in the Union?

The Commission clearly investigates and fines violations of EU competition law on an **extraterritorial basis**. So far, the ECJ has managed to arrive at similar results, sometimes by slightly different reasoning. In the *Dyestuffs* Case (→ *9.3, 9.6*), Case 48/69 *Imperial Chemical Industries Ltd* v. *Commission* [1972] ECR 619, it found that the actions of a UK firm, at a time before the UK had joined the Community, were **carried on** directly **within the Community** because, as a result of the **'single economic unit'** doctrine (→ *9.6*), the actions of its European subsidiary could be attributed to the parent:

> "The fact that a subsidiary has separate legal personality is not sufficient to exclude the possibility of imputing its conduct to the parent company.
>
> "Such may be the case in particular where the subsidiary, although having separate legal personality, does not decide independently upon its own conduct on the market, but carries out, in all material respects, the instructions given to it by the parent company."

In the later *Wood Pulp* Case, Joined Cases 89, 104, 114, 116–17, 125–9/85 *Ahlström Oy* v. *Commission* [1993] ECR I-1307 (→ *9.3*), it found that where foreign wood pulp producers sold directly to purchasers in the EC and engaged in price competition to win orders from those customers, such activity constituted competition **'within'** the internal market. The ECJ further distinguished between formation and implementation of agreements and held that the place where they are implemented was 'decisive'.

9.10 Is the extraterritorial application of EU competition law permissible under public international law?

As a matter of principle, each state, or other entity exercising state-like legislative functions such as the EU in the field of competition law, has the **power to regulate** things and persons situated **within its territory**. This so-called jurisdiction to prescribe may sometimes also extend beyond a state's territory when protecting core state interests, for example, against espionage or the counterfeiting of its currency, under the **'protective principle'**. Another enlargement of the territorial principle of jurisdiction to prescribe is the so-called **effects doctrine**, used mainly in international criminal law, according to which a state may regulate behaviour abroad if that behaviour **produces effects** within its territory. The famous gun-shot across a state border is the textbook example.

In international economic law, this **effects principle** is increasingly accepted in the field of **anti-trust/competition law**. This, of course, makes perfect business sense because otherwise national or EU competition law might be easily avoided by managers simply flying off to a remote place outside the Union in order to fix their restrictive agreements. It remains, however, a conceptual challenge to the prevailing territoriality principle of international law, allocating to states jurisdiction to prescribe along mainly territorial lines.

In 1991 the US and the EC entered into an agreement regarding the application of their competition rules which aimed at avoiding conflicts over enforcement activities resulting from mutual extra-territorial claims. Each party stipulated, in particular, to take into account the relative significance of the conduct and its effect on the other party. It was replaced by a 1998 Agreement between the European Communities and the Government of the United States of America regarding the application of their competition laws after it had been annulled by the ECJ in Case 327/91 *France* v. *Commission* [1994] ECR I-3641 for competence reasons (→ *11.7*).

? 9.11 Are all economic activities covered by the prohibition of Article 101(1) TFEU?

In addition to express exceptions like Article 346 TFEU (ex Article 296 TEC) relating to national security and, to a more limited extent, for services of **general economic interest** under Article 106(2) TFEU (ex Article 86(2) TEC) (→ *9.32*), the ECJ has clarified that **certain agreements** fall **outside** the scope of **EU competition law**.

In Joined Cases C-115/97, C-116/97 and C-117/97 *Brentjens' Handelsonderneming BV* v. *Stichting Bedrijfspensioenfonds voor Handel in Bovwmaterialen* [1999] ECR I-6025, it found that **collective bargaining** agreements are excluded from EU competition law because:

> "the social policy objectives pursued by such agreements would be seriously undermined if management and labour were subject to [Article 101(1)] of the Treaty when seeking jointly to adopt measures to improve conditions of work and employment."

In Case C-309/99 *Wouters* v. *Algemene Raad van de Nederlandse Orde van Advocaten* [2002] ECR I-1577, the Court held that a national regulation prohibiting so-called multidisciplinary partnerships between lawyers and accountants 'adopted by a body such as the Bar of the Netherlands does not infringe [Article 101(1)] of the Treaty, since that body could reasonably have considered that that regulation, despite the effects restrictive of competition that are inherent in it, is necessary for the proper practice of the legal profession, as organised in the Member State concerned'. In Case C-519/04 P *Meca Medina and Majcen* v. *Commission* [2006] ECR I-6991, the Court found that even if anti-doping rules of sports associations are to be regarded

> "as a decision of an association of undertakings limiting the appellants' freedom of action, they do not [...] necessarily constitute a restriction of competition [...] since they are justified by a legitimate objective. Such a limitation is inherent in the organisation and proper conduct of competitive sport and its very purpose is to ensure healthy rivalry between athletes."

Whether, and to what extent, other Treaty aims and national interests may be held to be generally exempted from EU competition law remains to be seen. What is clear, however, is the fact that Article 101 TFEU itself provides for certain exceptions from its prohibition.

? 9.12 Under what condition may a cartel be exempted from the prohibition of Article 101(1) TFEU?

Union law provides for the permissibility of restrictive agreements which may encourage competition in another way. Article 101(3) TFEU makes such **exemptions** conditional upon the requirement that the agreement in question

> "contributes to improving the production or distribution of goods or to promoting technical or economic progress, while allowing consumers a fair share of the resulting benefit, and which does not:

(a) impose on the undertakings concerned restrictions which are not indispensable to the attainment of these objectives;

(b) afford such undertaking the possibility of eliminating competition in respect of a substantial part of the products in question.''

While in the early days of EU Competition Policy Article 101(3) TFEU **exemptions** always had to be granted by the Commission either on an **individual** or on a **general** basis, the reform of EU competition law pursuant to Regulation 1/2003 (→ *9.16*) makes Article 101(3) TFEU **directly applicable** (→ *4.4*) and, thus, leaves the assessment whether an agreement may benefit from the exemption or not to the affected companies themselves and to **national competition authorities**. While economic efficiency is the major consideration in determining whether an agreement 'contributes to improving the production or distribution of goods or to promoting technical or economic progress', the practice of the EU institutions shows that also other Union interests, such as environmental or industrial policy goals, may play a certain role in this assessment.

9.13 What is the purpose of 'group exemptions'?

In 1965 the Council authorised the Commission in Regulation 19/65 to formulate group 'declarations of inapplicability' under Article 101(3) TFEU. These declarations, also referred to as **'group'** or **'block exemptions'**, eliminated the notification requirement for entire groups of agreements and, thus, reduced the administrative burden for the Commission. These regulations typically included a **'black list'** of prohibited restrictions and a **'white list'** of permissible provisions. Agreements falling under such 'group' or 'block exemptions' did not need to be notified to the Commission; they were instead exempted automatically.

The economic justification for exempting certain agreements from the cartel prohibition of Article 101(1) TFEU is not always free from controversy (→ 9.1). With regard to exclusive distribution agreements, for example, it has been argued that they facilitate costly market access to newcomers and thereby foster the idea of the internal market. They are further considered to be beneficial because the exclusive retailers will add marketing efforts to sell a manufacturer's brand and, thus, increase so-called inter-brand competition. At the same time, the exclusive distribution agreement will discourage customers from seeking pre-sales services from exclusive retailers and then buying from cheaper competitors. This elimination of so-called intra-brand competition prevents free-riders from benefiting from the exclusive retailers' increased marketing efforts.

On the other hand, exclusive distribution agreements with territorial protection may disintegrate the internal market – as was recognised in the 1966 *Consten and Grundig* Case (→ 9.5). Sometimes pre-sales services may be unwanted by consumers and merely increase the price of the products they are seeking. Additionally, exclusive distribution agreements may prevent competing manufacturers from entering a market.

? 9.14 Which kind of EU legislation is used to grant 'group exemptions'?

Contrary to **individual exemptions**, which were granted in the form of **decisions**, the Commission enacts **'group exemptions'** in the form of **regulations**. Since the first block exemption, Regulation 67/67 on exclusive purchasing agreements, such exemptions have been laid down in a series of Community regulations, exempting among others certain research and development agreements (Regulation

2659/00), specialisation agreements (Regulation 2658/00) and technology transfer (Regulation 240/96) among others.

The block exemptions system had the advantage of avoiding the slow individual exemption route. However, since it basically required parties to structure their agreements according to the permissible clauses contained in the various block exemption regulations it was increasingly criticised as being too formalistic and narrow and providing a strait-jacket for business partners. Thus, by the mid-1990s the Commission revised its competition policy on vertical restraints. The regulations concerning exclusive distribution agreements (Regulation 1983/83), exclusive purchasing agreements (Regulation 1984/83) and franchise agreements (Regulation 4087/88) expired by the end of 1999 and were replaced by the so-called **Vertical Restraints Block Exemption Regulation** 2790/1999. This regulation entered into force on 1 June 2000 and covers most vertical agreements involving the sale of goods or services. It rendered the prohibition of Article 101(1) TFEU inapplicable to vertical agreements entered into by companies with market shares not exceeding 30 per cent. Further, Regulation 2790/1999 still contains a 'black list' of prohibited clauses, such as price fixing or most territorial protection clauses. It also prohibits a number of non-compete obligations aimed at preventing access to a distribution network by competitors. In response to the charge of having been too legalistic in the past, the Commission noted in its Guidelines on Vertical Restraints, OJ 2000 C291/1, that it will adopt an **'economic approach'** in the application of Article 101 TFEU to vertical restraints.

9.15 Outline the basic procedure under Regulation 17

For a long time, **Regulation 17/62**, adopted by the Council in 1962, provided the procedural framework for the **enforcement** of

European Competition Law **by the Commission**. It rested on broad **notification** requirements imposed on companies, **complaints** by competitors and sweeping **investigation** powers given to the Commission.

According to the Regulation, agreements contrary to Article 101(1) TFEU had to be notified to the Commission. The Commission then had a number of options from which to choose: it could issue a so-called **comfort letter**, an informal statement asserting that it saw no reason to intervene in opposition to the activities notified; it could give a **'negative clearance'** certifying that 'on the basis of the facts in its possession, there are no grounds ... for action'; or it could grant **individual exemptions** to the parties by declaring Article 101(1) TFEU inapplicable according to Article 101(3) TFEU (→ *9.12*).

Individual exemptions thus granted by the Commission were open to **modification** by subsequent Commission decisions in case of:

(1) a change in any of the facts which were basic to the making of the decision;
(2) a breach of any obligation attached to the decision;
(3) a decision was based on incorrect information or was induced by deceit; or
(4) an abuse of the exemption.

If the Commission concluded that the notified agreement **contravened** Article 101(1) TFEU, it had the power to **prohibit** it and **impose fines** on the offending firms.

For all Commission competition decisions, **judicial review** was available through the ECJ. Since 1989 such challenges first go to the CFI (now the General Court) and can reach the ECJ on appeal (→ *5.3, 5.6*). In the past, the European courts have repeatedly reduced the fines imposed by the Commission. For instance, in the *Cement Cartel* Case, Joined Cases T-25/95 *Cimenteries CBR SA and others*

v. *Commission* [2000] ECR II-491, the CFI reduced the total fine of approximately €250 million to around €110 million.

9.16 Outline the reform of EU competition law enforcement

Regulation 17/62 was replaced by **Regulation 1/2003** on the implementation of the rules on competition laid down in Articles 81 and 82 (now Articles 101 and 102) of the Treaty which entered into force in May 2004. It embodies a radical reform by **decentralising** and **simplifying** the existing **competition law procedure**. Regulation 1/2003 abolishes the Commission's power to grant individual exemptions. Instead, business firms have to ensure that their agreements do not violate Article 101(1) TFEU or, in case they do, that the restrictive practices qualify under Article 101(3) TFEU ($\rightarrow$ *9.12*). There is thus greater reliance on **block exemptions**. At the same time, the Commission is partly replaced by **national competition authorities**. This became legally feasible by making the provisions of Article 101(3) TFEU directly applicable ($\rightarrow$ *4.4, 9.12*), allowing enforcement of the rules governing restrictive practices by national competition authorities and national courts. By 2002 the Commission and the national competition authorities had already created a network of competition authorities, the **'European Competition Network'**, which provides for the allocation of cases according to the principle of the best-placed authority and ensures investigation cooperation between its members.

There are a number of safeguards in the new regulation to ensure cooperation, while at the same time providing an ultimate 'watchdog' role for the Commission. Regulation 1/2003 provides, for instance, that the Commission be consulted before decisions applying Articles 101 or 102 TFEU are taken. Moreover, there are rules on suspending parallel national proceedings once the Commission or a national competition authority have commenced **investigations** in a particular case. Finally, the Commission has the opportunity to continue to deal with cases affecting more than three Member States, and the Commission's investigatory powers have been broadened. Under the control of national judges, its search rights also extend to private homes of business executives if there is a reasonable suspicion that business records, which may be relevant to prove a serious violation of Article 101 or Article 102 TFEU, are kept there.

9.17 How does EU competition law regulate dominant market power?

The second main pillar of EU competition law is the prohibition of **abuse** of a **dominant market** position found in Article 102 TFEU. It provides as follows:

> ''Any **abuse** by one or more undertakings of a **dominant position** within the internal market or in a substantial part of it shall be **prohibited** as incompatible with the internal market insofar as it may affect trade between Member States.
>
> "Such abuse may, in particular, consist in:
>
> (a) directly or indirectly imposing unfair purchase or selling prices or other unfair trading conditions;
> (b) limiting production, markets or technical development to the prejudice of consumers;
> (c) applying dissimilar conditions to equivalent transactions with other trading parties, thereby placing them at a competitive disadvantage; and
> (d) making the conclusion of contracts subject to acceptance by the other parties of supplementary obligations which,

by their nature or according to commercial usage, have no connection with the subject of such contracts."

9.18 When does an undertaking enjoy a 'dominant position'?

Article 102 TFEU is very clear in **not** making **monopoly** (or oligopoly) power **illegal** *per se*. Instead, it requires an **abuse** of a dominant position which may also be held collectively. However, otherwise abusive practices under Article 102 TFEU may not be prohibited if engaged in by a firm lacking market dominance.

Thus, for any analysis under Article 102 TFEU, it is crucial to determine the existence of **market dominance**, which remains undefined in the Treaty. In one of the Banana cases, Case 27/76 *United Brands* v. *Commission* [1978] ECR 207, the ECJ defined this concept as:

> "a position of **economic strength** enjoyed by an undertaking which enables it to **prevent** effective **competition** being maintained on the relevant market by giving it the power to **behave** to an appreciable extent **independently** of its competitors, its customers and ultimately of the consumers."

In practice, the Commission has prosecuted in instances where market share is 40 per cent, such as in the *United Brands* Case (→ *9.19*, *9.23*). However, even a market share of more than 40 per cent may not be sufficient for a finding of dominance in the absence of other factors, as the Court held in Case 85/76 *Hoffmann-La Roche* v. *Commission* [1979] ECR 461. According to the *Michelin* Case, Case 322/81 *Nederlandse Banden-Industrie Michelin NV* v. *Commission* [1983] ECR 3461, it depends upon the 'relative economic strength'

of a company, which means that dominance will depend upon the
market shares of the **competitors**, and, as the Court has held in the
United Brands Case, even a low market share may imply dominance
if there are significant entry barriers to (potential) competitors.

? 9.19 What is the relevant market in order to determine a dominant position?

Market dominance is not only an economic concept, sometimes
difficult for lawyers to grasp, it is also a relative concept relating to:
(1) a **product market** and (2) a **geographical market** and comprising (3) a **temporal factor**.

Legal battles have been fought over the scope of the relevant product market which may be decisive for a finding of dominance and,
thus, the applicability of Article 102 TFEU. The Commission and
the Court have focused on the **interchangeability** of products. From
a demand side, this requires that high **cross-elasticity** be shown, that
is, the willingness of buyers to substitute product B for product A
if the price of product A has been raised. There may be other factors in determining a product market, such as a product's **objective
physical characteristics**. Obviously, it is sometimes not so easy to
make a choice. The ECJ's reasoning in the abovementioned *United
Brands* Case (→ *9.18, 9.23*) offers some of the most entertaining
reading in EU jurisprudence. In finding that the banana market was
sufficiently distinct from the other fresh fruit market, the Court made
the following remarks:

> "The banana has certain characteristics, appearance, taste,
> softness, seedlessness, easy handling, a constant level of
> production which enable it to satisfy the constant needs
> of an important section of the population consisting of
> the very young, the old and the sick ... It follows from
> all these considerations that a very large number of

> consumers having a constant need for bananas are not
> noticeably or even appreciably enticed away from the
> consumption of this product by the arrival of fresh fruit on
> the market and that even the seasonal peak periods only
> affect it for a limited period of time from the point of view
> of substitutability."

From a supply-side perspective products will be considered inter-
changeable if they can be produced by a simple change in the production process, as was demonstrated in the *Continental Can* Case
(→ *9.20*).

? 9.20 Why is the *Continental Can* Case so important to EU competition law?

Case 6–72 *Europemballage Corporation and Continental Can
Company Inc.* v. *Commission* [1973] ECR 215, is another leading case
on **market definition**. The Court annulled a Commission decision
differentiating between separate markets for preserved meat, shellfish
cans and metal tops which did not state the difference in markets for
containers of other goods (for example, fruit and vegetables). The ECJ
focused on **interchangeability** from a supply-side and held that:

> "In order to be regarded as constituting a distinct market,
> the products in question must be individualized, not only
> by the mere fact that they are used for packaging certain
> products, but by particular characteristics of production
> which make them specifically suitable for that purpose.
> Consequently, a dominant position on the market for light
> metal containers for meat and fish cannot be decisive, as
> long as it has not been proved that competitors from other
> sectors of the market for light metal containers are not in a
> position to enter this market, by a simple adaptation, with
> sufficient strength to create a serious counterweight."

The *Continental Can* Case was also important for the Community's **merger control** before the 1989 Merger Regulation was adopted (→ *9.26–30*). The Commission found an abuse of a dominant position in Continental Can's acquisition of a Dutch metal can producer after having already acquired a dominant position on the relevant market by acquiring 85 per cent in a German metal can producer.

? 9.21 Which other factors are important for market definition?

While the relevant **geographical market** may in some cases be the entire internal market, technical and practical obstacles in product distribution may require a narrower concept of the relevant market. It may be the territory of a single Member State or even parts of it, as long as the objective conditions of competition applying to certain products are identical for all traders.

Equally, a **temporal element** may be important, since certain product markets may be seasonally determined or even more generally subject to change due to technological progress and shifting consumer preferences.

In order to make the arcane subject of market definition somewhat more transparent and accessible, the **Commission** published a **Notice** on the **Definition of the Relevant Market** for the Purposes of Community Competition Law, OJ 1997 C372/5, which primarily follows a demand-side substitutability test. According to the Commission:

> "the question to be answered is whether the parties' customers would switch to readily available substitutes or to suppliers located elsewhere in response to a hypothetical small (in the range of 5 to 10 per cent) but

permanent relative price increase in the products and areas being considered. If substitution were enough to make the price increase unprofitable because of the resulting loss of sales, additional substitutes and areas are included in the relevant market. This would be done until the set of products and geographical areas is such that small, permanent increases in relative prices would be profitable.''

? 9.22 What kind of behaviour amounts to an 'abuse' in the sense of Article 102 TFEU?

Article 102 TFEU itself provides a number of examples of an **abuse**, such as imposing unfair prices and trading conditions, limiting production, applying dissimilar conditions to equivalent transactions (discriminatory pricing, etc.) and subjecting contracts to unconnected supplementary obligations (tying). However, the precise scope of abusive practices made illegal by the Treaty is difficult to ascertain and has been refined by the practice of the Commission and the European courts. While most of the examples listed in the non-exhaustive enumeration of Article 102 TFEU (→ *9.17*) are forms of so-called exploitative abuse, primarily harming consumers as a result of unrivalled monopoly or quasi-monopoly power, European competition law practice has equally used Article 102 TFEU in order to fight so-called exclusionary abuse whereby dominant firms try to eliminate competitors from the market (→ *9.1*). An example of the latter type of anti-competitive behaviour can be seen in Case C-95/04 P *British Airways* v. *Commission* [2007] ECR I-2331, where the Court confirmed the Commission's finding that an airline's practice to offer travel agents bonuses if they specifically promoted their tickets had exclusionary effect.

9.23 Which were the abusive practices of *United Brands?*

In addition to its importance with regard to market definition ($\rightarrow$ *9.19*), Case 27/76 *United Brands* v. *Commission* [1978] ECR 207, is one of the leading competition law cases concerning **abusive behaviour**. It involved the largest banana producing firm which owned, among others, the brand 'Chiquita'. The trade restrictive activities, for which United Brands was fined by the Commission, comprise a textbook sample of abusive practices:

(a) **Unfair pricing** According to the Commission, the difference between actual costs and price was excessive. This point was, however, rejected by the Court since it was not adequately proven by the Commission. The Court accepted that the sales in Ireland might have been made at a loss to gain market access.

(b) **Refusal to deal** United Brands refused to supply a Danish distributor with Chiquita bananas because he had also become the sole distributor of competing 'Dole' bananas. The ECJ regarded such behaviour as inconsistent with Article 102(b) and (c) TFEU 'since the refusal to sell would limit markets to the prejudice of consumers and would amount to discrimination which might in the end eliminate a trading party from the relevant market'.

(c) **Discriminatory pricing** United Brands charged its Irish distributors 50 per cent less than its Danish one. In a not wholly uncontroversial ruling, the ECJ upheld the Commission's finding of abusive price discrimination, obviously inspired by the goal of creating a single market: 'a rigid partitioning of national markets was thus created at price levels which were artificially different, placing certain distributors/ripeners at a comparative disadvantage, since compared with what it should have been competition had thereby been distorted.'

9.24 What is the 'essential facilities doctrine'?

As in *United Brands*, the ECJ found an abuse of a dominant position in a **refusal to supply** a customer in the *Commercial Solvents* Case, Joined Cases 6 and 7/73 *Istituto Chemioterapico Italiano SpA* v. *Commission* [1974] ECR 233. It was a special aspect of this case that the customer had also become a competitor of the dominant firm as a result of the latter's decision to move into the production of pharmaceuticals originally only made by the customer. What was important in this case was the fact that the raw materials that were subject to the refusal to supply were 'essential' to the customer's production.

Based on such cases, the Commission developed a practice according to which refusal to grant **access** to an **'essential facility'** may constitute **abuse**. In particular, the transport and telecommunications sector was targeted by the Commission. The problem lies in defining the scope of such a facility, because it basically refers to something owned or controlled by a dominant firm to which others need access in order to provide products or services to their customers. In Case C-7/97 *Oscar Bronner* v. *Mediaprint* [1998] ECR I-7791, the ECJ held that a newspaper home delivery service maintained by a dominant publisher did not constitute an 'essential' facility for the distribution of newspapers to which a competing publisher with a small market share would have to be granted access. According to the ECJ's very restrictive standard in *Bronner*, the dominant firm's refusal to supply its delivery service to a competitor would be abusive only if it were likely to eliminate the competitor from the market, if access was 'indispensable', if there was no available alternative and if there was no objective justification for refusing to cooperate. In addition, one should not overlook the fact that the *Bronner* Case concerned a situation where a dominant firm refused to establish commercial relations with a competitor, whereas a case like *Commercial Solvents* concerned a refusal to continue such relations.

In the *Microsoft* Case, Case COMP/C 3/37.792 *Microsoft-Antitrust* [2004] EC Comm. 1, the Commission reverted to the 'essential facilities' doctrine and found that Microsoft had abused its dominant position by not disclosing 'inter-operability information' which would have allowed competitors to design competing products in the 'work groups server' market. Microsoft's challenge of the Commission decision before the CFI in Case T-201/04 *Microsoft* v. *Commission* [2007] ECR II-3601, was largely unsuccessful.

? 9.25 What is 'predatory pricing'?

'Predatory pricing' is the internal equivalent to what would constitute **'dumping'** in the context of external trade ($\rightarrow$ *11.2*). The leading case is Case C-62/86 *AKZO Chemie* v. *Commission* [1991] ECR I-3359, in which a dominant firm targeted the customers of its competitor, offering them extremely low prices (below cost) in order to eliminate the competitor. Such elimination may result even if the competitor is just as efficient as the dominant firm but lacks comparable financial resources to sustain the 'price war'. In theory, undertakings engaging in predatory pricing will recoup their losses after having successfully excluded competitors through subsequent price increases. In Case C-202/07 P *France Télécom SA* v. *Commission* [2009] ECR I-2369, the ECJ has rejected the view that 'proof of the possibility of recoupment of losses suffered by the application, by an undertaking in a dominant position, of prices lower than a certain level of costs constitutes a necessary precondition to establishing that such a pricing policy is abusive'. Below-cost sales are often financed through a form of **cross-subsidisation** as in Case C-333/94P *Tetra-Pak* v. *Commission* [1996] ECR I-5951. Tetra-Pak had a dominant position in the market for aseptic packaging cartons for food and used its profits made there in order to subsidise its below-cost sales of non-aseptic cartons. According to the CFI in Case T-228/97 *Irish Sugar plc* v. *Commission* [1999] ECR II-2969, a dominant firm may, however, justify its aggressive pricing policy if it is intended to protect its market position, is based on efficiency and is in the interests of the consumers.

9.26 Are mergers and acquisitions prohibited by the TFEU?

The issue of **mergers** is **not expressly mentioned in the TFEU** and, while, for a long time, Member States were unable to agree on secondary legislation to fill this gap, the European competition law enforcers and the ECJ helped out by applying the existing competition rules contained in Articles 101 and 102 TFEU in a broad fashion.

It clearly was a matter of contention in Case 6/72 *Europemballage Corporation and Continental Can Company Inc.* v. *Commission* [1973] ECR 215, when the Commission objected to a control bid for a Dutch competitor by Continental Can, a firm which already enjoyed a dominant position in the market (→ *9.20*). The ECJ upheld this decision stating that:

> "abuse may therefore occur if an undertaking in a dominant position strengthens such position in such a way that the degree of dominance reached substantially fetters competition, i.e. that only undertakings remain in the market whose behaviour depends on the dominant one."

In 1987 the ECJ held in the *Philip Morris* Case, Joined Cases 142 and 156/84 *British American Tobacco Co. Ltd and R. J. Reynolds Industries Inc.* v. *Commission* [1987] ECR 4487, that Article 101 TFEU could also apply to the acquisition of shares in a competitor if that acquisition could influence the behaviour in the marketplace of the companies involved.

? 9.27 Describe the main features of the Commission's merger control

In December 1989, the time was finally ripe for **Community legislation** in the field of **mergers**, which are referred to as **'concentrations'** in EU law. Council Regulation 4064/89 on the Control of Concentrations between Undertakings, as amended by Regulation 1310/97 and now embodied in Regulation 139/2004, empowers the **Merger Task Force** of the Commission to **oppose** large-scale (EU relevant) **mergers and acquisitions**. It sets out the following procedure:

(1) Intended concentrations must be **notified** to the Commission within one week after the agreement to merge, announcement of a takeover bid, or the like. Any proposed merger is on hold while being investigated by the Commission.

(2) A substantive **Common Market compatibility check** is carried out by the Commission in two stages: first, it decides within one month whether a proposed concentration falls under the Regulation, whether it is compatible with the Common Market or, if there are serious doubts about that, whether an investigation should be initiated. Second, the Common Market compatibility will be investigated during a period usually not exceeding four months.

Commission decisions blocking or conditioning mergers upon the fulfilment of burdensome prerequisites are subject to judicial review ($\rightarrow$ 5.3, 5.6). The European courts have adopted a **strict scrutiny standard** for merger cases. As explained in Case C-12/03 *Commission* v. *Tetra-Laval* [2005] ECR I-987, they will not only 'establish whether the evidence relied on is factually accurate, reliable and consistent but also whether that evidence contains all the information which must be taken into account in order to assess a complex situation and whether it is capable of substantiating the conclusions drawn from it'. Thus, where, in Case T-310/01 *Schneider Electric SA* v. *Commission* [2002] ECR II-4071, for example, they found 'errors, omissions and inconsistencies ... in the Commission's analysis of undoubted gravity' they annulled Commission decisions to block mergers.

? 9.28 What are 'concentrations'?

The EU law term for **mergers and acquisitions** is **'concentrations'**. According to the Merger Regulation, any kind of acquiring control over a firm, for example, a merger agreement, a stock or asset purchase, may qualify as concentration. A particular problem is posed by various forms of so-called **joint ventures** which cover all kinds of arrangements between firms, from loose cooperation, to strategic alliances, to strict integration. It is fairly obvious that only **'concentrative'** joint ventures are subject to the Merger Regulation, while **'cooperative'** joint ventures remain subject to Article 101 TFEU. The real problem lies in distinguishing between the two forms in practice. According to Article 3(2) of the Merger Regulation, 'the creation of a joint venture performing on a lasting basis all the functions of an autonomous economic entity shall constitute a concentration ...'. The Commission has shed some further light on this concept in its Notice on Full Function Joint Ventures, OJ 1998 C66/1.

? 9.29 How does EU law ensure that only Union relevant mergers and acquisitions are regulated by the Merger Regulation?

The Merger Regulation contains **quantitative** Union **thresholds** triggering its application. According to the one-stop shop principle, once the Merger Regulation applies there is no need to seek approval from national authorities in the Member States. According to Article 1(2) of the Merger Regulation a concentration has a **Union dimension** if: (a) the combined world-wide turnover of all affected undertakings exceeds €5 billion; and (b) the Union-wide turnover of each of at least two affected undertakings exceeds €250 million, unless each of the undertakings achieves more than two-thirds of its aggregate Union-wide turnover within one and the same Member State. This rule is supplemented by alternative (lower) thresholds for companies operating in more than two Member States.

In addition there are rules providing for some **flexibility** as regards the question of who should investigate mergers and acquisitions:

According to the so-called **'German clause'** in Article 9 of the Merger Regulation, the Commission may refer a Union relevant merger to national authorities, if a distinct market exists within the Member State and the concentration 'threatens to create or strengthen a dominant position [therein] as a result of which effective competition would be significantly impeded'. In practice, the number of referrals to national competition authorities under this clause has been low.

Pursuant to the **'Dutch clause'** (the Netherlands, like Belgium and Italy, did not have merger control legislation in the early 1990s) of Article 22 of the Merger Regulation, the Commission may enforce the Merger Regulation even below the relevant thresholds at a Member State's request. Article 21 of the Merger Regulation also mentions certain 'legitimate interests' of Member States, such as 'public security, plurality of the media and prudential rules', as possible reasons to exempt certain concentrations from its merger rules.

9.30 Under what conditions may 'concentrations' be approved?

Under Article 2(1) of the Merger Regulation the Commission will take into account the following criteria in order to assess the **Common Market compatibility** of a proposed merger:

(a) the need to maintain and develop effective competition within the common market in view of, among other things, the structure of all the markets concerned and the actual or potential competition from undertakings located either within or outwith the Community [now Union];

(b) the market position of the undertakings concerned and their economic and financial power, the alternatives available to suppliers and users, their access to suppliers or markets, any legal or other barriers to entry, supply and demand trends for the relevant goods and services, the interests of the intermediate and ultimate consumers and the development of technical and economic progress provided that it is to consumers' advantage and does not form an obstacle to competition.

The **Common Market compatibility** test basically means to ascertain whether the planned concentration would constitute a '**significant impediment to effective competition**'. In its Guidelines on the Assessment of Horizontal Mergers under the Council Regulation on the Control of Concentrations between Undertakings, OJ 2004 C31/5, the Commission has specified the methods it intends to use in order to scrutinise a proposed merger's Common Market compatibility.

If, on the basis of such an assessment, the **Commission** concludes that a proposed concentration would 'create or strengthen a dominant position as a result of which effective competition would be significantly impeded in the Common Market', Article 2(3) of the Merger Regulation provides that it has the power to **declare** it **incompatible** with the Common Market. Out of the numerous merger proposals filed under the Merger Regulation's regime, only a few have been actually blocked.

More frequently, the Commission imposes **conditions** on the **structuring** of a proposed deal in order to give its clearance. In a 2001 Notice on Remedies Acceptable under Regulation 4064/89, the Commission provided some guidance on what it would consider appropriate, such as partial divestiture in order to create or strengthen competition.

The formal criteria of the Merger Regulation may in practice be supplemented by other considerations, such as industrial policy concerns or the like.

? 9.31 Is EU competition law also binding for state-owned or specially privileged enterprises?

Although competition law is not applicable to activities connected with the exercise of official powers, as the ECJ held in the *Eurocontrol Case* (→ *9.6*), Article 106(1) TFEU (ex Article 86(1) TEC) clearly provides that with regard to 'public undertakings and undertakings to which Member States grant special or exclusive rights', Member States shall not enact any measures contrary to the Treaty's competition law rules. In Cases 188–190/80 *France, Italy and the United Kingdom* v. *Commission* [1982] ECR 2545, the ECJ accepted the Community legislator's definition of **'public undertaking'** as 'any undertaking over which the **public authorities** may **exercise** directly or indirectly a **dominant influence**', for instance, if they 'hold the major part of the undertaking's subscribed capital, control the majority of the votes, or can appoint more than half of the members of its administrative, managerial or supervisory body'.

An illustration of the ECJ's approach to Article 106(1) TFEU can be found in Case 18/88 *RTT* v. *GB-Inno-BM SA* [1991] ECR 5941. In that case, the Court found that Article 106(1) TFEU, in conjunction with Article 102 TFEU, 'preclude[s] a Member State from granting to the undertaking which operates the public telecommunications network the power to lay down standards for telephone equipment and to check that economic operators meet those standards when it is itself competing with those operators on the market of that equipment'.

? 9.32 Are there special competition law rules for utilities or other services in the general interest?

In most Member States, certain businesses of **general economic interest**, such as postal, electricity, information and other services, are granted exclusive rights in order to compensate for their service obligations in non-profitable areas. The Treaty accepts this practice in the rather ambiguous Article 106(2) TFEU which provides:

> "Undertakings entrusted with the operation of services
> of general economic interest or having the character of
> a revenue-producing monopoly shall be subject to the
> rules contained in the Treaties, in particular to the rules
> on competition, insofar as the application of such rules
> does not obstruct the performance, in law or in fact, of
> the particular tasks assigned to them. The development of
> trade must not be affected to such an extent as would be
> contrary to the interests of the Union."

Although the ECJ has interpreted this exception restrictively, it upheld it in case of firms with **universal** or quasi-universal **service obligations**. It thereby prevented private sector competitors from exploiting the profitable parts of an activity since this would make it financially impossible for the public service provider to fulfil its tasks. This was the main reasoning for the ECJ in the *Corbeau* Case, Case C-320/91 *Criminal proceedings against Paul Corbeau* [1993] ECR I-2533, where the Court upheld the Belgian postal monopoly which prevented a competitor operating a fast delivery service.

The Article 106(2) TFEU defence was also successfully invoked in Case C-475/99 *Ambulanz Glöckner* v. *Landkreis Südwestpfalz* [2001] ECR I-8089, where the Court held that this provision 'allows Member States to confer, on undertakings to which they entrust the operation of services of general economic interest, exclusive rights which may hinder the application of the rules of the Treaty on competition insofar as restrictions on competition, or even the exclusion of all competition, by other economic operators are necessary to ensure the performance of the particular tasks assigned to the undertakings holding the exclusive rights'. In the particular case, the exclusive right to provide a profitable service in the field of non-emergency ambulance transports was given to a firm which also provided emergency transports that were not profitable.

? 9.33 Does the Treaty prohibit Member States granting subsidies to private companies?

Article 107(1) TFEU (ex Article 87(1) TEC) provides that:

> ''any **aid** granted by a Member State or through State resources in any form whatsoever which **distorts** or threatens to distort **competition** by favouring certain undertakings or the production of certain goods shall, insofar as it affects trade between Member States, be **incompatible** with the internal market.''

Article 107(2) TFEU, however, does **exempt** the following types of subsidies:

(a) aid having a social character, granted to individual consumers, provided that such aid is granted without discrimination related to the origin of the products concerned;

(b) aid to make good the damage caused by natural disasters or exceptional occurrences; and

(c) aid granted to the economy of certain areas of the Federal Republic of Germany affected by the division of Germany, insofar as such aid is required in order to compensate for the economic disadvantages caused by that division. Five years after the entry into force of the Treaty of Lisbon, the Council, acting on a proposal from the Commission, may adopt a decision repealing this point.

While the Treaty does not define what constitutes 'state aid', the notion of aid used by the Commission and the European courts closely follows the GATT/WTO concept of a subsidy ($\rightarrow$ *11.2*). Thus, in order to qualify as **'aid'** a measure must **confer** an economic or financial **advantage** upon an undertaking. A benefit may also consist in tax holidays or reduced public charges, preferential interest rates or other advantageous loan conditions. There will be no 'financial advantage' where payments are received to offset public service obligations. Thus, in Case C-280/00 *Altmark Trans GmbH* [2003] ECR I-7747, the ECJ held that:

> "where a State measure must be regarded as compensation
> for the services provided by the recipient undertakings
> in order to discharge public service obligations, so that
> those undertakings do not enjoy a real financial advantage
> and the measure does not have the effect of putting
> them in a more favourable competitive position than the
> undertakings competing with them, such a measure is not
> caught by [Article 107(1)] of the Treaty."

The advantage must be granted **by** a **Member State** or 'through State resources' which is broadly interpreted. In order to assess state participation in undertakings a market investor test is applied.

According to the *Tubemeuse* Case, Case C-142/87 *Belgium* v. *Commission* [1990] ECR I-959, 'to determine whether such measures are in the nature of State aid, the relevant criterion is ... whether the undertaking could have obtained the amounts in question on the capital market'. Prohibited aid must be **'specific'** (Article 107 TFEU speaks of 'favouring certain undertakings or the production of certain goods'), which implies that measures broadly benefiting all market operators are usually not aid.

Article 107(3) TFEU further provides that the following types of subsidies may be declared compatible with the internal market by the Commission:

> (a) aid to promote the economic development of areas where the standard of living is abnormally low or where there is serious underemployment;
>
> (b) aid to promote the execution of an important project of common European interest or to remedy a serious disturbance in the economy of a Member State;
>
> (c) aid to facilitate the development of certain economic activities or of certain economic areas, where such aid does not adversely affect trading conditions to an extent contrary to the common interest;
>
> (d) aid to promote culture and heritage conservation where such aid does not affect trading conditions and competition in the Union to an extent that is contrary to the common interest; and
>
> (e) such other categories of aid as may be specified by decision of the Council on a proposal from the Commission.

In this way, Article 107 TFEU clearly attempts to complement the competition law rules addressed to private undertakings by proscribing state measures which would equally distort competition within the EU market.

10 Selected EU policies

The initial **European Economic Community** was largely about the creation of a **Common Market**, comprising a customs union and providing for the unhampered free movement of goods, persons, services and capital. Over the years, Community/Union competences have been considerably **extended** into other fields, called **policies** in EU jargon. This chapter will briefly address those EU policies which have gained significantly in importance, such as the **Common Agricultural Policy (CAP)**, **environmental** and **social policy**, with particular regard to **non-discrimination** issues. All were hardly visible in the original TEC and grew only as a consequence of **judge-made** law, EU **legislation** and **Treaty amendments**.

10.1 What are the objectives of the CAP?

According to Article 39(1) TFEU (ex Article 33(1) TEC) the aims of the CAP are:

(a) to increase agricultural productivity by promoting technical progress and by ensuring the rational development of agricultural production and the optimum utilisation of the factors of production, in particular labour;

(b) to ensure a fair standard of living for the agricultural community, in particular by increasing the individual earnings of persons engaged in agriculture;

(c) to stabilise markets;

(d) to ensure the availability of supplies; and

(e) to ensure that supplies reach consumers at reasonable prices.

Under the so-called *lex specialis* principle, which provides that specialised rules prevail over more general ones, CAP rules take precedence over other Treaty rules, such as those on the free movement of goods. According to Article 38(1) TFEU (ex Article 32(1) TEC), the CAP applies to **agricultural products** defined as 'products of the soil, of stockfarming and of fisheries and products of first-stage processing directly related to these products'.

? 10.2 What principles is the CAP based on?

By the time of the Stresa Conference in 1958 the following principles of the CAP were laid down:

- single market/**market unity** (replacing national markets via free movement);
- **Community/Union preference** (through import regulating instruments, subsidies and other measures); and
- **financial solidarity** (transfer payments between states involving net-payers vs. net receivers, the creation of the European Agricultural Guidance and Guarantee Fund, within which the Guidance Section finances structural measures and the Guarantee Section finances common market organisations).

? 10.3 How is the CAP put into operation?

Article 40 TFEU (ex Article 34 TEC) provides for the creation of 'a common organisation of agricultural markets', which may include the 'regulation of prices, aids for the production and marketing of the various products, storage and carryover arrangements and common machinery for stabilising imports or exports'.

Such **Common Market Organisations** were created for **different products** (for example, cereals, oil seeds and protein crops, beef and veal, dairy products and others), which typically provided for both **external protection** in the form of levies, increasing the cheaper import price to the threshold price set by the Union, as well as for **internal intervention** arrangements according to which agencies had to buy if the market price fell under a pre-set intervention price. This costly system clearly guaranteed a minimum income to producers. In practice, most of the enormous CAP spending, which in 2000 accounted for almost half of the entire Union expenses, supports the income of European farmers.

10.4 Is there an end in sight for CAP reform?

A major **CAP reform** was initiated in 1992, which, among other things, **reduced guaranteed prices**, provided for compensatory payments on the basis of factors of production, not of production, foresaw early retirement schemes for farmers, offered set-aside premiums for taking agricultural land out of production and encouraged the restructuring of farms and ecological concerns. In 1997, CAP reform plans were re-emphasised in the **AGENDA 2000**, which proposed further price support cuts and a shift to direct aid for farmers.

A number of these plans were adopted in the 2003 reform which provided for the payment of subsidies independently of the volume of production. So-called 'single farm payments' were linked to respecting environmental, food safety and animal welfare standards.

In 2008, this CAP reform was subjected to a 'health check' assessing its effect and trying to reinforce the plan to reduce market intervention by the EU.

? 10.5 What does the *Mulder* Case stand for?

The *Mulder* Case illustrates the difficulties of implementing CAP principles when they collide with **general principles of EU law** (→ *ch. 6*) and may trigger the EU's **non-contractual liability** (→ *4.9*).

The case arose from an attempt to reduce the excess production of milk in the Community. In the first *Mulder* Case, Case 120/86 *Mulder* v. *Minister van Landbouw en Visserij* [1988] ECR 2321, a Dutch farmer, who had agreed not to market milk for a five-year period, applied for a production quota after that period. The Dutch authorities rejected his request because under Dutch implementing legislation, based on a 1984 Council Regulation, quotas were issued on the basis of the production levels of the previous year. In a preliminary reference from an action against the Dutch authorities, the ECJ held this to be a violation of the producer's legitimate expectations and annulled the Council Regulation (→ *6.5*). In the second *Mulder* Case, Joined Cases C-104/89 and 37/90 *Mulder* v. *Council and Commission* [1992] ECR I-3061, the ECJ found an entitlement to lost profits on the basis of Article 340(2) TFEU (ex Article 288(2) TEC) which provides that:

> "in the case of **non-contractual liability**, the Union shall, in accordance with the **general principles** common to the laws of the Member States, make good any **damage caused** by its **institutions** or by its servants in the performance of their duties."

? 10.6 Does the EU have its own fisheries policy?

The **Common Fisheries Policy** is part of the CAP (Article 38(1) TFEU). The first Common Market Organisation for Fish was established in 1970. It provided for marketing standards (quality controls), a producer organisation and the setting of guide prices by the Community (if the market price falls below withdrawal prices production is withdrawn from sale).

The Common Fisheries Policy is based on the principle of **non-discrimination** between Union nationals with regard to **access to fishing grounds**, except for a 12-nautical miles coastal band reserved for local fishers. It further provides for **conservation measures** within the 200-nautical miles exclusive economic zone, expressed in annually fixed 'total allowable catches', which are in turn divided among the Member States in the form of quotas for specific fish species.

? 10.7 How did environmental protection in the Union start?

Since the 1972 EC Paris summit, which coincided with the UN Stockholm Conference on the Environment, five-year non-binding **'Environmental Action Programmes'** have been adopted by the Parliament and the Council. The Sixth Community Environment Action Programme (2002–2012) emphasised the four priority areas of natural resources and waste, environment and health, nature and biodiversity and climate change. What was initially a mere 'service' in the Commission for environmental and consumer issues subsequently became a Directorate-General for the

Environment, Nuclear Safety and Civil Protection and is now the **Environment Directorate-General** supporting the Commissioner for Environment.

10.8 What is the legal basis for Union legislation on the environment?

The legal basis for the Union's **environmental legislation** is complex and has been subject to numerous amendments. Before the inclusion of express environmental powers by the SEA 1986, the harmonisation of the laws of Member States concerning the internal market provided for in then Article 100 TEC (now Article 115 TFEU) and the Community's implied powers clause of then Article 235 TEC (now Article 352 TFEU) (→ *3.2, 3.4*) served as the legal basis for early environmental legislation. The practical drawback of both provisions was that they required **unanimity** (→ *2.3*), which involved the danger of simply reaching the lowest common denominator. The SEA introduced a title on environment that included Article 130s TEC (now Article 192 TFEU), which required unanimity but authorised the Council to define (unanimously) those matters on which decisions were to be taken by a qualified majority. Article 130t TEC (now Article 193 TFEU) contained a safeguard clause according to which Community measures 'shall not prevent any Member State from maintaining or introducing more stringent protective measures' compatible with the Treaty.

Under the Maastricht Treaty, environmental legislation became subject to the ex Article 252 TEC procedure, which required a qualified majority on the Council and co-operation with the European Parliament (→ *3.8*). Today, environmental legislation is subject to the ordinary legislative procedure of Article 294 TFEU (→ *3.9*).

? 10.9 Give examples of EU legislation in the environmental field

Since the 1970s, the EU has adopted an impressively wide range of environmental legislation, mostly in the form of **directives**, aiming at **harmonisation** instead of unification brought about by regulations.

The main focus of early Community legislation was on **combating pollution** and **environmental damage**, through clean water objectives (by limiting discharge of dangerous substances), clean air legislation (through limiting sulphur dioxide, lead and other pollutants), noise reduction (for example, lawnmowers), risk control for chemicals and biotechnology, as well as on nature and resources conservation, through banning pesticides, adopting the wild birds directive and various waste management directives since 1975, and by becoming signatory to international environmental agreements such as the 1989 Basle Convention concerning cross-border movements of dangerous waste.

In 1985, Directive 85/337 introduced an **'environmental impact assessment'** procedure requiring a preventive policy approach for public and private projects.

? 10.10 What are the principles of EU environmental action?

According to Article 191(1) TFEU (ex Article 174(1) TEC), the Union's **environmental policy** pursues the objectives of 'preserving, protecting and improving the quality of the environment; protecting human health; prudent and rational utilisation of natural resources; promoting measures at international level to deal with regional or worldwide environmental problems, and in particular combating climate change'.

Article 191(2) TFEU (ex Article 174(2) TEC) further ensures that:

> "Union policy on the environment shall aim at a **high
> level** of **protection** taking into account the diversity of
> situations in the various regions of the Union. It shall
> be based on the **precautionary principle** and on the
> principles that **preventive action** should be taken, that
> environmental damage should as a priority be rectified at
> source and that the **polluter should pay.**"

**? 10.11 Under what conditions are Member States
permitted to adopt environmental rules that
might restrict the free movement of goods?**

In the so-called *Danish Beverage Container* Case, Case 302/86
Commission v. *Denmark* [1988] ECR 4607, the Commission instituted an infringement action against Denmark because it considered the Danish deposit and return system for drink containers to
be contrary to the free movement of goods (→ *ch. 7*). The Danish
return system for beer and soft drink containers had two distinctive
features: first, marketing was permitted only in re-usable containers that had to be approved by a national agency; and second, non-
approved containers could be used by foreign producers for up to
3,000 hectolitres with a deposit-and-return system. Building on its
judgment in the *Cassis* Case (→ *7.5*), the ECJ held that:

> "in the absence of common rules relating to the marketing
> of the products in question, obstacles to free movement
> within the Community resulting from disparities between
> the national laws must be accepted insofar as such rules
> are, applicable to domestic and imported products without
> distinction, may be recognized as being necessary in
> order to satisfy mandatory requirements recognized by
> Community law. Such rules must be proportionate to the
> aim in view."

On that basis, the Court concluded that **environmental protection** was a **mandatory requirement** and that the deposit-and-return system was proportionate. The restriction of the quantity of imported products inherent in the system for non-approved containers, however, was disproportionate.

10.12 What was the so-called *Walloon Waste* Case?

In Case C-2/90 *Commission* v. *Belgium* [1992] ECR I-4431, the Belgian region of Wallonia restricted the **import** of foreign non-toxic **waste** and prohibited its deposit there. These rules violated a directive as far as hazardous waste was concerned. With regard to non-hazardous waste, which was not covered by common Community rules, the Court found that they contravened Article 34 TFEU (→ 7.3), but that they were justified as **'mandatory requirements'** (→ 7.5) even if discriminatory. In fact, the ECJ apparently dispensed with the element of discrimination inherent in an import ban by asserting rather cryptically that:

> "taking into account differences between waste produced in one place and that produced in another and of the link between waste and the place of its production, the challenged measures cannot be considered discriminatory."

10.13 What kind of activities has the Union undertaken in the field of consumer protection?

Consumer protection was introduced into the TEC by the 1992 Maastricht Treaty which in ex Article 129a(2) TEC authorised specific action under the co-decision (now ordinary legislative) procedure ($\rightarrow$ *3.9*). Previously, consumer protection legislation consisted mainly of harmonisation measures, although the **First Consumer Protection Action Programme** had been adopted in 1975. It provided for basic consumer rights, covering, for example, health and safety protection, the protection of economic and legal interests, the right of redress, the right to information and the right of representation.

The 1986 SEA introduced the notion of the **consumer** into the Treaty. Then Article 100a TEC entitled the Commission to propose measures designed to protect consumers, taking as a base a 'high level of protection'. Today, Article 169(1) TFEU (ex Article 153(1) TEC) mandates the Union to:

> "contribute to **protecting** the health, safety and economic interests of **consumers**, as well as to promoting their right to information, education and to organise themselves in order to safeguard their interests."

In particular in the health and safety area, important standards for consumer products were laid down in numerous directives, such as Directive 85/734 on Defective Products or Directive 92/59 on General Product Safety. With regard to the economic and legal interests of consumers, directives on misleading advertising, door-step sales, product liability, consumer credit, package holidays, unfair terms in consumer contracts and other issues have been adopted. Further, important consumer rights are the two-year guarantee for the sale of all consumer goods anywhere in the EU (Directive 99/44), or the compensation rules for air passengers (Regulation 261/2004).

? 10.14 What is the legal basis for the Union's social policy legislation?

The **Social Policy Chapter** of the Treaty, starting with Article 151 TFEU (ex Article 136 TEC), does not contain general legislative powers for the Union. Rather, according to Article 153(1) TFEU (ex Article 137(1) TEC) it is mostly intended to 'support and complement the activities of the Member States in [various] fields'.

For a long time, Community action in the field of social policy was thus based on general **harmonisation legislation**, such as a number of directives adopted under (old) Article 100 TEC which required unanimity in the Council and consultation of the Parliament (→ *3.8*). The 1986 SEA introduced (old) Article 118a TEC, which expressly mentioned a legislative competence in the field of 'health and safety of workers'. This is the core of the current Article 153(2) TFEU (ex Article 137 TEC) power of the Union to adopt minimum requirements by way of directives, which are now generally adopted according to the ordinary legislative procedure (→ *3.9*).

However, measures in the areas of social security and social protection of workers, protection of workers where their employment contract is terminated, representation and collective defence of the interests of workers and employers, and conditions of employment for third country nationals legally residing in Union territory may be adopted in accordance with a special legislative procedure after consulting the Parliament and the Economic and Social Committee as well as the Committee of the Regions.

The 1997 Amsterdam Treaty also added specific legislative powers in the field of **anti-discrimination law**. Article 157(3) TFEU (ex Article 141(3) TEC) gives the Council and the Parliament the power to adopt measures according to the ordinary legislative procedure in the field of 'equal opportunities and equal treatment of men and women in matters of employment and occupation' beyond the strict 'equal pay' principle laid down in Article 157(1) TFEU (ex Article 141(1) TEC) (→ *10.18*).

In addition, Article 19 TFEU (ex Article 13 TEC) permits the adoption of provisions on **non-discrimination**, and authorises the

Council, acting unanimously, to 'take appropriate action to combat discrimination based on sex, racial or ethnic origin, religion or belief, disability, age or sexual orientation'.

? 10.15 Describe the major results of the Social Action Programme 1974

In common with other policy areas, the Community initially used its harmonisation competence in order to adopt various social policy goals. The measures taken pursuant to the 1974 **Social Policy Programme** are a good example of such Community legislation aimed at fighting unemployment. The programme led to three particularly important directives:

- Directive 75/129 on **collective redundancies**, now codified in Directive 98/59, which requires advance (thirty days) notice for mass lay-offs (10 per cent of the workforce), as well as for 'consultations' with workers' representatives leading to possible government-proposed 'solutions';
- Directive 77/187 on the **safeguarding of employees' rights** in the event of **transfer of undertakings**, businesses, or parts of businesses, now codified in Directive 2001/23, which entitles employees to keep their employment relationship when all or part of the entity by which they were employed is transferred; and
- Directive 80/987 on the **protection of employees** in the event of **insolvency** of their employer, the famous '*Francovich* directive' (→ *4.9*), now codified in Directive 2008/94, which requires the setting up of 'guarantee institutions' with assets independent of the employers' capital to provide for payment of wages and benefits for a certain period after insolvency.

10.16 Which other measures were taken by the EU on the basis of its social policy powers?

On the basis of the 1989 Framework Directive 89/391, a number of directives relating to the prevention and protection of the health and safety of workers were adopted. In addition to the above-mentioned Directive 75/129 on collective redundancies, directives concerning working conditions, including working time, part-time and fixed-term work, and posting of workers were approved.

Similarly, the Treaty based 'equal pay' principle ($\rightarrow$ *10.18, 10.19*) was enlarged by EU legislation relating to equal treatment at work, pregnant workers, maternity leave, parental leave, as well as legislation countering discrimination on grounds of sex, race, religion, age, disability and sexual orientation ($\rightarrow$ *10.20*).

10.17 What is the Union's Social Charter?

This **non-binding instrument** was adopted at the Strasbourg European Council in 1989 as the **'Community Charter of the Fundamental Social Rights of Workers'**. Its objectives were to be translated into proposals in a Commission Action Plan, which led to a number of Council **directives** on health and safety standards, mutual recognition and other issues. The Union's Social Charter should not be confused with the 1961 European Social Charter of the Council of Europe, which is referred to in Article 151 TFEU (ex Article 136 TEC) as a source of inspiration for EU social policy measures.

The Union's Social Charter was transformed into a binding **Protocol on Social Policy** added to the **Maastricht Treaty** to promote employment, improve working conditions and foster dialogue between management and labour, etc. The Social Policy Protocol contained complicated decision-making provisions with special qualified majority quorums because, initially, the UK abstained from it (→ *1.6*). With the Treaty of Amsterdam the Protocol was incorporated into the TEC and now forms Title X, Articles 151–161 TFEU (ex Articles 136–145 TEC).

? 10.18 May an individual rely directly upon the Treaty's 'equal pay' principle?

Article 157(1) TFEU (ex Article 141(1) TEC) provides that 'each Member State shall ensure that the principle of **equal pay** for male and female workers **for equal work** or work of equal value is applied'. However, the wording of this Treaty provision was not always that clear and precise and, thus, gave rise to questions as to its **direct effect**. The original Article 119(1) TEC was formulated as follows: 'Each Member State shall during the first stage ensure and subsequently maintain the application of the principle that men and women should receive equal pay for equal work.'

In a landmark decision in 1976, Case 43/75 *Defrenne* v. *Sabena* [1976] ECR 455 (→ *4.5, 5.10*), the ECJ held that – after the first stage which had expired in December 1961 and despite its language – this provision had **'horizontal direct effect'** in cases of 'direct and overt discrimination'. According to the ECJ:

> "the principle that men and women should receive equal pay, which is laid down in Article 119, may be relied on before national courts. These courts have a duty to ensure the protection of the rights which that provision vests in individuals, in particular in the case of those forms of discrimination which have their origin in legislative provisions or collective labour agreements, as well as where men and women receive unequal pay for equal

work which is carried out in the same establishment or
service, whether private or public.''

10.19 What exactly is covered by the concept of 'equal pay' in Article 157(1) TFEU?

Since **'pay'** is **not defined** in the Treaty it was left to the ECJ to determine the scope of the equal pay principle. The Court, not surprisingly,
has arrived at a rather **broad definition** regarding any consideration
that a worker receives directly or indirectly in respect of employment
from his or her employer as 'pay'. In its case law, the ECJ has qualified
as 'pay', among other things, travel concessions (Case 12/81 *Garland*
v. *British Rail Engineering* [1982] ECR 359), pension schemes (Case
170/84 *Bilka-Kaufhaus GmbH* v. *Karin Weber von Hartz* [1986] ECR
1607), redundancy payments (Case C-262/88 *Barber* v. *Guardian
Royal Exchange Assurance Group* [1990] ECR I-1889), maternity
pay (Case C-342 *Gillespie* v. *Northern Health and Social Services
Board* [1996] ECR I-457), and compensation for unfair dismissal
(Case C-167/97 *R.* v. *Secretary of State for Employment, ex parte
Seymour-Smith and Perez* [1999] ECR I-623).

10.20 Outline the major legislative acts of the EU's non-discrimination policy

Initially, most Community legislation in the field of non-discrimination related to **gender discrimination**, such as the Equal Pay, the
Equal Treatment, and the Social Security Directive.

The so-called **Equal Pay Directive** 75/117 basically implemented
Article 119 TEC (now Article 157 TFEU). It specified the concept
of 'equal work' including 'work of equal value' which was not covered by the old Article 119 TEC, but is now covered by Article 157
TFEU (ex Article 141 TEC). Article 1(1) of the Directive provided:

> "The principle of equal pay for men and women outlined
> in Article 119 of the Treaty, hereinafter called 'principle
> of equal pay', means, for the same work or for work to
> which equal value is attributed, the elimination of all
> discrimination on grounds of sex with regard to all aspects
> and conditions of remuneration."

The **Equal Treatment Directive**, Directive 76/207, amended by
Directive 2002/73, covered 'hiring, promotion, all working conditions, and vocational training'. Its Article 2(1) provided that:

> "For the purposes of the following provisions, the principle
> of equal treatment shall mean that there shall be no
> discrimination whatsoever on grounds of sex either
> directly or indirectly by reference in particular to marital
> or family status."

Similar equal treatment provisions can be found in Directive 86/613
regarding those who are self-employed.

In 2006, these separate directives were replaced by a single **Equal
Treatment Directive**, Directive 2006/54 on the implementation of
the principle of equal opportunities and equal treatment of men and
women in matters of employment and occupation, which left the
substance largely unchanged.

The **Social Security Directive**, Directive 79/7, extends non-discrimination to the fields of social security and social protection to
workers and in Directive 86/378 to the self-employed.

In addition, the Community has legislated against race and ethnic
discrimination in the so-called **Race Directive**, Directive 2000/43,
and against various other forms of discrimination on the basis of
religion, belief, disability, age and sexual orientation in the so-called
Framework Directive, Directive 2000/78 establishing a general
framework for equal treatment in employment and occupation.

The latter directive gained particular prominence even before the
implementation period into national law had expired ($\rightarrow$ 4.8) in the
controversial *Mangold* case. In Case C-144/04 *Mangold* v. *Helm*

[2005] ECR I-9981, the ECJ found that most of the directive's age-discrimination rules were expressions of a general principle of EU law. Thus, the Court boldly concluded that it was

> "the responsibility of the national court, hearing a dispute involving the principle of non-discrimination in respect of age, to provide, in a case within its jurisdiction, the legal protection which individuals derive from the rules of Community law."

As a result, the Court found that the German prohibition of fixed-term employment contracts only for employees of a certain age was contrary to the principle of age-discrimination.

Both the Race and the Framework Directive are based on the broader general **non-discrimination** provision of Article 19 TEU (ex Article 13 TEC) which was introduced by the Amsterdam Treaty. Its first paragraph runs as follows:

> "Without prejudice to the other provisions of the Treaties and within the limits of the powers conferred by them upon the Union, the Council, acting unanimously in accordance with a special legislative procedure and after obtaining the consent of the European Parliament, may take appropriate action to combat discrimination based on sex, racial or ethnic origin, religion or belief, disability, age or sexual orientation."

? 10.21 Does the general exclusion of part-time employees from an employer's private pension plan constitute indirect discrimination if most part-time employees are women?

Sometimes, rules and regulations which appear neutral on their face may constitute indirect discrimination, if, *de facto*, they primarily affect members of a particular group. According to Article 2(1) of the **Equal Treatment Directive**, Directive 76/207 amended by Directive 2002/73, now Directive 2006/54:

> "**indirect discrimination** shall be taken to occur where an **apparently neutral provision**, criterion or practice would **put** persons of [a protected group] at a particular **disadvantage** compared with other persons, unless that provision, criterion or practice is objectively justified by a legitimate aim and the means of achieving that aim are appropriate and necessary."

As this legislative definition demonstrates, there is a specific justification for some forms of indirect discrimination, that is, if they serve legitimate aims and fulfil a proportionality test (→ *10.22*).

Since women are more likely to be part-time employees than men, any provisions favouring full-time over part-time employees regularly result in forms of indirect discrimination. This conclusion was drawn by the Court on the basis of today's Article 157 TFEU and not the Equal Treatment Directive in Case 170/84 *Bilka-Kaufhaus GmbH* v. *Karin Weber von Hartz* [1986] ECR 1607. There, the ECJ held that a private pension plan constituted 'pay' in the sense of Article 157 TFEU and that the exclusion of part-time workers from it might infringe Article 157 'where that exclusion affects a far greater number of women than men, unless the undertaking shows that the exclusion is based on objectively justified factors unrelated to any discrimination on grounds of sex'. (This shift of the burden of proof has been codified in Directive 97/80/EC on the burden of proof in cases of discrimination based on sex and is now contained in the Equal Treatment Directive 2006/54.) However, the Court acknowledged that the measure might pursue a legitimate aim if it was intended to have staff working at all times including weekends and evenings. Similarly, in Case 96/80 *Jenkins* v. *Kingsgate* [1981] ECR 911, the ECJ found that a lower wage for part-time than for full-time workers was not an illicit discrimination *per se*. Rather, where more women were affected than men, it might be lawful through an 'objective justification' which could lie in an incentive to take up full-time employment.

? 10.22 Are discriminatory employment practices always contrary to EU law?

EU non-discrimination legislation aims at eliminating discrimination. Nevertheless, it recognises that in certain circumstances, discriminatory practices may be justified. For instance, the 1976 Equal Treatment Directive – like the Race Directive and the Framework Directive (→ *10.20*) – provides that differences in treatment may be justified 'where, by reason of the nature of the particular occupational activities concerned or of the context in which they are carried out, such a characteristic constitutes a genuine and determining occupational requirement, provided that its objective is legitimate and the requirement is proportionate'. This provision permits a theatre to hire exclusively females for the role of a tragic heroine or the Catholic Church to employ only Catholics as priests.

The boundaries of the **'genuine occupational requirement'** have been tested in a number of cases concerning access to the armed forces by women. In Case C-273/97 *Sirdar* v. *Army Board and Secretary of State for Defence* [1999] ECR I-7403, the ECJ upheld the exclusion of women from a segment of the UK armed forces, the Royal Marines, because this army group had a policy that every member had to have the ability to fight at any time. In a very controversial judgment, in Case C-285/98 *Kreil* v. *Germany* [2000] ECR I-69, however, the Court held that German constitutional law barring women outright from army jobs involving the use of arms was contrary to the principle of equal treatment for men and women. While the Court found that derogations remained possible where sex constituted a determining factor for access to certain special combat units, it held that a general exclusion of women was a disproportionate discrimination.

? 10.23 Does Union law permit positive discrimination in the sense of affirmative action programmes?

One of the most difficult and controversial issues of non-discrimination law is the question of whether and to what extent the law should permit **temporary discrimination** in favour of historically disadvantaged groups in order to achieve an equality of results. Examples are hiring practices systems favouring the under-represented sex or race which have been used in many states in various **affirmative action programmes**.

Their legitimacy was already recognised in Article 2(4) of the 1976 Equal Treatment Directive (→ *10.20*), which provided an exception to the general equal treatment principle in respect of measures intended 'to promote equal opportunity for men and women, in particular by removing existing inequalities which affect women's opportunities'. The 1997 Amsterdam Treaty inserted a new paragraph 4 to Article 141 TEC (now Article 157(4) TFEU) which clarifies that Member States may maintain or adopt:

> "measures providing for specific advantages in order to make it easier for the underrepresented sex to pursue a vocational activity or to prevent or compensate for disadvantages in professional careers."

In Case C-450/93 *Kalanke* v. *Freie Hansestadt Bremen* [1995] ECR I-3051, the ECJ held, however, that such **affirmative action measures** may **not** take the form of **strict quotas** or include a system whereby a job would automatically go to a woman in cases of equal qualification. In Case C-409/95 *Hellmut Marschall* v. *Land Nordrhein-Westfalen* [1997] ECR I-6363, the ECJ stated that a qualification introduced by a saving clause which enabled male candidates to be made the subject of an objective assessment excluded absolute and unconditional priority for women. The Court concluded that priority given to equally qualified women – which was designed to restore the balance – was not contrary to EU law provided that an objective assessment of each individual candidate, irrespective of the sex of the candidate in question, was assured and that the promotion of a male candidate was not excluded from the outset.

This case law was confirmed in Case C-407/98 *Abrahamsson and Anderson* v. *Fogelqvist* [2000] ECR I-5539. In that case the Court held that Swedish legislation which automatically favoured access for women to public posts, even where their qualifications were not equal to those of their male candidates, was contrary to EU law. The Court pointed out that priority for women where their qualifications were equal – as a way of restoring balance – was not contrary to EU law provided that an objective assessment of each candidature was guaranteed.

10.24 Is an earlier retirement age for women than for men contrary to EU law?

Social security questions, and in particular **pension schemes**, are frequently the result of very controversial public policy choices of the various Member States. Thus, such issues were initially considered to be outside the reach of EU law. Article 119 TEC (now Article 157 TFEU) originally covered only 'pay', and even secondary EC law such as the Social Security Directive 79/7 ($\rightarrow$ *10.20*) expressly provided in its Article 7 that states might 'exclude from its scope the determination of pensionable age'.

Nevertheless, different **retirement ages** soon became the subject of litigation before the ECJ and the Court gradually acted more assertively in its scrutiny. In Case 19/81 *Burton* v. *British Railways Board* [1982] ECR 555, a case concerning a man who alleged discrimination on receiving lower redundancy dismissal benefits than women at the same age, the ECJ held that a private plan, paralleling the state social security system as far as different pensionable age was concerned, did not violate equal treatment.

In 1986, however, the ECJ held that different retirement ages were unlawful in Case 152/84 *Marshall* v. *Southampton and SW Hampshire Area Health Authority* [1986] ECR 723, a leading case denying horizontal direct effect and limiting it to the vertical relationship between individuals and Member States (→ *4.8*). Marshall complained that she had been discriminatorily dismissed at age 62, while men were retired at 65. According to the ECJ, Article 5(1) of the Equal Treatment Directive 76/207 (→ *10.20*), regulating 'working conditions, including the conditions governing dismissal', 'must be interpreted as meaning that a general policy concerning dismissal involving the dismissal of a woman solely because she has attained the qualifying age for a state pension, which age is different under national legislation for men and women, constitutes discrimination on grounds of sex, contrary to that directive'. The Court had first found that the case did not concern access to a retirement scheme, which would probably have been covered by the Social Security Directive 79/7, but rather the fixing of an age limit pursuant to a general policy concerning dismissal, which was covered by the Equal Treatment Directive.

Finally, in Case C-262/88 *Barber* v. *Guardian Royal Exchange Assurance Group* [1990] I-1889, the Court found 'an age condition which differs according to sex in respect of pensions paid under a contracted-out scheme [early retirement pension for men at age 55, women at age 50], even if the difference between the pensionable age for men and that for women is based on the one provided for by the national statutory scheme' contrary to Article 157 TFEU requiring 'equal pay'. The case concerned a man who was dismissed at age 52 and who did not receive an early retirement pension because it was generally offered to men at the age of 55. Because such an early retirement pension was generally offered to women at the age of 50 he successfully sued for discrimination.

It should be noted that **age discrimination** is now included in the abovementioned Framework Directive, Directive 2000/78 ($\rightarrow$ *10.20*).

10.25 How did the Lisbon Treaty affect Police and Judicial Cooperation in Criminal Matters?

The integration of the former third intergovernmental pillar of **Police and Judicial Cooperation in Criminal Matters** (PJCC) into the supranational TFEU is one of the most far-reaching changes accomplished by the Lisbon Treaty. This policy sector started out as intergovernmental cooperation in the fields of Justice and Home Affairs (JHA) under the Maastricht Treaty, focusing on visa, asylum and immigration matters. With the Amsterdam Treaty these matters became subject to supranational law-making, while further areas were added. However, the basic intergovernmental approach still applied which meant that unanimous decision-making in the Council prevailed, Parliament's role was merely consultative, and the ECJ had only very limited jurisdiction.

With the Lisbon Treaty this changed fundamentally. Today, the enlarged PJCC is part of a new Title V of the TFEU entitled **'Area of Freedom, Security and Justice'** which now comprises the policies on border checks, asylum and immigration; judicial cooperation in civil matters; judicial cooperation in criminal matters and police cooperation.

10.26 What has been accomplished in the field of Judicial Cooperation in Civil Matters?

Since Article 81 TFEU (ex Article 65 TEC) expressly ties the EU's competence in the field of Judicial Cooperation in Civil Matters to such matters 'having cross-border implications' most EU measures relate to **private international law** or **international civil procedure law**. Based on the Treaty-mandated **'principle of mutual recognition of judgments'**, many harmonisation measures have attempted to apply this integration principle to the new field of EU policy.

One of the major steps in this area was the replacement of the 1968 Brussels Convention on Jurisdiction and the Enforcement of Judgments in Civil and Commercial Matters by the so-called **Brussels I Regulation** 44/2001. According to its rules on **jurisdiction**, in general the courts of the Member State in which a defendant is domiciled, regardless of nationality, shall be competent to hear a case. However, consumers may also sue in their own country. Pursuant to its special jurisdiction rules, contractual disputes shall be dealt with by the courts of the place of performance, while tort claims shall be brought before the courts of the place where the harmful event occurred. The mutual **recognition of judgments-**obligation may only be avoided as a result of limited grounds, like being contrary to public policy, lack of proper service or where the matter has already been decided (*res judicata*). The so-called Brussels II Regulation 2201/2003 contains rules on jurisdiction and enforcement in family law matters; while additional measures aim at improving cooperation between Member States with regard to the taking of evidence in legal proceedings (Regulation 1206/2001), create a simplified European order for payment procedure (Regulation 1896/2006), standardise service of process methods (Regulation 1393/2007), or promote mediation (Directive 2008/52).

In the field of private international law proper, the 1980 Rome Convention on the Law Applicable to Contractual Obligations, containing harmonised conflict-of-law rules in civil and commercial matters, was transformed into EU legislation by the so-called **Rome I Regulation** 593/2008. It basically respects the parties' freedom to select the applicable law and provides for some residual rules in the absence of a **choice-of-law**. Similar rules are contained in the Rome

II Regulation 864/2007 with regard to no-contractual liability, such as product liability.

10.27 Is there an EU criminal law policy?

Though still couched in terms of 'judicial cooperation in criminal matters' the EU has made use of its legislative powers to extend the common market principle of **mutual recognition** ($\rightarrow$ *7.5*) to the field of criminal law (Article 82(1) TFEU) and to adopt **harmonisation measures** in criminal law matters 'having a cross-border dimension' (Article 82(2) TFEU).

The most important outcome in the former area is the replacement of traditional extradition principles by an expedited surrender procedure based on the recognition of **European Arrest Warrants** ($\rightarrow$ *10.28*), while the legislator's harmonisation powers in the latter field have been used to set up minimum rules concerning the definition and penalties for **serious cross-border crimes** such as terrorism, money laundering, trafficking in drugs, arms and human beings, corruption and organised crime.

10.28 What is the European Arrest Warrant?

Pursuant to the Framework Decision 2002/584/JHA, a directive-type of law-making act applicable to the Justice and Home Affairs field before Lisbon, a **European Arrest Warrant** is 'a **judicial decision** issued by a Member State with a view to the **arrest and surrender** by another Member State of a requested person, for the purposes of conducting a **criminal prosecution** or executing a custodial sentence or detention order'. The issuance of a European Arrest Warrant in one EU Member State in principle obliges all other Member States to surrender the requested person within short time limits.

The underlying premise of **mutual trust** in the fairness of criminal proceedings has led to a number of problems. Many national constitutions contain **due process guarantees** which require that extraditions are only granted where it is ensured that 'the rule of law is observed' in the requesting state. According to the German Constitutional Court in the *European Arrest Warrant Case*, BVerfG, 2 BvR 2236/04 of 18 July 2005, though limitations on such guarantees are permissible they 'must at least put the executing authorities in a position ... to weigh the citizen's confidence in the German legal system, which is protected in this respect, in the individual case according to these constitutional principles'. It thus voided the German implementing act of the European Arrest Warrant Framework Decision, admonishing that 'putting into effect a strict principle of mutual recognition, and the extensive statement of mutual confidence among the states that is connected with it, cannot restrict the constitutional guarantee of the fundamental rights'.

With regard to thirty-two particularly serious crimes, the European Arrest Warrant eliminates the traditional **double criminality** principle which in extradition law requires that the offence for which the surrender of person is requested must be punishable not only in the requesting, but also in the requested state. This abolition has been challenged as an infringement of the general principle of law and fundamental rights standard (→ *6.5, 6.7*) of *nullum crimen sine lege* (legal certainty in criminal matters) according to which no one shall be prosecuted unless on the basis of clearly defined offences. In Case C-303/05 *Advocaten voor de Wereld* [2007] ECR I-3633, the ECJ rejected such challenges by stating that 'the definition of those offences and of the penalties applicable continue to be matters determined by the law of the issuing Member State, which ... must respect fundamental rights and fundamental legal principles as enshrined in Article 6 TEU, and, consequently, the principle of the legality of criminal offences and penalties'.

Further, the implementation of the European Arrest Warrant Framework Decision has required some Member States to disregard their **constitutional law guarantees** prohibiting the **extradition** of their own **citizens**.

? 10.29 Is there already a harmonised EU criminal law?

In addition to the cooperation in criminal law, Article 83(1) TFEU empowers the Union legislator to use the ordinary legislative procedure in order to adopt directives to 'establish minimum rules concerning the **definition of criminal offences** and sanctions in the areas of particularly **serious crime** with a **cross-border dimension**'. The Lisbon Treaty also expressly codified some areas where the Union has already adopted **harmonisation** measures, mostly under the previous PJCC powers in the form of framework decisions, among them, terrorism, trafficking in human beings and sexual exploitation of women and children, illicit drug trafficking, illicit arms trafficking, money laundering, corruption, counterfeiting of means of payment, computer crime and organised crime.

The Framework Decision on Combating Terrorism 2002/745/JHA is an example of the far-reaching and often controversially exercised powers of the EU under the PJCC. Its **definition of terrorist acts** has given rise to criticism by criminal lawyers as well as human rights activists for being overly broad.

EU action to counter terrorism is not limited to criminal law action in the field of the PJCC. In implementing UN Security Council resolutions, the EU has also adopted **preventive measures** like the **freezing of assets** of persons and entities suspected of terrorism. These measures are now taken on the basis of an express competence in Article 75 TFEU. Before the Lisbon Treaty, however, it was less clear whether the then Community had the power to adopt freezing legislation, although in Joined Cases C-402/05 P and C-415/05 P *Kadi and Al Barakaat* v. *Council and Commission* [2008] ECR I-6351 the ECJ affirmed that (→ *3.4*).

❓ 10.30 How do the police cooperate in the EU?

Article 87(1) TFEU calls for the establishment of '**police cooperation** involving all the Member States' competent authorities, including police, customs, and other specialised law enforcement services in relation to the **prevention, detection and investigation of criminal offences**'. The Union has adopted a number of legislative measures like the Framework Decision on Simplifying the Exchange of Information and Intelligence between Law Enforcement Authorities in the Member States of the EU 2006/960/JHA which provides for a speedy **exchange of information**. In order to safeguard privacy rights, acts like the Framework Decision on the Protection of Personal Data 2008/977/JHA stipulate that personal data may be collected by the competent authorities only for 'specified, explicit and legitimate purposes'.

Since personal data relevant for police investigation may also be contained in databases run by financial, telecommunications or transport service providers, the EU has also enacted legislation to ensure that such data may be used for police purposes. For instance, the so-called **Money Laundering Directive** 2005/60 requires financial institutions to report suspicious transactions, while the **Data Retention Directive** 2006/24 requires electronic communications providers to store data for a certain period of time and to make it available to law-enforcement authorities.

Finally, the EU has created its own police cooperation entity in the form of **Europol** which was originally set up by a 1995 treaty between the EU Member States. It is now based on the Framework Decision establishing the **European Police Office** (Europol) 2009/371/JHA which provides for a largely supportive role of Europol in joint investigations of Member State authorities. Europol also handles its own **Europol Information System** which may include ID and social security numbers, records about criminal offences, DNA profiles and fingerprints.

11 The EU as an international actor

One of the main achievements of the Lisbon Treaty, already envisaged in the 2004 **Draft Constitution Treaty** in its endeavour to simplify European law and, thus, to make it more accessible to EU citizens, is the **abolition** of the **three pillar** structure under a common EU roof. Instead, **one single EU** replaced the existing supranational Community (Article 1 TEU). This new European Union pursues both the supranational former Community policies as well as the inter-governmental areas of cooperation, such as the CFSP. With the entry into force of the Lisbon Treaty, one EU, endowed with **legal personality** in Article 47 TEU, is expressly empowered to enter into **international agreements** with third countries and international organisations (Article 37 TEU and Article 216 TFEU) and is the sole actor on the international plane. However, even though all external relations of the EU are now governed by common principles, the CFSP retained some of its distinct features and remains separated in the TEU, rather than the TFEU.

When dealing with the EU as an international actor, the analysis of its competence is always twofold. The first important question is, whether a **competence** for the Union to act externally exists at all. In a second step, it is crucial whether an existing competence is **exclusive** to the EU or **shared** with the Member States.

This final chapter tries to provide a brief overview of the different aspects of the activities of the EU on the international plane.

? 11.1 What is the common constitutional framework of EU external action?

On the international plane, the complex three pillar structure was particularly hindering for the EU to become a visible actor with a consistent and coherent foreign policy. The CCP ($\rightarrow$ *11.5*), association agreements and other external dimensions of the former Community policies were pursued by the Community whereas the former second pillar, the CFSP was pursued by the Union ($\rightarrow$ *11.17*). Hence, the merger of the three pillars was also intended to simplify matters in EU external relations law.

All external relations of the Union are now governed by a single set of principles outlined in Article 21 TEU, which states:

"(1) The Union's action on the international scene shall be guided by the principles which have inspired its own creation, development and enlargement, and which it seeks to advance in the wider world: democracy, the rule of law, the universality and indivisibility of human rights and fundamental freedoms, respect for human dignity, the principles of equality and solidarity, and respect for the principles of the United Nations Charter and international law.

[…]

"(3) The Union shall respect the principles and pursue the objectives set out in paragraphs 1 and 2 in the development and implementation of the different areas of the Union's external action covered by this Title and by Part Five of the [TFEU], and of the external aspects of its other policies."

According to Article 22 TEU, the **European Council**, as a major actor in EU external relations, is empowered to adopt **unanimous decisions** in order to 'identify the **strategic interests and objectives** of the Union', which 'shall relate to the common foreign and security policy and to other areas of the external action of the Union'.

However, even though there are common provisions that govern all external action of the EU, the CFSP retained some of its distinct features and remains separated in the TEU, rather than being integrated into the TFEU. The CFSP in particular is subject to different institutional and procedural rules (→ *11.17–20*). Generally, whereas the external relations powers of the TFEU continue to be dominated by the Commission, the CFSP is still significantly shaped by the Council.

? 11.2 Who is the High Representative of the Union for Foreign Affairs and Security Policy?

As outlined above (→ *11.1*), the complexity of the institutional structure of the EU was particularly evident in its external relations. Depending on the subject matter, it was either the Commission or the Council who spoke for the EU. This was not only detrimental for the coherence and consistency of EU external relations (→ *11.1*) but it also complicated issues for those who wanted to interact with the EU on the international plane. This is often illustrated by reference to the famous quote of Henry Kissinger: 'Who do I call if I want to call Europe?'

The Lisbon Treaty created the office of the High Representative of the Union for Foreign Affairs and Security Policy (hereinafter **'High Representative'**), who would have been called 'Foreign Minister' under the Constitutional Treaty. It succeeds the post of the former High Representative for the Common Foreign and Security Policy, introduced by the 1997 Amsterdam Treaty. Pursuant to Article 18 TEU the High Representative is appointed by the European Council, with the agreement of the President of the Commission and is assisted by the European External Action Service (EEAS). At the time of writing, the office is held by the British politician Catherine Ashton.

Apart from the merger of the three pillars and the definition of common policies and objectives of all EU external relations, the creation of the office of a High Representative with a 'double hat' is intended to enable the EU to 'speak with one voice'. The High Representative is 'double-hatted' because, on the one hand, the office consists of the chair of the Foreign Affairs Council (Article 18(3) TEU; → *2.2*) and the conduct of the Common Foreign and Security Policy (Article 18(2) TEU; → *11.17–20*). However, on the other hand, it also encompasses the role as a Vice-President of the European Commission, responsible for external relations (Article 18(4) TEU; → *2.7*). According to Article 15(2), the High Representative furthermore takes part in the work of the European Council (→*2.1*). These provisions meant to ensure the consistency and coordination of the EU's external action.

? 11.3 How does the EU enter into international agreements?

According to the standard treaty-making procedure laid down in Article 218 TFEU (ex Article 300 TEC), the **Commission**, upon authorisation from the Council, conducts treaty **negotiations** with third states or organisations, while the **Council concludes** international **agreements**. In the CFSP field, the High Representative, instead of the Commission, negotiates treaties.

The Lisbon Treaty has enhanced the role of the **Parliament**. In addition to cases where it is merely **consulted**, its **consent** is now required for the accession of new Member States, association agreements, the accession to the ECHR (→ *6.8*), agreements setting up a specific institutional framework or with important budgetary implications and agreements covering fields to which either the ordinary legislative procedure applies, or the special legislative procedure where consent by the EP is required (Article 218(6)(a) TFEU). Hence, the extension of the ordinary legislative procedure to new areas has also strengthened the Parliament's role in the conclusion of international agreements (→ *2.17*).

As a matter of principle, the **Council** acts on the basis of **qualified majority** (→ *2.3*). However, in the case of association agreements (→ *11.14–16*), accession treaties with new Members, the EU accession to the ECHR (→ *6.8*) and agreements covering fields for which unanimity is required for the adoption of internal rules, the Council has to act unanimously. Similarly, certain types of CCP treaties require unanimity on the Council, among, them some relating to GATS, TRIPS or foreign direct investment (Article 207(4) TFEU; → *11.6, 11.13*).

? 11.4 What is the legal basis of the EU's external relations based on the TFEU?

The **external relations** of the then EC were traditionally limited to **trade relations** with third countries, conducted either on the basis of unilateral measures, such as anti-dumping or countervailing duties, or through trade agreements. For both types of 'external' activities, the **Common Commercial Policy** (CCP) powers expressly mentioned in ex Article 133 TEC (now Article 207 TFEU) provided a solid legal basis (→ *11.5*). The other traditional Community (now EU) competence concerning external relations is the power found in ex Article 310 TEC (now Article 217 TFEU) to enter into **association agreements**, which are frequently pre-accession relations going beyond mere trade relations (→ *11.14–16*). These agreements should not be confused with the association with overseas countries and territories of Member States, such as Greenland, French Polynesia or the British Virgin Islands, provided for in Article

198 TFEU (ex Article 182 TEC). Parallel to the extension of the Community's internal competences, its **treaty-making power** was gradually extended to include research and technology, environment and development policy (since the 1986 SEA), monetary and foreign exchange matters, education, culture, health and trans-European networks (since the 1992 Maastricht Treaty). Also the Amsterdam and the Nice Treaty amendments further extended these express powers. The Lisbon Treaty added a new investment power to the CCP which remains controversial in its precise form and extent (→ *11.6*). Moreover, Article 198 TFEU (ex Article 302 TEC) states that the Union shall maintain appropriate relations with the UN and other **international organisations** (→ *2.12*).

In addition to these express powers, the ECJ developed a rather complex case law of so-called **implied external powers**, outlined below (→ *11.8–13*).

? 11.5 How does the EU pursue its CCP?

The Union's activities under Article 207 TFEU (ex Article 133 TEC) are not limited to treaty-making powers with regard to trade matters. Rather, they also cover **unilateral external trade measures**, such as the imposition of a **common customs tariff**, Union rules on **anti-dumping** and **countervailing duties** against **subsidies**, as well as other **trade measures**. The establishment of a **common external tariff** is one of the essential features of the European customs union, and it involves applying uniform customs duties to products imported from third countries (→ *7.1*). The customs union envisaged in the original 1957 EEC Treaty and completed in 1968 requires the elimination of all customs duties and restrictions among the Member States of the Union and the introduction of a common customs tariff (an external tariff which applies to third-country goods).

Since 1988 the imposition of a Union-wide **common customs tariff** has been based on the so-called **'combined nomenclature'**, originally laid down in Council Regulation (EEC) 2658/87 of 23 July 1987 on the tariff and statistical nomenclature and on the common customs tariff. This combined nomenclature classifies goods for customs and statistical purposes. Every year the Commission adopts a Regulation reproducing a complete version of the combined nomenclature and common customs tariff duty rates.

In addition, the EU's external trade is regulated by a number of **unilateral** measures **restricting** the import (such as safeguard measures) or **export** of goods (such as restrictions covering radio-active waste or culturally, artistically or historically important products). Unilateral export restrictions are also laid down in Regulation 428/2009 for so-called dual use goods, that is, products that may serve military purposes in addition to their primary civilian use.

The **Anti-dumping Regulation** 384/96, which implemented the relevant 1994 GATT code, is now codified in Council Regulation 1225/2009. It permits the Commission to impose anti-dumping duties on imported products if they are dumped, that is, **sold below** their **normal value**, and if such dumping causes **injury** to a Union **industry**. These Commission decisions, adopted in the form of regulations, can be challenged before the General Court through annulment actions (→ 5.6).

Pursuant to **Regulation** 597/2009 on **protection** against **subsidised imports** from countries which are not members of the European Union, the Union may also take trade measures against subsidies granted by foreign states to their exporters which cause harm to European producers. A **subsidy**, or **'state aid'** in Union terminology (→ 9.33), is defined as a **financial contribution** by a government or any other **public body** which **confers** a **benefit**. Examples of less obvious subsidies are, for instance, tax holidays, export credits, or transport benefits. The Union's CCP power to adopt measures against subsidised imports from third countries, usually in the form of so-called **countervailing duties**, should not be confused with the rules on state aid in Articles 107–109 TFEU, which prohibit Member States from subsidising firms and thereby distorting competition within the internal market (→ *9.33*).

Finally, the EU may also counteract other 'obstacles to trade' on the basis of the so-called **Trade Barriers Regulation** 3286/94, which provides for the initiation of dispute settlement under the WTO rules, the imposition of duties or quotas and the like as a reaction to other unfair trade practices of third parties.

? 11.6 Does the EU have the power to enter into international investment agreements?

For decades individual EU Member States have concluded **bilateral investment treaties** (BITs) mostly with third countries, containing standards of fair and equitable treatment, full protection and security, most-favoured-nation and national treatment as well as guarantees against uncompensated expropriation. In addition, such treaties often permit investors of one Contracting Party to institute arbitration directly against the other Contracting Party which made the substantive standards of protection highly effective. Already in the past, the Commission was keen on including investment chapters to free trade agreements it negotiated with third states.

The **Lisbon Treaty** now adds an express treaty-making power with regard to **foreign direct investment** to the CCP. The fact that this EU power is expressly limited to 'foreign direct investment' implies that future investment agreements which usually comprise both direct and portfolio investment are likely to be concluded as **mixed agreements** (→ *11.12*). It appears that this addition, already anticipated in the Draft Constitution Treaty, was not thoroughly discussed by the EU's Member States, some of which were taken by surprise that they have now lost their power to conclude BITs.

Meanwhile the Commission has proposed a draft Regulation on transitional arrangements for BITs between Member States and third countries and adopted a Communication on a comprehensive **European international investment policy**. For a transitional period Member States are still competent to maintain and even enter into investment treaties with third states.

? 11.7 Was the Commission competent to conclude an international agreement involving competition law?

In the division of powers system of the EU, it is the task of the Commission to negotiate and of the Council to conclude international agreements. The **Commission's own 'treaty-making power'** was always strictly limited to **privileges and immunities** according to the Privileges and Immunities Protocol and 'administrative agreements' with the UN and other international organisations according to Article 220 TFEU (ex Article 302 TEC).

Thus, as a consequence, in Case 327/91 *France* v. *Commission* [1994] ECR I-3641, the ECJ struck down a 1991 EC–US agreement for mutual cooperation and assistance in matters of anti-trust enforcement concluded by the Commission with the US Department of Justice (→ *9.10*). In 1998 it was, however, in substance, 're-concluded' by the Council as 'Agreement between the European Communities and the Government of the United States of America regarding the application of their competition laws' and supplemented by the 'Agreement between the European Communities and the Government of the United States of America on the application of positive comity principles in the enforcement of their competition laws'.

? 11.8 Does the Union also possess implied powers to enter into international agreements?

As already noted, an express treaty-making competence of the then EC was originally contained only in Articles 133 and 310 TEC (now Articles 207 and 217 TFEU) with regard to the CCP and association agreements (→ *11.4, 11.14*). The gradual elaboration of the **implied powers doctrine** (→ *3.2*) in the area of external relations (now codified in Article 216 TFEU; → *11.10*) enabled the Union to enter into agreements in other fields where it had an **internal competence to legislate**. An apt description of this reasoning can be found in the ECJ's Opinion 2/91, *ILO Convention No. 170* [1993] ECR I-1061 where it was stated that:

> "Authority to enter into international commitments may not only arise from an express attribution by the Treaty, but may also flow implicitly from its provisions ... **whenever** Community law created for the institutions of the Community **powers** within its **internal system** for the purpose of attaining a specific objective, the Community had **authority** to **enter** into the **international commitments** necessary for the attainment of that objective even in the absence of an express provision in that connection."

? 11.9 Where did the ECJ find the Union's power to enter into international agreements according to the *ERTA* judgment?

The groundwork for such an extensive reading of the then Community's external powers was laid in the Court's case law of the early 1970s. In the so-called *ERTA* Case, Case 22/70 *Commission v. Council* [1971] ECR 263, the Court had to decide whether the Commission (for the Community) or the Member States (on their own behalf) had the competence to negotiate a European Road Transport Agreement (ERTA) with third countries.

The ECJ took as a starting point that ex Article 281 TEC provided for the (international) **legal personality** of the Community (now Article 47 TEU for the EU). It continued to reason that in order to establish the Community's treaty-making power in a specific case it is necessary to look at the **whole scheme** of the Treaty and not only at single substantive provisions. The Court then reaffirmed the **implied powers** doctrine by stating that the authority to enter into international agreements 'arises not only from an **express conferment** by the Treaty but may equally flow **implicitly** from other provisions of the Treaty, from the act of accession and from measures adopted within the framework of those provisions, by the Community institutions'. Finally, the ECJ concluded that:

> "each time the Community, with a view to implementing a common policy envisaged by the Treaty, adopts provisions laying down common rules, whatever form these may take, the Member States no longer have the right, acting individually or even collectively, to undertake obligations with third countries which affect those rules. As and when such common rules come into being, the Community alone is in a position to assume and carry out contractual obligations towards third countries affecting the whole sphere of application of the Community legal system. With regard to the implementation of the provisions of the Treaty the system of **internal Community** measures may **not** therefore be **separated** from that of **external relations**."

? 11.10 For its power to enter into agreements is it necessary that the EU has already exercised its internal legislative competence?

The *ERTA* Case seems to make exclusive **external powers dependent** upon the prior adoption of 'common rules', that is, **EU legislation**.

In the *Rhine Navigation* Case concerning a Draft Agreement Establishing a Laying-up Fund for Inland Waterway Vessels, Opinion 1/76 [1977] ECR 741, the Court clarified, however, that the then EC was competent to enter into an agreement for the control of river traffic, although it had not yet exercised its internal competence to regulate inland waterway traffic based on its **power to regulate transport** 'insofar as the participation of the Community in the international agreement is, as here, necessary for the attainment of one of the objectives of the Community'. It is likely that the Court found an exclusive external competence of the Community in this very specialised field because it felt that individual Member State action could have threatened the common Community objective.

In later rulings the ECJ seemed to retreat from such broad assertions of Community/Union powers. In Opinion 1/94, *WTO Agreement* [1994] ECR I-5267 (→ *11.13*), it made clear that external and internal powers are **not co-extensive** and that 'save where internal powers can only be effectively exercised at the same time as external powers (see Opinion 1/76), internal competence can give rise to exclusive external competence only if it is exercised'.

In Case C-476/98 *Commission* v. *Germany (Open Skies)* [2002] ECR I-9855, the ECJ reaffirmed the notion that an 'implied external competence exists not only whenever the internal competence has already been used in order to adopt measures for implementing common policies, but also if the internal Community measures are adopted only on the occasion of the conclusion and implementation of the international agreement'. However, it rejected an implied Community competence to conclude air transport agreements with third countries because that was not necessary in order to adopt internal rules.

The Treaty of Lisbon attempted to codify the major concepts of the Court's jurisprudence on implied treaty-making powers in Article 216(1) TFEU which provides as follows:

> ''The Union may **conclude** an **agreement** with one or
> more third countries or international organisations where

the Treaties **so provide** or where the conclusion of an
agreement is **necessary** in order to **achieve**, within the
framework of the Union's policies, one of the **objectives**
referred to in the Treaties, or is **provided for** in a legally
binding **Union act** or is likely to **affect common rules** or
alter their scope.❜❜

> **? 11.11 Does the treaty-making power of the EU**
> **• preclude the Member States from entering**
> **into agreements in the fields concerned?**

In the case of an **'exclusive'** Union competence, such as the CCP
under Article 207 TFEU (ex Article 133 TEC), Member States have
lost their power to enter into international agreements. The Lisbon
Treaty has clarified in Article 3(2) TFEU that exclusive competence
exists also 'for the conclusion of an international agreement when
its conclusion is provided for in a legislative act of the Union or is
necessary to enable the Union to exercise its internal competence,
or insofar as its conclusion may affect common rules or alter their
scope'.

In the case of a **'shared'** Union competence, however, this is
different. In the *Kramer* Case, Joined Cases 3, 4 and 6/76 *Officier
van Justitie* v. *Kramer and others* [1976] ECR 1279, Dutch rules
on fish conservation according to the North-East Atlantic Fisheries
Convention were upheld. The Court stated that 'it follows from
the ... duties and powers ... on the internal level [fisheries were a
common EC policy (→ *10.6*)] that the Community has authority to
enter into international commitments for the conservation of [sea
resources]'. However, 'the Community not yet having fully exercised its functions in the matter ... the Member States had the power
to assume commitments'. This shared authority of the EU's Member
States is transitional, that is, valid until the EU resumes its authority,

and limited by the Union principle of loyalty of ex Article 10 TEC (now Article 4(3) TEU) which required states to respect the common EU position.

11.12 Was the Community competent to conclude the International Rubber Agreement?

In addition to the complex issue of **express** and **implied** (external) **powers** of the Union (→ *3.2, 11.8*), students of European law have to live with the notion that the treaty-making power of the EU does not always lie exclusively with the Union, but is more often **shared** with its Member States (→ *3.3*). In these cases of shared external competence, both the Union and its Member States have to become parties to what is known in EU law as a **'mixed agreement'**.

One of the leading cases in this field is the ECJ's Opinion 1/78 [1978] ECR 2817, on the procedure to be followed in order to enter into the International Rubber Agreement, which was negotiated under UNCTAD auspices as part of an Integrated Programme for Commodities. Commodity agreements aim at price and income stabilisation for developing countries. The Commission wanted to negotiate alone, claiming an exclusive Community competence under the Common Commercial Policy, while the Council recommended joint negotiations with the Member States because it regarded the agreement as a 'mixed' agreement.

The Court held that the agreement, 'a more structured instrument in the form of an organisation of the market', required direct financial contributions from the Member States and was thus 'characteristic of development aid'. As a result, it could **not** be **entirely based** on ex Article 133 TEC (now Article 207 TFEU) and, **therefore**, was to be concluded as a **'mixed agreement'**.

> **11.13 Who had the power to conclude the GATS and TRIPs agreements resulting from the Uruguay Round negotiations?**

In 1994 the GATT Uruguay Round negotiations came to an end. The 1947 **General Agreement on Tariffs and Trade** (GATT), dealing with trade in goods, was incorporated largely unchanged into the GATT 1994. In addition, however, the Uruguay Round negotiations produced a new international organisation, the **World Trade Organization** (WTO), and resulted in numerous side agreements to the GATT, addressing matters such as anti-dumping, countervailing duties, etc., as well as two major treaties transcending strict trade in goods: the 1994 **General Agreement on Trade in Services** (GATS), and the 1994 **Agreement on Trade-Related Intellectual Property Rights** (TRIPs).

As a result of its exclusive competence in the field of external trade stemming from the Common Commercial Policy the EC had already taken over the external trade obligations of its Member States under the GATT well before the Uruguay Round, as the ECJ recognised in Case 21–24/72 *International Fruit Company* v. *Produktschap voor Groenten en Fruit* [1971] ECR 1219 (→ *4.13*), where it found that:

> "insofar as under the EEC Treaty the Community has assumed the powers previously exercised by Member States in the area governed by the General Agreement, the provisions of that agreement have the effect of binding the Community."

In 1994, the fundamental issue arose whether the then still Community also had the **power** to **conclude** the **WTO** and the other **new agreements** on services and intellectual property. Again the ECJ's advice was sought. In Opinion 1/94, *WTO Agreement* [1994] ECR I-5267 (→ *11.10*), the Court held that only the **GATT** 1994, not **GATS** and **TRIPs** fell under the Community's exclusive competence. Thus, the latter two treaties had to be concluded as '**mixed agreements**'.

To understand the Court's reasoning one has to be aware of the GATS differentiation between different types of providing services according to four so-called **modes of supply**: cross-border, commercial presence or movement of either provider or consumer to the other WTO member. According to the ECJ, only **'cross-frontier supply'** situations were not unlike trade in goods and, thus, covered by ex Article 133 TEC (now Article 207 TFEU) ($\rightarrow$ *11.5*), whereas **'consumption abroad'** and **'commercial presence'** – matters touching on such politically sensitive issues as entry rights for foreign nationals – related more to 'measures concerning the entry and movement of persons' where the Community did not have exclusive competence. Also with regard to TRIPs the ECJ adopted a middle way. It held that, with the exception of provisions concerning the prohibition of the release into free circulation of counterfeit goods ('measures to be taken by the customs authorities at the external frontiers of the Community'), TRIPs measures did not fall within the scope of the Community's CCP.

While the precise legal reasoning of the Court may sometimes be a little arcane, the outcome clearly reflects the political will of the Member States which had rejected proposals for a broad Community external economic policy competence suggested by the Commission during the Maastricht negotiations ($\rightarrow$ *1.8*).

One of the political consequences of Opinion 1/94 was the introduction of a new paragraph to ex Article 133 TEC during the Amsterdam Intergovernmental Conference. According to this provision the Council was able to unanimously, after consulting the European Parliament, extend the scope of the Community's Common Commercial Policy to services and intellectual property. Since no action followed in the Council, the Nice Treaty wrote the Community powers with regard to these areas directly into ex Article 133 TEC. Now the Lisbon Treaty further broadens the external trade powers of the EU by the inclusion of foreign direct investment in Article 207 TFEU ($\rightarrow$ *11.6*).

? 11.14 What is the legal basis for association agreements?

Article 217 TFEU (ex Article 310 TEC) provides for the Union's power to enter into **agreements establishing an association** involving 'reciprocal rights and obligations, common action and special procedure'. As a rule, association agreements are more than just free trade agreements, often including rules on the free movement of persons, on investments, development aid, or other economic issues. They regularly provide for special (legislative and administrative) procedures and set up joint bodies, such as Association Councils ($\rightarrow$ *4.12*).

The first association agreement was concluded with Turkey in 1963 in order to establish a customs union in three stages. It moved on to the third stage in March 1995. In 1971 and 1973, association agreements providing for two-stage customs unions were concluded with Malta and Cyprus. So-called **cooperation agreements**, legally also association agreements, were concluded with Maghreb (Algeria, Tunisia, Morocco) and Mashrek (Egypt, Jordan, Lebanon, Syria) states as well as with Israel and the West Bank and Gaza Strip. '**Europe Agreements**' were concluded with central and eastern European states, indicating that those were association agreements for states that were likely to soon become members of the EU.

Such agreements were usually signed in the framework of two EU policies, the Stabilisation and Association Process and the European Neighbourhood Policy. The former is particularly aimed at candidates or potential candidates for accession, whereas the latter mainly covers Maghreb and Mashrek states as well as Eastern Europe and the Southern Caucasus.

In 2004, at the EU–Latin America and Caribbean summit, the EU and the Central American region agreed to negotiate a new Association Agreement. The negotiations were concluded in 2010 and the new agreement was initialed in March 2011. In 2010, negotiations for an Association Agreement between the EU and the Mercosur (Argentina, Brazil, Paraguay, Uruguay; Venezuela is currently integrating into the Mercosur) were re-launched, after the first attempt, which had already started in 1999 was suspended in 2004. These negotiations are still ongoing.

Based on the EU–Russia relations in the 'common spaces', a new treaty is also being negotiated in order to extend cooperation with Russia in areas such as trade, investment and energy as well as visa-free travel and Russia's application to join the WTO.

? 11.15 What is the significance of the Cotonou Agreements?

Starting with the first **Yaoundé Agreement** in 1963 and followed by Yaoundé II in 1969, the then EEC embarked on designing a web of cooperation agreements with the so-called **ACP** (African, Caribbean and Pacific) countries, many of which were former colonies of the EU Member States. Since 1975 relations between the ACP states and the Community have been governed by the **Lomé Conventions**, which established a far-reaching and complex partnership, focusing on economic and development cooperation. Through a system of non-reciprocal trade preferences certain manufactured and mostly agricultural products (such as bananas, rice and sugar) entering the Community were exempted from EC customs duties and quantitative restrictions.

Lomé IV, the last Lomé Convention, was concluded in 1989 for a ten-year period. It emphasised development via self-reliant economies and sustainable development. It also introduced the promotion of human rights and respect for democracy as key elements of the partnership in so-called **human rights conditionality** clauses which have remained controversial politically. Human rights clauses make the observance of certain human rights standards an 'essential element' of the respective agreement. Pursuant to the rules of treaty law, their breach entitles the other party to suspend or even terminate the agreement. After the expiry of Lomé IV in 2000 ACP–EC relations were replaced by the **Cotonou Agreement**, which builds on the existing institutional and financial instruments of cooperation. Under the Cotonou Agreement, which has been concluded for a period of twenty years, the group of ACP countries has risen to seventy-seven.

? 11.16 Which other association agreements have been entered into by the Union?

The Union's enlargement process after the fall of the Iron Curtain (→ *1.7*) was supported by the conclusion of so-called **Europe Agreements** with Eastern European countries in 1991 (Poland, Hungary and CSFR), 1993 (Czech Republic, Slovakia, Romania, Bulgaria) and 1995 (Estonia, Latvia, Lithuania). They aimed at establishing a free-trade area for industrial products by 2002 and preparing for accession by covering the main areas in which the *acquis communautaire* (→ *1.6*) was to be adopted.

Also, the EEA (**European Economic Area**) Agreement, concluded between the then EC and the remaining individual EFTA countries (today Iceland, Liechtenstein and Norway, but not Switzerland which rejected EEA membership in a popular referendum), is an association agreement. The EEA basically extends all four freedoms and other Union policies and provides for a sophisticated institutional framework.

? 11.17 How did European Political Cooperation evolve?

The informal meetings of the **heads of state and government** of the EU Member States, today assembled in the 'European Council'

($\rightarrow$ *2.1*), starting with The Hague summit in 1969, led to a form of **political cooperation** which was first recognised in the 1986 SEA. It endorsed the foreign policy cooperation actually practised and provided that the Member States 'shall endeavour jointly to formulate and implement a European foreign policy' by 'informing and consulting each other'. A **political committee**, consisting of the political directors of the foreign ministries of the Member States, with its own secretariat in Brussels was formed. This Committee largely substituted for COREPER ($\rightarrow$ *2.6*) in preparing for European Council meetings.

The 1992 Maastricht Treaty formally established the **Common Foreign and Security Policy** (CFSP) with the following **objectives** laid down in the TEU:

- to safeguard the **common values**, fundamental interests, independence and integrity of the Union in conformity with the principles of the United Nations Charter;
- to strengthen the **security** of the Union in all ways;
- to preserve **peace** and strengthen **international security**, in accordance with the principles of the United Nations Charter, as well as the principles of the Helsinki Final Act and the objectives of the Paris Charter, including those on external borders;
- to promote international **co-operation**; and
- to develop and consolidate **democracy** and the **rule of law**, and respect for **human rights** and fundamental freedoms.

Article 3(5) TEU now formulates these aims in slightly different terms. It states:

> "In its relations with the wider world, the Union shall uphold and promote its values and interests and contribute to the protection of its citizens. It shall contribute to peace, security, the sustainable development of the Earth, solidarity and mutual respect among peoples, free and fair trade, eradication of poverty and the protection of human rights, in particular the rights of the child, as well as to the strict observance and the development of international

law, including respect for the principles of the United
Nations Charter."

With regard to the Union's external action Article 21 TEU specifies
a more limited set of values (→ *11.1*).

? 11.18 How do the EU and its Member States act in the CFSP field?

Although the Lisbon Treaty abolished the pillar structure of the
EU and integrated the former intergovernmental policies CFSP and
PJCC into one single EU, the CFSP remains 'subject to specific
rules and procedures'. The loose, **intergovernmental** form of cooperation in the **CFSP** is reflected in the relatively weak instruments
available to the EU when acting in this area. The most important
EU acts are as follows. According to Article 26 TEU the **European
Council** identifies the Union's strategic interests, determines the
objectives of and defines the **'general guidelines'** of the Union's
CFSP. On this basis, the Council may then adopt decisions defining
and implementing the **CFSP**.

These decisions replace the old dichotomy between 'common
positions' and 'joint actions'. Article 28 TEU (ex Article 14 TEU)
provides with regard to what was formerly termed 'joint actions':

"Where the international situation requires operational
action by the Union, the Council shall adopt the necessary
decisions. They shall lay down their objectives, scope, the
means to be made available to the Union, if necessary their
duration, and the conditions for their implementation."

In a similar way, pursuant to Article 29 TEU (ex Article 15 TEU)
the Council adopts 'decisions which shall define the approach of the
Union to a particular matter of a geographical or thematic nature'
corresponding to the former common positions.

The **Council** clearly has the decisive role. Although Member
States and the High Representative, either on her own or with the

Commission's support, may make proposals (Article 30 TEU (ex Article 22 TEU)), it is the Council which decides, on the basis of 'general guidelines' of the European Council ($\rightarrow$ *2.1*), whether there should be 'action' at all and on the scope, objective and other issues.

The first CFSP 'joint action' was the sending of election observers to Russia in December 1993. Many country-focused joint actions concerned the former Yugoslavia. Others address non-proliferation issues, in particular with respect to nuclear weapons, or bans on anti-personnel mines. Recent actions include the imposition of sanctions on Syria and the suspension of the cooperation, restrictive measures against certain individuals in Afghanistan, Iran, Egypt, Libya, Tunisia and other countries, restrictive measures and the extension of measures relating to Article 96(2)(c) of the ACP–EU Partnership Agreement with regard to Zimbabwe as well as restrictive measures against other countries.

Not expressly mentioned in the TEU are **declarations** which give public expression to a position, request or expectation of the EU. This flexible instrument enables the EU to react very quickly to international incidents and to state the Union's point of view vis-à-vis a third country or any international question. They are usually called 'Declarations by the High Representative on behalf of the European Union'. The EU regularly issues more than a hundred declarations per year. Recent Declarations included reactions of the EU to the elections in the Democratic Republic of Congo, the death penalty, the escalation of violent repression in Syria, on the situation in Libya, in Iran, as well as on the alignment of third states with various Declarations of the EU on different political issues.

11.19 Why is the CFSP usually referred to as an 'intergovernmental' form of cooperation?

As opposed to the majority voting usually applied in the supra-national area of EU activity under the TFEU, the intergovernmental policy of the CFSP still rests largely on the principle of **unanimity** (→ 2.3). Article 31(1) TEU (ex Article 23(1) TEU) confirms that, in principle, decisions on CFSP matters are taken unanimously (→ 2.3). The Lisbon Treaty added that in the CFSP the adoption of legislative acts (→ 3.1) is excluded. Though many CFSP critics have long demanded a departure from this form of intergovernmental decision-making to supranational majority voting for the sake of a more effective EU foreign policy, the unanimity principle has been only slightly modified. The Lisbon Treaty largely retains two major modifications introduced by the Amsterdam Treaty, allowing some qualified majority voting and a so-called constructive abstention.

Article 31(2) TEU (ex Article 23(2) TEU) permits **QMV** in cases of **implementing decisions**, such as 'adopting a decision defining a Union action or position on the basis of [an Article 22 TEU European Council] decision [identifying] the Union's strategic interests and objectives', 'adopting a decision defining a Union action or position' on a High Representative proposal or 'adopting any decision implementing a decision defining a Union action or position'. If, however, 'a member of the Council declares that, for vital and stated reasons of national policy, it intends to oppose the adoption of a decision to be taken by qualified majority' no vote shall be taken and, if a conciliation attempt by the High Representative (→ 11.2) remains unsuccessful, the matter will be referred to the **European Council** for unanimous decision making. It is obvious that this 'procedural emergency brake' was inspired by the 1966 Luxembourg Compromise (→ 2.5).

A second modest erosion of the unanimity principle of Article 31(1) TFEU (ex Article 23(1) TEU)) can be found in its complex rules on **abstention**. Article 31(1), subparagraph 2 TFEU maintains what has euphemistically been called a **'constructive abstention'**. It provides that a Member State, when abstaining, 'may qualify its abstention by making a formal declaration'. This formal abstention implies that the abstaining Member State 'shall not be obliged to apply the decision, but shall accept that the decision commits the Union'. While the 'constructive' abstention leads to an effective opting-out, the abstaining Member State must 'refrain from any action likely to conflict with or impede Union action'. At the same time, the other EU Member States must respect the abstaining Member's position. If the combined weighted votes of Member States wishing to abstain under this provision represent one-third of the Member States comprising at least one-third of the population of the Union, the 'constructive' abstention turns 'destructive' by preventing the adoption of a decision.

11.20 Does the EU have treaty-making power in the CFSP field?

Ex Article 24 TEU on the **conclusion** of **international agreements** in the field of the **CFSP** was an outstanding example of **intentional ambiguity**. On the one hand, it provided that agreements in the CFSP sphere were **negotiated** by the **Presidency** and 'concluded by the **Council** on a recommendation from the Presidency' – which indicated that these were **EU treaties**. On the other hand, it stated that 'no agreement shall be binding on a Member State whose representative in the Council states that it has to comply with the requirements of its own constitutional procedure' – which could have been taken to mean that these were, in fact, **treaties** concluded by the Council **on behalf of the Member States**. Apparently, the Member States could not agree on this issue and thus arrived at a compromise formulation which may be interpreted both ways.

With the abolition of the pillar structure and the creation of one single EU succeeding to the EC, Article 37 TEU, which also forms part of the Treaty's CFSP chapter, has put these discussions to rest by simply stating that 'the Union may conclude agreements with one or more States or international organisations in areas covered by this chapter'.

? 11.21 How does the EU implement economic sanctions?

The adoption of **economic sanctions** against third states for **political purposes** provides a good example of the complex interrelationship between the former **first** and the **second pillar**, the former governed by the supranational law of the Community and the latter by the inter-governmental rules of the Union (→ *1.5*, *2.6*). Since sanctions are of a hybrid nature – they are economic measures for political goals – both the TEC's **Common Commercial Policy** and the TEU's **CFSP** were potentially relevant.

In practice, the Treaties had codified a **compromise procedure** already developed under the European Political Cooperation (→ *1.8*, *11.17*). First, a CFSP 'common position' or 'joint action' was adopted (→ *11.18*). Then, according to ex Article 301 TEC (now Article 215 TFEU), the Council, by a qualified majority on a proposal from the Commission, took the 'necessary urgent measures', usually regulations aimed at banning imports and/or exports from the targeted countries.

The Lisbon Treaty, even though adapting it to the new circumstances, did not substantially change this mechanism. Article 215(1) TFEU now provides:

> "(1) Where a decision, adopted in accordance with Chapter 2 of Title V of the Treaty on European Union, provides for the interruption or reduction, in part or completely, of economic and financial relations with one or more third countries, the Council, acting by a qualified majority on a joint proposal from the High Representative of the Union for Foreign Affairs and Security Policy and the Commission, shall adopt the necessary measures. It shall inform the European Parliament thereof."

Since both UN-mandated as well as unilateral EU sanctions are increasingly adopted as so-called targeted sanctions, aimed not at states, but rather at individuals and groups, the Lisbon Treaty added a specific EU power to impose **financial measures**, such as asset freezes, on natural and legal persons in Article 75 TFEU in order to prevent the financing of terrorism. Previously, the existence of such a power was controversial, however, upheld by the ECJ in the *Kadi* case (→ *3.4*).

? 11.22 Does the EU possess a European Security and Defence Policy?

According to Article 42(1) TFEU (ex Article 17(1) TEU), the 'common security and defence policy shall be an integral part of the common foreign and security policy and shall provide the Union with an operational capacity drawing on civilian and military assets'. According to Article 42(2) TFEU, it shall include 'the progressive framing of a common Union defence policy'. This provision is the core of a still infant **European Security and Defence Policy** (ESDP), which is in constant danger of being marginalised by **NATO**, on the one hand, and by being effectively 'neutralised' by the interests of **neutral Member States**, on the other hand. The latter interests are protected by the rather cryptic **'Irish' clause** of Article 42(2), second subparagraph TFEU (Article 17(1) TEU), according to which, the ESDP 'shall not prejudice the specific character of the security and defence policy of certain Member States'.

The Amsterdam Treaty provides that ESDP includes the so-called **Petersberg tasks**, that is, '**humanitarian** and rescue tasks, **peacekeeping** tasks and tasks of combat forces in **crisis management**, including peacemaking'. In 2003, the first ESDP missions took place on the basis of unanimously approved joint actions, among them the European Police Mission in Bosnia and Herzegovina, 'Operation Concordia' in the Former Yugoslav Republic of Macedonia and

'Operation Artemis', the first EU peace-keeping mission outside Europe, in the Democratic Republic of the Congo.

? 11.23 Who pays for CFSP and ESDP?

According to Article 41 TEU (ex Article 28 TEU), **administrative expenditure** is charged to the **budget** of the **EU**. Since the 1997 Amsterdam Treaty, the same applies in principle to **operational expenditure**. However, operational expenditure 'arising from operations having military or defence implications', that is, **ESDP** costs, are borne by the **Member States**, as a rule, 'in accordance with the gross national product scale'. Member States having exercised their right to 'constructive abstention' ($\rightarrow$ *11.19*) are exempted from contributing.

Index

Abbé de Saint Pierre, 2
abusive behaviour, 196
acquis communautaire, 7, 8, 77, 256
acquisitions and mergers, *see* merger control
acte clair doctrine, 96, 98
Action Plans, 40
actions for annulment, 77
Adeneler and others v. *ELOG* [2006], 68
administrative expenditure, 264
administrative law, principles of, 106
advisory committees, 30
advisory opinions, 97
advocates-general, 78
role of, 79
Agreement on the European Economic Area, 8
agricultural levies, 36
Aklagaren v. *Mickelsson and Roos* [2009], 136
Alighieri, Dante, 2
Alliance of Liberals and Democrats for Europe (ALDE), 32
amicus curiae, 79
Amsterdam Bulb BV Case [1977], 63
Amsterdam Treaty (1997), 5, 10, 50, 52, 118, 219, 263
annulment actions, 108
Antici Group, 24
anti-competitive activities, 171–173, 176–177
abuse of dominant market position, 195

effect on trade between Member States, 179–180
anti-discrimination law, 219
anti-dumping duties, 84, 243
Anti-dumping Regulation, 82, 244
anti-trust law, 170
A-points, 24
approximation of laws, *see* harmonisation of laws
arbitral tribunals, 96
Assembly, *see* European Parliament (EP)
asset freezing, 45
association agreements, 9
legal basis for, 254–255
other agreements by European Union, 256
Association Councils, 75
autonomous external trade policy, 123
'avis', 8

bankruptcy, 90
Barroso Commission (2004), 27
Becker v. *Finanzamt Münster-Innenstadt* [1982], 65
bilateral investment treaties (BITs), 245
'black list' of prohibited restrictions, 185
Bonn Basic Law, 112
Bosman Case, 146
B-points, 24
Branntwein (German for *Brandy*) Case [1963], 88
Briand, Aristide, 3

Broekmeulen v. *Huisarts Registratie Commissie* [1981], 95
Bronner Case, 197
Brown v. *Secretary of State for Scotland* [1988], 152
Brussels I Regulation, 232
Brussels Treaty (1948), 5
Bulmer v. *Bollinger* [1974], 98
Buy Irish Case, 126, 145

cabinet, 26
cartel law, 170
Cassis Case, 122, 126, 127–128
charges equivalent to customs duties, 121, 123–125
Charter of Fundamental Rights of the European Union (CFR), 100, 119–120
choice-of-law, 232
Churchill, Winston, 3
Cinéthèque v. *Fédération Nationale des Cinémas Français* [1985], 116
citizens' initiative, 28
Civil Service Tribunal, 15, 79–80
Codorniu SA v. *Council* [1994], 84
collective bargaining agreements, 183
collective responsibility, principle of, 27
collegiality, principle of, 27
comfort letter, 188
comitology, 56
Comitology Decision 1999/468/EC, 30
'comitology' scheme, COREPER, 24
'comitology' scheme comitology', notion of, 30–32
Commission Action Plan, 221
Commission Notice on Agreements of Minor Importance (1986), 180
Commission proposals, 51
Commission v. *Belgium* [1983], 93
Commission v. *Germany* [1988], 125
Commission v. *Greece* [1988], 92
Commission v. *Greece* [2000], 92
Commission v. *Italy* [2003], 93
Commission v. *Luxembourg and Belgium* [1964], 93

Commission v. *United Kingdom* [1983], 138
Commission v. *United Kingdom* [1991], 93
Committee of Inquiry, 35, 54
Committee of Permanent Representatives (COREPER), 257
  Antici Group, 24
  comitology scheme, 24
  Mertens Group, 24
  structure and tasks of, 24
  working groups, 24
Committee of the Regions, 15, 37
Common Agricultural Policy (CAP), 20, 22
  agricultural products, for, 210
  implementation of, 210–211
  Mulder case, 212
  objectives of, 209–210
  principles of, 210
  reforms, 211–212
Common Commercial Policy (CCP), 43, 121, 242, 243–245, 252, 262
Common Customs Tariff, 36, 121, 243, 244
common external customs tariff, 123
common external tariff, 243
Common Fisheries Policy, 213
Common Foreign and Security Policy (CFSP), 8, 12, 40, 257, 264
  EU's treaty-making power, 261
  intergovernmental form of cooperation, as, 259–261
common market, 63, 123
Common Market compatibility test, 203
Common Market Organisations, 211, 213
common position, adoption by the Council, 49
Community Charter of the Fundamental Social Rights of Workers, 221
companies, 162–164
competition policy
  abuse of a dominant position, 191–192

collective bargaining agreements, 183
concerted practices, 173–174
Consten and Grundig Case, 176–177
Continental Can Case, 193–194
dominant market position, 190–191
economic rationales for, 171
effects principle, 181–182
enforcement, 189–190
exceptions to prohibition, 184–185
extraterritorial application, 182–183
group exemptions, purpose of,
 185–186
international agreement involving,
 246
legal consequences of a violation of,
 174–175
prohibition of anti-competitive
 activities, 171–173
protective principle, 182
'single economic unit' doctrine, 181
'single enterprise doctrine', 178
state-owned enterprises, applicability
 to, 204–205
subsidies, 206–208
undertaking, meaning of, 177–179
utilities, applicability to, 205–206
concerted practices, 173–174
Conciliation Committee, 51
Conegate Ltd v. *Customs and Excise
 Commissioners* [1986], 132
Conference of Presidents, 33
conferral, principle of, 40–42, 44
conferred powers, principle of, 40
Consten and Grundig Case, 176–177,
 179, 186
Constitutional Convention, 11
constructive abstention, 260
consumer protection, 217–218
Continental Can Case, 193–194
Convention for the Protection of
 Human Rights and Fundamental
 Freedoms, 110
cooperation agreements, 254
COREPER, *see* Committee of
 Permanent Representatives
 (COREPER)

cornerstone principle of Community
 law, 72
Costa v. *ENEL*, 71–73
Cotonou Agreement, 255–256
Coudenhove-Kalergi, Count Richard
 Nikolaus, 3
Council for Economic and Financial
 Affairs, 17
Council of the EU, 5, 99
 difference with the European
 Council, 16–17
 indirect legitimacy, 56
 representatives of, 17–18
 right to bring annulment actions, 77
 voting procedures, 18–20
countervailing duties, 245
 against subsidies, 243
country-of-origin principle, 168
Court of Auditors
 Annual Report, 37
 functions of, 36–37
Court of First Instance (CFI), 79
criminal law, cooperation in, 235–236
criminal offences, definition of, 235
criminal prosecution, 233
crisis management, 263
cross-border cooperation, 37
cross-border crimes, 233
cross-border services, 166–167
cross-subsidisation, 198
customs
 common tariff, *see* Common
 Customs Tariff
 duties, 36
customs union, establishment of, 121,
 123

Danish Beverage Container
 Case, 216
Dassonville Case, 122, 125–126
Data Retention Directive, 236
de minimis rule, clarification of,
 180–181
declaratory judgments, 91
Defrenne Case [1976], 90
Defrenne v. *Sabena* [1976], 62, 68

delegation procedures of the
    Commission, 27
Demirel v. *Stadt Schwäbisch Gmünd*
    [1987], 116
democratic deficit, notion of, 56–57
derogations, 116
diplomatic settlement, 90
direct discrimination, on the basis of
    nationality, 143
direct effect of law
    association and cooperation
        agreements, 74
    characteristic of, 59
    Costa v. *ENEL*, 71–73
    decentralised law enforcement, 60
    denial of, 76
    difference to direct applicability,
        59–60
    directives, 64–66
    equal pay legislation, 90
    Europe agreements, 74
    free trade agreements, 74
    GATT provisions, 75–76
    horizontal direct effect, *see* horizontal
        direct effect of legislation
    individual rights, 62
    international agreements, 74–75
    meaning of, 58–59
    means of federalism, and, 64
    objective requirements, 63
    rationale, 60
    regulations, 63
    Simmenthal Case, 73–74
    teleological interpretation, 62
    treaty provisions, 61–62
        limits to, 62–63
    vertical direct effect, 66
    WTO agreements, 75–76
directives
    grant of rights to individuals, 69
    horizontal direct effect for, 66
    indirect (horizontal) effect of, 67
    interpretation maxim of, 67
    preliminary references for
        interpretation of, 94
    provisions of, 65

remedies for damage caused by,
    69–71
role in harmonisation, 64
Directorate-General for Competition,
    170
Directorates-General (DGs), 26, 27
discriminatory internal taxation, 137
discriminatory pricing, 196
double criminality principle, 234
double majority system, 21
Draft Constitution Treaty (2004), 42,
    72, 109
    abolition of three pillars, 238
    single EU proposal, 238
Draft Treaty establishing a Constitution
    for Europe, 11
Dubois, Pierre, 2
due process guarantees, 234
dumping, 198
'Dutch clause' (merger control), 202
Dyestuffs Case, 173, 178, 181

EC Treaty
    advocates-general, role of, 79
    association and cooperation
        agreements, 74
    bodies recognised as tribunals, 95–96
    in CFSP field, 261
    charges equivalent to customs duties,
        121, 123–125
    Commission's supervisory powers, 90
    consumer protection, 217–218
    duty to state reasons for laws, 46
    equal pay, 90
    free movement of goods, 130
    free movement of persons, 123
    freedom of establishment, 158–159
    freedom to provide services, 158,
        164–165
    general scheme of, 61
    individuals' right to request judicial
        review, as to, 46
    infringement proceedings, 90
    infringements of, 87
    lack of competence, 87
    law-making activities, 46

plea of illegality, as to, 85–86
spirit of, 61
violation of Union law by, 69
ECOFIN, *see* Council for Economic
and Financial Affairs
Economic and Social Committee
(ESC), *see* European Economic
and Social Committee (EESC)
economic sanctions, 262–263
EC–Portugal Free Trade Agreement, 74
effet utile, 41, 60, 62, 64, 65, 66, 72, 148
Einfuhr- und Vorratsstelle v. *Köster
et al.* (1970), 30
Elleniki Radiophonia Tiléorassi (ERT)
v. *Dimtiki (DEP)* [1991], 116
employment policy, *see* social policy
empowerment procedure of the
Commission, 27
enhanced cooperation for integration, 7
Enlargement Protocol (2004), 20, 25
enumerated powers, 40, 81, 87
Environment Directorate-General, 214
Environmental Action Programmes,
213–214
environmental action, principles of,
215–216
Environmental Council, 17
environmental damage, 215
environmental impact assessment, 215
environmental legislation
examples of, 215
legal basis for, 214
equal pay, 62, 90, 221, 222–223
concept of, 223
definition of, 223
Equal Pay Directive, 223
Equal Treatment Directive, 224, 226,
227, 230
equal treatment, case law, 106
ERTA case, 248
*Essay Towards the Present and Future
Peace of Europe, An* (1693), 2
essential facilities doctrine, 197–198
essential procedural safeguards,
infringement proceedings,
87–89

estoppel, 23, 65, 66
Eurocontrol case, 177, 204
Europe Agreements, 9, 74, 254, 256
Europe of Freedom and Democracy
Group (EFD), 33
European Arrest Warrants, 233–235
European Atomic Energy Community
(EURATOM), 1, 5, 11
European Coal and Steel Community
(ECSC), 1, 4, 11
European Commission (EC)
assessment of accession candidates
('avis'), 8
collegiate body of, 27
Common Commercial Policy, 30
'as guardian of the treaties', 28
individuals indirect access, 90
international agreement involving
competition law, 246
letter of notice, 91
political cooperation, 256–258
powers of, 31
privileges and immunities, 246
procedure for adoption of proposal
in, 27
reasoned opinion, 91
Regulation 1/2003/EC, 29
right of initiative, 27–28
right to bring annulment actions, 77
role in the EU's external relations,
29–30
supervision and control, tasks of,
28–29
treaty-making power, 246
European Community (EC)
development of the institutional
structure of, 12
non-contractual liability, 70
powers of
asset freezing, 45
scope of, 45
targeted sanctions, 45
preaccession treaties, 8
steps undertaken to
enlarge, 8–9
European Competition Network, 189

European Conservatives and Reformists
    Group (ECR), 33
European Convention for the Protection
    of Human Rights and
    Fundamental Freedoms, 110
European Convention on Human Rights
    (ECHR), 6, 99, 108–110, 118
European Council, 10, 239, 260
    difference with Council of the EU,
        16–17
    Member States, selection of, 26–27
    Presidency of, 17
    voting system, 13, 18–20
    working group, 17
European Court of Human Rights
    (ECtHR), 6, 99, 103–104, 118
European Court of Justice (ECJ), 15,
    28, 33
    acquis communautaire, 77
    actions for annulment, 81
        Article 263 of TFEU, 81–82
        individuals, by, 82–85
    administration, 78
    advisory opinions, 97
    advocates-general, 78, 79
    annulment actions, 77
    appeals, 80
    Case 25/70 Einfuhr- und Vorratsstelle
        v. Köster et al. [1970], 30
    case law, 77
        according to direct effect of Union
            law, 59
    Civil Service Tribunal, 79–80
    composition, 78–79
    constitutional court, as, 77
    Court of First Instance, 79
    cross-border services, restrictions on,
        166–167
    declaratory judgments, 91
    delegated acts, 85
    disguised decisions, 84
    duty to re-consult the EP, 53
    effet utile role, 41
    enumerated powers of, 81
    ERTA judgment, 247–248
    exercise of sovereign powers, 178

four freedoms, 77
free movement of workers
    legislation, 147–149
full court, 79
General Court, 79–80
Grand Chamber of thirteen judges,
    79
human rights protection, 101
implementing acts, 85
infringement actions directed against
    Member States, 77
infringement proceedings, 90
    against Member States, 81
interpretation of ECHR rights,
    103–104
judges, 78
judicial review, 77
jurisdiction, 79–80
jurisprudence, 100
justiciability, principle of, 47
legal effects vis-à-vis third parties, 81
legality of legislative acts, review
    of, 81
plea of illegality, 85–86
powers of judicial review, 101
preliminary references, 81
preliminary rulings, 78
primacy doctrine, 101
privileged applicants, 82
publication of decisions, 78
questions of law, 80
registrar, 78
regulatory acts, 85
retroactive effect of decisions, 89–90
right to privacy, 103
role as a 'quasi-law-maker', 77
role in developing fundamental rights
    protection, 101–103
special legal interest, 82
staff disputes, 80
teleological interpretation (effet
    utile) of Article 7(2) Regulation
    1612/68, 148
transfer of preliminary rulings, 96–97
types of procedures before, 80–81
working language, 79

European Defence and Political Community, 9

European Defence Community, 4, 10, 99

European Economic and Social Committee (EESC), 15
tasks of, 37

European Economic Area (EEA), 256

European Economic Community (EEC), 1, 5, 11, 209

European External Action Service (EEAS), 14, 240

European Free Alliance (EFA), 33

European Free Trade Association (EFTA), 9

European General Court, 15

European integration, 1
between Treaties of Paris and Rome, 4–5
economic integration, 4
enhanced cooperation for, 7
federalism approach, 3–4
flexibility approach, 7
functionalism approach, 3–4
history of, 4–5
ideas for, *see* ideas for European integration
'multiple speed' approach, 7
plans for, 3
political integration, 2
post-war European organisations, 5–6
process of, 1
Schuman Plan (1950), 4
spill-over effect from economic to political integration, 4, 99
supranational aspects of, 4–5
variable geometry' approach to, 7

European international investment policy, 245–246

European legislation, 16

European Monetary System (1979), 10

European Monetary Union (EMU), 7, 50

European Parliament (EP), 8, 15, 48
actions for annulment or failure to act, 35
adoption of legislative act with the approval of the Council, 54
approval of nominations of Commission, 35
assent procedure, 34
budget, approval of, 36
Bureau, 33
Commission proposal for annual budget, 36
Committee of Inquiry, 35
common position on consideration of Council's proposals, 49
Conciliation Committee, 51
consent procedure, 34, 44
consultation procedure, 34
Council acting unanimously with the consent of, 53
counterweight to democratic deficit, as, 56–57
essential procedural safeguard, 53
five-year term, 32
international agreements, 29
investiture of Commission, assent to, 36
legislative powers, 33–34
motion of censure on Commission, 35
new Member States, assent to, 35
Ombudsman, 35
ordinary legislative procedure, 34, 50
President, 35
role in international agreement, 241
role in the Union's budgetary process, 36
situations requiring consent of, 35–36
special legislative procedure, 34
structure of, 32–33
supervisory powers, 34–35
veto power, 51

European Parliament v. *Council* [2006], 120

European People's Party (EPP), 32

European Police Office, *see* Europol

European Political Cooperation (EPC), 10

European political union, 10

European Recovery Program, 5
European Road Transport Agreement
　　(ERTA), 248
European Security and Defence Policy
　　(ESDP), 263–264
European Social Charter, 110
European Union
　　Common Fisheries Policy, 213
　　non-contractual liability, 212
European Union (EU), 2
　　anti-terrorism competence, 45
　　categories and areas of competence,
　　　42
　　Charter of Fundamental Rights, 6,
　　　119–120
　　Civil Service Tribunal, 80
　　Common Commercial Policy (CCP),
　　　43, 243–245
　　common constitutional framework,
　　　239–240
　　Common Foreign and Security Policy
　　　(CFSP), 258–259
　　competition law, 58
　　competition rules, 43
　　conferral, principle of, 44
　　conservation of marine biological
　　　resources, 43
　　constitution for, 11
　　criminal law policy, 233
　　customs union, 43
　　development of institutional structure
　　　of, 11–12
　　distribution of powers with Member
　　　States, 42
　　enlargement or internal enhancement
　　　of, 7
　　enumerated powers, 87
　　Environmental Action Programmes,
　　　213–214
　　exclusive and shared competences,
　　　42, 44
　　exclusive competence, 47
　　expansion of competences, 46
　　flexibility clause, 43–45
　　foreign affairs and security policy,
　　　representatives of, 240–241

free movement of workers
　　legislation, 147–149
fundamental rights, 100
Fundamental Rights Charter, 11
human rights, 100
implementation of economic
　　sanctions, 262–263
implied powers to enter into
　　international agreements, 247
internal decision-making process, 15
internal legislative competence,
　　248–250
international agreements, 241–242
International Rubber Agreement, 251
law-making, kinds of instruments
　　used for, 38–40
legal basis of external relations,
　　242–243
major steps towards, 9–10
monetary policy for the Member
　　States, 43
non-contractual liability, 70
policy definition of, 16
power to enter into international
　　investment agreements, 245–246
preaccession treaties, 8
revenue and expenditure, 36
rules governing the accession of new
　　members to, 8
security and defence policy, 263–264
shared competences with Member
　　States, 43
social and employment policy, 40
specific acts, adoption of, 42–43
trade protection legislation, 30
treaty-making power, 41, 250–251
　　in CFSP field, 261
European Union Agency for
　　Fundamental Rights, 119
European Union Civil Service Tribunal,
　　78
Europol, 237
Europol Information System, 237

fair hearing, breach of right, 88
fascism, 3

federalism approach to integration, 3–4
federalists, 9
Firma A. Racke v. *Hauptzollamt Mainz* [1979], 107
Firma Foto Frost v. *Hauptzollamt Lübeck-Ost* [1987], 94
First Art Treasures Case, 124
First Consumer Protection Action Programme, 218
'flexibility' approach to integration, 7
Foglia v. *Novello* [1980], 96
Foreign Affairs Council, 17
foreign direct investment, 245
fortress Europe, 7
Foster v. *British Gas* [1990], 67
Fouchet Plans (1961, 1962), 10
four freedoms, 121, 139
Framework Directive, 224
Francovich Directive, 69, 70
Franz Grad v. *Finanzamt Traunstein* [1970], 64
free movement of goods
  Cassis Case, 126, 127–128
  derogation from free movement obligations, 129
  final selling price as basis for 'VAT resource', 36
  and fundamental rights, 129–130
  German purity law of 1516, consistency with EC law, 130–131
  indecent items, 131–132
  Keck Case, 133–136
  measures having equivalent effect, 126, 134
  mutual recognition, 127
  obligations, 128
  obscene items, 131–132
  as one of the four freedoms, 121
  restrictions due to environmental policies, 128–129, 216–217
  Sunday trading restrictions, compatibility with EC law, 132–133
  tax aspects, 136–138
free movement of persons, 123

benefits from free movement rights, 142–143
common market, 123
freedom of establishment, 158–159, 162–164
freedom to provide services, 158, 164–165
job-seekers, 143
Lair Case, 152
language requirements for certain jobs, 144–145
lawyers, 159–160
non-discrimination law as to, 143–144, 145–147
passive services, 165–166
protection of workers' families' rights, 150–151
public policy, public security and public health expectations, 153–155
public service workers, 155–156
right of free movement, 140–142
rights to education, 151–153
Van Binsbergen Case, 165
workers, 142–143
  meaning of, 142
free trade agreements, 74, 122
freedom of establishment, 139
  community, of, 62
  companies, for, 162–164
  guarantee, 158–159
  lawyers, for, 159–160
  union legislation, 167–169
freedom to provide services, 139, 158, 164–165
  union legislation, 167–169
French National Assembly, 10
French Pleven Plan, 10
Frontini v. *Ministero delle Finanze* [1974], 114
functionalist approach to integration, 3–4, 99
fundamental freedoms, 116, 117
fundamental rights, 87, 99
  accepted in ECJ's jurisprudence, 104–106

fundamental rights (*cont.*)
  case law, 113
  Charter of Fundamental Rights,
      119–120
  cross-border services, 167
  differences in approach of ECJ and
      ECtHR, 103–104
  ECJ's role in protecting, 101
  in EU law, 101–103
  European Convention for the
      Protection of Human Rights and
      Fundamental Freedoms, 110
  and free movement of goods,
      129–130
  general principles of law, 100, 102,
      106–107
  infringement of, 99
  international treaties for the
      protection of, 102
  Internationale Handelsgesellschaft
      Case, 110–112
  jurisdiction of national courts, 108
  protection of, 100, 117
  relevance of, 102
  sanctions against Member States for
      violations of, 118–119
  Solange I Case, 112–113
  Solange II Case, 113–114
  Wachauf Case, 115–117

Geitling v. *High Authority* [1960], 101
gender discrimination, 223
General Affairs Council, 17
General Agreement on Tariffs and Trade
      (GATT), 75–76, 122
  conflict settlement provisions, 75
  Uruguay Round negotiations,
      252–253
General Court, 78, 79–80, 84
'general political' organisations, 5
Generalised Tariff Preferences Case
      [1995], 53
Genscher–Colombo Plan (1981), 10
geographical market, 192
German Beer Case, 130
German Beer Duty Act (1952), 130

'German clause' (merger control), 202
German Constitutional Court, 114
German Federal Constitutional Court,
      112
  supervisory powers, 114
German Foodstuffs Act (1974), 131
German purity law of 1516, consistency
      with EC law, 130–131
Germany v. *European Parliament and
      Council*, 42
GNP resource, 36
Grand Chamber of thirteen judges, 79
Gravier Case, 153
Groener v. *Minister for Education*
      [1989], 144
group exemptions
  EU legislation used to grant, 186–187
  purpose of, 185–186
Group of the Greens (The Greens), 33
Group of the Progressive Alliance of
      Socialists and Democrats in the
      European Parliament (S&D), 32

harmonisation of laws, 53, 64
Hauer v. *Land Rheinland-Pfalz* [1979],
      103
hierarchical test for legal basis of
      legislation, case law, 55
High Representative for the CFSP, 240
horizontal direct effect of legislation
  meaning of, 66–68
human dignity, 117
human rights, *see* fundamental rights
Humblot v. *Directeur des Services
      Fiscaux* [1985], 137
Hünermund v. *Landesapotheker Baden-
      Württemberg* [1993], 135

IBM v. *Commission* [1981], 81
ideas for European integration, 2–3,
      see also Dubois, Pierre
implied powers doctrine, 41, 247
indirect discrimination, 143
  language requirements for certain
      jobs, 144–145
Indirect Tax Recovery Case [2004], 54

indirect taxation, 53
individuals, *see* persons, rights of
infringement
    essential procedural safeguards, of,
      case law, 87–89
    rule of law, 70
intergovernmental conferences, 10
intergovernmental organisation, 6
internal taxes, 121
International Chemical Corporation v.
    Amministrazione delle Finanze
    dello Stato [1981], 86
international civil procedure
    law, 232
International Fruit Case, 75, 83
international law, legal order of, 61
international organisation, 15
International Rubber Agreement, 251
international treaties for the protection
    of human rights, 102
Internationale Handelsgesellschaft
    Case, 110–112
interpretation of Union acts, 94
invalidation of secondary legislation by
    national courts, case law, 86–87,
    94–95
Ioannina formula, 23
Isoglucose Case [1980], 53

job-seekers, 143
Joint Declaration on human rights, 109
joint ventures, 201
judges, appointment to ECJ, 78
Judicial Cooperation in Civil Matters,
    231–233
jurisdiction of national courts, 94–95

Kadi and Al Barakaat v. *Council and*
    Commission, 45
Kant, Immanuel, 3
Keck Case, 122, 133–136
Köbler v. *Austria* [2003], 70
Kolpinghuis Nijmegen case [1987], 68
Korean War (1952), 10
Kremzow v. *Austria* [1997], 157
Kupferberg Case [1982], 74

Laeken Declaration on Future Reform
    (2001), 11, 44
Lair Case, 152
law
    acquis communautaire, 8
    anti-dumping, 30
    approximation of laws, 53
    autonomous legal order, 71
    binding power of laws, 39
    causal link between the violation
      of, 69
    Commission proposals, 48, 51
    delegated acts, 39
    direct application, 39
    direct effect, 58–59
    effet utile, 60, 62, 65
    free movement of workers
      legislation, 147–149
    free movement rights, 142–143
    fundamental rights, 100,
      101–103
    general application, with, 39
    general international law, 59
    general principles of Community
      law, 102
    implementing acts, 39
    invalidation of secondary legislation
      by national courts, 63–64,
      86–87, 94–95
    language requirements for certain
      jobs, 144–145
    legal uniformity and effectiveness
      of, 72
    legislative acts, 39
    making, 38–40
    meaning of direct effect, 58–59
    non-legislative acts, 39
    passive services, 165–166
    primacy of EU law, 91
    primary law, 38
    regulations, 39
    right to sue
      Member States, 28
      other Community organs, 28
    rights to education, 151–153
    rule of law infringed, 70

law (*cont.*)
  sanctions against Member States
    for human rights violations,
    118–119
  secondary law, 38
  soft law instruments, 40
  supremacy of, 66, 71, 91
  uniform application of Community
    law, 60
  violations of, 69, 92–93
law-making procedures, 87
  assent procedure, 53
  co-decision procedure, 50
  consent procedure, 49, 53
  consultation procedure, 49, 52
  cooperation procedure, 49
  decentralisation of, 58
  declarations, 40
  general principles of, 48–49
  hierarchical test for legal basis of
    legislation, 55
  indirect legitimacy, 56
  'open method of coordination', 40
  ordinary legislative procedure, 48, 50
    choice of, 54–56
    working of, 50–52
  primary purpose of legislation,
    identifying, 55
  procedure shopping, prevention of,
    54
  shift from the consultation procedure
    to the ordinary legislative
    procedure, 49–50
  special legislative procedures, 48
    important forms of, 52–54
  specific legal act on the EC treaty, 46
  subsidiarity, principle of, 46–48
Lawrie-Blum v. *Land Baden
    Württemberg* [1986], 142
lawyers, 159–160
Lawyers' Establishment Directive, 162
League of Nations, 3
legal certainty principle in human rights
    cases, 107
legal persons, 82
legal profession, 160–162

legality of discrimination in
    employment, 227–228
legitimate expectations principle,
    human rights cases, 107
Les Verts v. *Parliament* [1986], 77
letter of notice, 91
Levin v. *Staatssecretaris van Justitie*
    [1982], 142
lex specialis principle, 210
linguistic knowledge, 144
Lisbon Reform Treaty, 13, 16
Lisbon Treaty, 6, 8, 19, 21, 25, 28, 34,
    42, 47, 48, 72, 100, 113, 120,
    245
  and development of the institutional
    structure of the EU, 11–12
  meaning of, 13–14
  and notion of 'comitology', 30–32
locus standi of individuals, 82, 84
Lomé Convention, 255
lump sum payment, for infringement of
    Community law, 92
Luxembourg Accord, 22–23
Luxembourg Compromise,
    see Luxembourg Accord

Maastricht Treaty on European Union
    (1992), 7, 10, 12, 17, 66
  consumer protection, 217–218
majority of Member States, 21
majority voting, 6
management committees, 30
market abuse, prohibition on, 170
market dominance, concept of, 192–193
market shares of the competitors, 192
Marleasing SA v. *La Comercial* [1990],
    67
Marshall Case [1986], 66, 67
Marshall Plan, 5
measures having equivalent effect, 126,
    134
Member States
  admission of foreign nationals,
    156
  annulment procedure to challenge
    Union acts, 92

bilateral investment treaties (BITs),
  245
cabinet, 26
comitology committees, 31
Common Foreign and Security Policy
  (CFSP), 258–259
competences, 44
constitutional, administrative or
  institutional difficulties in
  complying with EU law, 93
courts and administrative agencies
  of, 58
customs union, 121
duty to comply with EU law, 92
effect on trade because of anti-
  competitive activities, 179–180
enforcement action against, 90
environmental policies restricting
  free movement of goods,
  216–217
fundamental rights, 100, 115
general competence, 26
granting of subsidies, 207
implied powers, 41
indecent items, 131–132
independence of, 26
infringement proceedings against, 90
international law treaty-making
  powers, 38
intra-EU restrictions, 139
law-making procedures, 40
legal relationships between, 61
liability for damage, 70
limitation of the power of, 122
obscene items, 131–132
official seat of the Parliament, 33
penalty payment, 92
political cooperation between,
  256–258
'private capacity' as employers, 67
renewable five-year terms, 26
representation on Commission,
  25–26
right of free movement, 140
right of initiative, 28
right to bring annulment actions, 77

right to grant subsidies, 84
right to request a lump sum or
  penalty payment from, 29
right to sue a, 28
rule-making power, 122
sanctions against, for human rights
  violations, 118–119
selection of, 26–27
separation of powers, 93
specific acts, adoption of, 42–43
transfer of powers, 41
treaty-making power of the EU, and,
  250–251
violation of Union law by, 69, 92–93
merger control
  Commission guidelines, 201–202
  common market compatibility, 203
  concentrations
    approval of, 203–204
    meaning of, 200, 201
  'Dutch clause', 202
  'German clause', 202
  joint ventures, 201
  main features, 200
  Merger Task Force, 200
  scope of prohibition, 199–200
merger control legislation, 170
Merger Regulation (1989), 194
Merger Treaty (1965), 6, 12
Mertens Group, 24
Microsoft Case, 198
*Migration Policies, Germany and
  others* v. *Commission*, 41
misuse of powers as ground of
  invalidity, 87
Money Laundering Directive, 236
Monnet, Jean, 4
monopolies, 171
Moser v. *Land Baden Württemberg*
  [1984], 157
motion of censure on Commission by
  Parliament, 35
Mulder Case, 212
'multiple speed' approach to
  integration, 7
Mutual Recognition Directive, 168

mutual recognition of goods, 127
mutual recognition of judgments,
 principle of, 232
mutual recognition, principle of, 233
mutual trust, 234

NAAT ('no appreciable affectation of
 trade') test, 180
national competition authorities, 185
national courts, 94–95, 97–98, 114–115
National Panasonic v. *Commission*
 [1980], 103
nation-states, 1
 political concepts transgressing, 2
natural persons, 82
negative clearance, 188
Nice Conference (2000), 6
Nice European Council, 120
Nice Treaty (2001), 7, 10, 11, 80, 82, 94
Nold v. *Commission* [1974], 102
non-discrimination
 indirect discrimination, part-time
  employees' pension rights,
  225–227
 language requirements for jobs,
  144–145
 legal profession, 160–162
 legislative acts, 223–225
 part-time employees' pension rights,
  225–227
 permitted positive discrimination,
  228–229
 place of education, in, 143
 private parties bound by, 145–147
 public service, in, 143
 retirement age, 229–231
 reverse discrimination, 156–158
 scope of, 143–144
 social and tax issues, to, 148
 vocational training, in, 148
non-legislative acts, types of, 85
non-retroactivity principle, human
 rights cases, 107
North Atlantic Treaty Organization
 (NATO), 5
notices, 40

obligatory dispute settlement, 7
Ombudsman, 35, 54
operational expenditure, 264
Organization for Economic Cooperation
 and Development (OECD), 5
Organization for European Economic
 Cooperation (OEEC), 5

Pan-European Movement, 3
Paris summit (1972), 213
Paris Treaty (1951), 4
Parliament, *see* European Parliament
 (EP)
partnership agreements, 9
part-time employees' pension rights,
 non-discrimination as to,
 225–227
part-time workers, 142
passive services, concept of, 165–166
penalty payment
 for infringement of Community law, 92
 right to request from Member States,
  29
Penn, William, 2
pension schemes, 229
persons, rights of, *see also* free
 movement of persons
 direct concern, 83
 individual concern, 83
 locus standi, 82, 84
 request judicial review, to, case law, 82
Petersberg tasks, 263
pillars of the EU
 basis of EU, 12
 co-operation in Justice and Home
  Affairs (JHA), 12
 first pillar (Community), 12
 intergovernmental, 12
 second pillar (CFSP) , 12,
  see also Common Foreign and
  Security Policy (CFSP)
 supranational, 12
 third pillar (PJCC), 12, 28,
  see also Police and Judicial
  Cooperation in Criminal Matters
  (PJCC)

Plato Plastik v. *Caropack* [2004], 97
Plaumann test, 83
plea of illegality, case law, 85–86
Police and Judicial Cooperation in
    Criminal Matters (PJCC), 12,
    28, 231
police cooperation, establishment of,
    236–237
political bargaining, 20
pollution control, 215
Polydor Case [1982], 74
Portugal v. *Council* [1999], 76
positive discrimination, affirmative
    action programmes, 228–229
predatory pricing, 198–199
preliminary references, 94
preliminary rulings, 78, 96–97
Presidency of the Council, 17
President (Parliament), 26
price war, 198
primacy doctrine, 71, 101
primary law, concept of, 38
private capacity of Member States as
    employers, 67
private international law, 232
privileged applicants, 82
procedure shopping, prevention of, 54
Procureur du Roi v. *Dassonville* [1974],
    126
product market, 192
professional qualifications, 168
proportionality
    case law, 106
    principle, 47, 106, 111
protective internal taxation, 137
Protocol on Social Policy, 221
public morality, 131
Public Prosecutor, 54
public undertaking, 204
publicity campaign, 126
Punto Casa v. *Sindaco del Comune di
    Capena* [1994], 135

qualified majority, 21
qualified majority voting (QMV)
    development and prospects of, 20–22

as form of decision making within
    the Council, 19
legislative procedures requiring, 54
tension with unanimity, 23
quantitative restrictions on imports and
    exports, 121

Race Directive, 224, 225, 227
Ratti Case [1979], 65
registrar of the ECJ, 78
Regulation 17, competition law
    enforcement under, 187–189
regulatory acts, meaning of, 85
regulatory committees, 31
relevant market as to dominant market
    position, 194–195
reservation of preliminary ruling, case
    law, 96–97
retirement ages, non-discrimination law
    as to, 229–231
reverse discrimination, 156–158
Reyners v. *Belgium* [1974], 62
Reynolds Tobacco v. *Commission*
    [2006], 120
Rhine Navigation Case, 249
right of free movement, 140–142
right to privacy, 103
rights of residence, 141
rights to education, 151–153
Road Taxes Case [1996], 53
Rome I Regulation, 232
Rome, Treaty of (1957), 2, 5, 11, 38,
    48, 99
Roquettes Frères SA v. *Council* [1980],
    87
Rousseau, Jean Jacques, 3
Rutili v. *Ministre de l'Intérieur* [1975],
    155

Schmidberger v. *Austria* [2003], 117,
    130
Schuman Plan (1950), 4
Schuman, Robert, 4
secondary law, concept of, 38
separation-of-powers, 15
Services Directive, 168

Sgarlata v. *High Authority* [1965], 101
Simmenthal Case, 73–74, 86
simple majority voting system, 19, 27
'single economic unit' doctrine, 181
single enterprise doctrine, 178
Single European Act (SEA, 1986), 16,
        30, 214
    consumer protection, 218
single farm payments, 211
single market, four freedoms, 121
Skimmed Milk Case [1977], 106
Sociaal Fonds voor de
        Diamantarbeiders v. *SA Ch.*
        Brachfeld & Sons [1969], 124
Social Action Programme (1974), 220
social policy
    Action Programme, 220
    equal pay, case law, 90, 221
    EU Framework Directive, 221
    legal basis of legislation, 218–220
    Social Charter, 221–222
Social Policy Chapter, 218
Social Policy Protocol, 50
Social Security Directive, 224, 229, 230
social security insurance, 178
soft law instruments, 40
Solange I Case, 110, 112–113
Solange II Case, 111, 113–114
Sotgiu v. *Deutsche Bundespost* [1974],
        156
Spanish Strawberries Case, 127, 130,
        145
spill-over effect from economic to
        political integration, 4, 99
Spinelli draft Treaty, 10
standard of living, 63
state aid, *see* subsidies
state liability, principle of, 69
state-like entity, 15
state-owned enterprises, applicability of
        competition law to, 204–205
Stauder v. *Stadt Ulm* [1969], 101
Stork v. *High Authority* [1959], 101
Strasbourg European Council, 221
Stresa Conference (1958), 210
'Study Group on European Union', 3

subsidiarity, principle of, 46–48, 57
subsidies, 84, 206–208, 243
Sunday trading restrictions,
        compatibility with EC law,
        132–133
supranational organisation
    and aspects of European integration,
        4–5
    characteristics of, 6–7
    supremacy of EU law, 72, 114–115

targeted sanctions, 45
Tariff Preferences, Case 45/86
        Commission v. *Council* [1987],
        46
'temple with three pillars', 12
terrorist acts, definition of, 235
Tindemans Report (1975), 10
Titanium Dioxide Case [1991], 55
Tobacco Advertising Directive, Case
        C-376/98, 42
Töpfer Case [1965], 84
Torfaen Borough Council v. *B & Q plc*
        [1989], 132
Trade Barriers Regulation, 30, 245
Trade-Related Intellectual Property
        Rights (TRIPs), 252–253
Traghetti del Mediterraneo v. *Italy*
        [2006], 70
'transatlantic' organisations, 5
transnational party affiliations, 32
Treaty on European Union (TEU), 12,
        13
    Article 13 of, 15
    Article 15 of, 16
    Article 16 of, 17
    Article 17(7) of, 26
Treaty on the European Community
        (TEC), 13
Treaty on the Functioning of the
        European Union (TFEU), 13
    Article 18 of, 153
    Article 30 of, 124
    Article 34 of, 125, 126–127
    Article 36 of, 128
    Article 45(2) of, 143–144

horizontal effect of, 145, 147
Article 101(1), 171–173
  economic activities covered by
    prohibition of, 183–184
  legal consequences of a violation
    of, 174–175
Article 102 of, 195
Article 110 of, 136–138
Article 258 of
  legal effect of, 91–92
  stages leading to, 90–91
Article 263 of, 81–82
Article 267 of, 94, 95–96
Article 294 of, 50
Article 352 of, 41, 44, 45
tribunals, 95–96
triple majority, 21

ultra vires acts, 87
unanimity
  amendments to Commission
    proposals, 49
  tension with QMV, 23
  voting procedure, 19
undertaking, meaning of, 177–179
unfair pricing, 196
Union legislative acts, 27
United Brands Case, 192, 196
Uruguay Round, 252–253
utilities, applicability of competition
  law to, 205–206

Van Binsbergen Case, 165, 167
Van Duyn Case, 65, 66, 154
Van Gend Case, 59–61, 99
'variable geometry' approach to
  integration, 7
VAT resource, 36
Verband Sozialer Wettbewerb v. *Clinique
  Laboratories* [1994], 135
vertical agreements, prohibition
  of, 176

Vertical Restraints Block Exemption
  Regulation, 187
veto power, of Parliament, 51
voting
  double majority system, 21
  Member States' allocation of votes, 20
  political bargaining, 20
  procedures, 18–20
  QMV, *see* qualified majority voting
    (QMV)
  qualified majority, 21
  simple majority, 19, 27
  tension between QMV and unanimity
    procedure, 23
  triple majority, 21
  unanimity, 19
  vote of consent, 26

Wachauf Case, 115–117
Waste Directive Case [1993], 55
waste management, *Walloon Waste*
  Case, 217
Western European Union (WEU), 5
'white list' of permissible provisions,
  185
'widening vs deepening' debate, 7–8
Wood Pulp Case, 174, 181
workers, meaning of, 142
working groups, COREPER, 24
World Trade Organisation (WTO), 29,
  75–76, 252
World War
  first, 3
  second, 3
written procedure of the Commission, 27
Wünsche Handelsgesellschaft [1987],
  see Solange II Case

Yaoundé Agreement (1963), 255

Zaera v. *Instituto Nacional de la
  Seguridad Social* [1987], 63